The BIG
Astrology Guide

Volume Two

The BIG Astrology Guide

Volume Two

A wide-ranging, thoroughly fascinating and educational book, all about the key branches of Astrology.

Volume One covers:

Sun Signs

Rising Signs & the Midheaven

The Planets

Aspects

~~~

Volume Two covers:

Moon Signs

Predictive Astrology

A Miscellany of Interesting Facts

The BIG
Astrology Guide

Volume Two

Sasha Fenton

Zambezi Publishing Ltd

Published in 2021 by
Zambezi Publishing Ltd
22 Second Avenue, Camels Head,
Plymouth, Devon PL2 2EQ (UK)
www.zampub.com   email: zambezipub@gmail.com

Text: copyright © 2021 Sasha Fenton
Cover design: copyright © 2021 Jan Budkowski
Certain images/part-images, on cover and within:
with much appreciation, courtesy of NASA.
Other images © Dreamstime.com, Pixabay.com

Sasha Fenton has asserted her moral right
to be identified as the author of this work in terms of
the Copyright, Designs and Patents Act 1988.

British Library Cataloguing-in-Publication Data:
A catalogue record for this book is available from
the British Library

Typeset by Zambezi Publishing Ltd, Plymouth UK
Printed and bound in the UK by Lightning Source (UK) Ltd
(Volume 1) ISBN: 978-1-903065-93-8
(Volume 2) ISBN: 978-1-903065-94-5

The Big Astrology Guide is a revised and updated, **two-volume** compilation of the following books, with additional content:
Sasha Fenton's Moon Signs (ISBN: 978-1-903065-74-7)
Sasha Fenton's Rising Signs (ISBN: 978-1-903065-75-4)
Sasha Fenton's Planets in Astrology (ISBN: 978-1-903065-76-1)
Sasha Fenton's Reading the Future (ISBN: 978-1-903065-77-8)

All rights reserved. No part of this publication may be reproduced, stored in a retrieval system, or transmitted in any form or by any means, electronic, mechanical, photocopying, recording, digital or otherwise, without the prior written permission of the publisher. This book is sold subject to the condition that it shall not, by way of trade or otherwise, be lent, resold, hired out, reproduced or otherwise circulated, without the publisher's prior written consent or under restricted licence issued by the Copyright Licensing Agency Ltd, London, fully or partially, in any binding, cover or format other than in which it is originally published, and without a similar condition being imposed on the subsequent purchaser.
This book is intended to provide information regarding the subject matter, and to entertain. The contents are not exhaustive and no warranty is given as to accuracy of content. The book is sold on the understanding that neither the publisher not the author are thereby engaged in rendering professional services, in respect of the subject matter or any other field. If expert guidance is required, the services of a competent professional should be sought.
The reader is urged to read a range of other material on the book's subject matter, and to tailor the information to your individual needs. Neither the author nor the publisher shall have any responsibility to any person or entity regarding any loss or damage caused or alleged to be caused, directly or indirectly, by the use or misuse of information contained in this book. If you do not wish to be bound by the above, you may return this book in sound condition to the publisher, with its receipt, for a refund of the purchase price.

About the Author

Sasha turned a childhood interest in palmistry and astrology into a career when she was in her twenties, later adding Tarot and developing her psychic abilities. She worked as a professional consultant from 1974 onwards, learning her trade in the best way possible - by doing readings for clients. She reduced her workload when her writing career took off, and over the past twenty-five years, has mainly concentrated on writing and publishing, but she still does the occasional professional reading to keep her skills relevant.

At present, Sasha's tally is 140 books, published by a number of mainstream publishers around the world. This now includes her three Tudorland novels.

The author wrote the stars page for Woman's Own magazine for six years and for the Sunday People's Weekend Magazine for a couple of years before that. She wrote a syndicated column for many local papers and about 3,000 articles and columns for papers and magazines of all kinds, mainly for the UK market but some for Australia.

Sasha has broadcast on many BBC and independent radio stations in the UK, with several regular spots that carried on for many years. She had her own spot on United Artists television for five years. Sasha now broadcasts from time to time on internet radio stations and podcasts around the world.

Sasha has given talks and workshops at hundreds of festivals in the UK and overseas, including the large Mind, Body and Spirit festivals in London and Australia.

Former President of the British Astrological and Psychic Society (BAPS)
Former Chair of the Advisory Panel on Astrological Education (APAE)
Former member of the Executive Council of the Writers' Guild of Great Britain

Together with her husband, Jan Budkowski, Sasha opened Zambezi Publishing in November 1996, and the company has since published over 300 books as an independent publisher. Most of their work is now co-editions and packaging projects. We have worked with Sterling Publishing Inc, HarperCollins/Thorsons, Carlton, Collins & Brown, Red Wheel Weiser, Charlesbridge, Parragon, Welbeck and Quarto.

Other Books by the Author

Astrology
Astrology East and West
Astrology for Living
Astrology for Wimps
Astrology in Focus: Decans and Dwaads
Astrology in Focus: How to Find Your Rising Signs
How to Read Your Star Signs
In Focus: Astrology – *(Writing as Roberta Vernon)*
Sasha Fenton's Moon Signs
Sasha Fenton's Planets
Sasha Fenton's Reading the Future
Sasha Fenton's Rising Signs
Sun Signs
Ten years of contributions to Llewellyn's Sun Sign Book
The Hidden Zodiac
The Magic of Astrology
The Moon in Focus
Understanding Astrology
Understanding the Astrological Vertex

Astrology / Numerology
Astro-Numerology: A Small Handbook
In Focus: Numerology

With the Late Jonathan Dee
Astro-guides – from 1995 to 2000 *(72 full sized books)*
Forecasts 2001
Forecasts 2002
Star*Date*Oracle
Sun Signs Made Simple
The Moon Sign Kit
Your Millennium Forecasts

Palmistry
Hand Reading
In Focus: Palmistry
Learning Palmistry
Living Palmistry
Modern Palmistry
Simply Palmistry
The Book of Palmistry
The Living Hand

Tarot
Elementary Tarot
Fortune-Telling by Tarot Cards
How to Find Love in the Tarot - *(ebook only)*
Super Tarot
Tarot in Action!
Tarot Masters *(chapter contribution)*
The Tarot

Chinese
Chinese Divinations
Elementary I Ching
Feng Shui for the Home
The Flying Stars

Health
In Focus: Chakra Healing – *(writing as Roberta Vernon)*
Diabetes: An Everyday Guide
Simply Chakras

Divination
Body Reading
Dream Meanings
Dreams *(with Jan Budkowski)*
Fortune-Teller's Handbook
Fortune-Teller's Workbook

Fortune-Telling by Tea Leaves
How to Be Psychic
Spells
Spells in Focus
Tea Cup Reading
The Aquarian Book of Fortune Telling

Publishing, Business and Finance
Prophecy for Profit *(with Jan Budkowski)*
Self-Publishing with Stellium
The Money Book *(with Jan Budkowski)*

Fiction – The Tudorland Series
Sophie's Inheritance *(book one)*
Lucy's Dilemma *(book two)*
Emily's Mistake *(book three)*

In Progress
Understanding Planetary Cycles in Astrology
Maisie – *(the fourth Tudorland novel)*
Revised Tarot in Action

Contents

MOON SIGNS 1
Moon Data 3
The Moon in Astrology 5
The Zodiac 11
Moon in Aries 18
Moon in Taurus 24
Moon in Gemini 30
Moon in Cancer 36
Moon in Leo 42
Moon in Virgo 48
Moon in Libra 54
Moon in Scorpio 60
Moon in Sagittarius 66
Moon in Capricorn 73
Moon in Aquarius 79
Moon in Pisces 86
Find Your Ascendant 93
The Astrological Houses 95
The Moon through the Houses 100
The Progressed Moon 105
Other Predictive Techniques 123
Moon and Planet Conjunctions 127
Moon Phases 134
Eclipses and Occultations 140
Weighting and Aspects 144
The Nodes of the Moon 146
Connections 151
Sun/Moon Combinations 153
Information and Suggestions 172

PREDICTIVE ASTROLOGY 175
Introduction and Beginners' Section 177
Transits 179
Progressions 183
Other Techniques 186
Hand Calculations to Progress a Chart 189
Further Methods, Ideas and Information 191

The Interpretation Maze 195
Progression & Transit Aspects 202
Solar Arcs & Returns 207
Moon Phases & Eclipses 209
The Cycles of Time 211
Recap: The Right Method for each Job 218
Astrology and the Body 220
Signs of the Zodiac 224
The Sun through the Signs & Houses 229
The Moon through the Signs & Houses 236
Solar Aspects 244
Lunar Aspects 253
Planetary Aspects 261
The Slower Moving Planets 274

A MISCELLANY OF INTERESTING FACTS 280

INDEX 289

The BIG Astrology Guide

Volume Two

MOON SIGNS

Moon Data

The Moon's average distance from the Earth, surface to surface, is 376,284 kilometres, or about 233,812 miles. It takes 27.32 days for the Moon to travel round the Earth and also 27.32 days for it to rotate on its axis, therefore it always has the same "face" pointing towards the Earth. Its diameter is 3476.6 kilometres and its temperature varies between plus 101° and minus 153° centigrade. The interior of the Moon is still hot enough to be made of molten rock and there are about 3,000 moonquakes per year. The surface of the Moon is fatter on the side that faces the Earth, and it's also warmer on the Earth side.

The Moon and Earth were both formed when the solar system came into being, roughly 4.5 billion (4,500,000,000) years ago. The Moon became attracted to the Earth's gravitational field and formed a double or binary planet system. Double planets spin round each other, rather like children swinging around each other on a rope; in this case, the relative sizes of the Earth and Moon mean that the Moon does most (not all) of the swinging. The first Moon landing was at 2.56 UT on the 20th July, 1969 by Armstrong, Aldrin and Collins in Apollo 11.

The Moon is about a quarter of the size of the Earth and its surface area is about the size of Asia. Nevertheless, its mountains reach 8,000 metres, which is higher than any on earth. There is no atmosphere on the Moon; therefore meteorites collide with it without being burned up by friction on their way down.

The Phases of the Moon

The Moon does not shed any light of its own, only the light that is reflected by the Sun. The phases of the Moon depend upon its position between the Earth and the Sun.

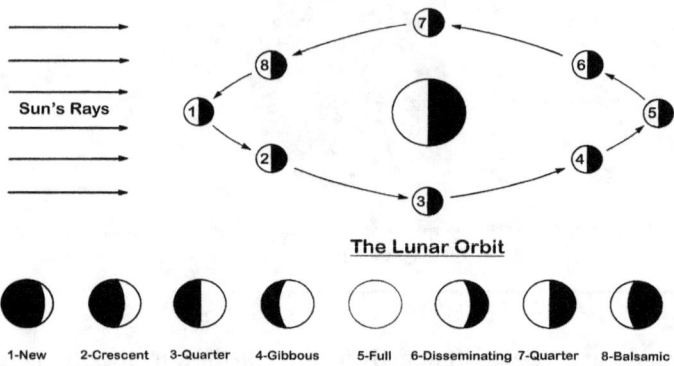

The Phases of the Moon

Eclipses

Eclipses of the Moon occur when the Earth is between the Moon and the Sun, and only when the Moon is full. Eclipses of the Sun occur when the Moon is between the Earth and the Sun, so this only happens when the Moon is dark or new. There are an average of two lunar and two solar eclipses each year, but not all can be seen from the same country and most of them are partial. Eclipses can last for a period of a few minutes to about an hour.

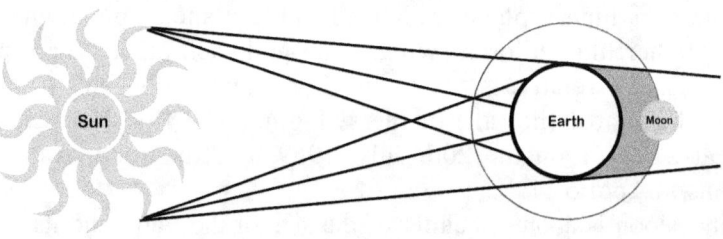

Lunar Eclipse

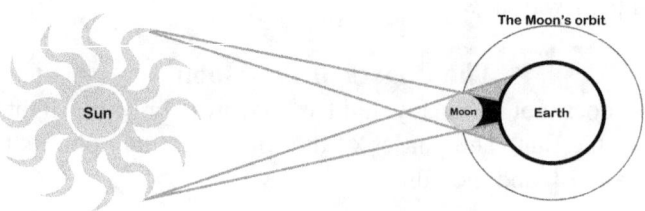

Solar Eclipse

Occultations
These occur when the Moon is directly between the Earth and a planet.

Tides
There are two high tides a day. At the time of the new Moon and the full Moon, when the Sun, Moon and Earth are in line, the tides are higher.

The Ecliptic or Zodiac
Until the discovery of the way that the solar system works, it was thought that the Sun orbited the earth and the line that the Sun appeared to take around the Earth is called the ecliptic. Interestingly, both astrologers and astronomers still use this "apparent" trajectory of the Sun to find their way around the sky. The constellations that make up our familiar zodiac are sited along or very close to, and touching, the ecliptic. The word zodiac comes from the Ancient Greek word for "animal" and is linked to the words "zoo" and "zoological".

Declination
The orbit of the Moon and the planets takes them above the ecliptic and below it as well.

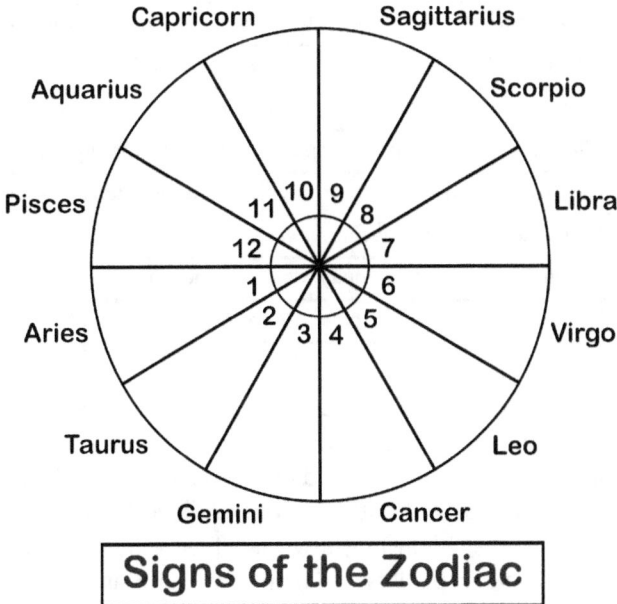

Signs of the Zodiac

The Moon in Astrology

Emotions

When I give a lecture on Moon signs, I start by asking the audience members what they think the Moon represents, and they invariably answer, "emotions". I then ask them what emotions they think the Moon might represent; for instance, are we talking about rage, jealousy, lust or hatred? The audience members often look puzzled while they mull this over. The problem is that all the planets in astrology represent emotional states of one kind or another, and here are some suggestions that show you what I mean:

PLANET	EMOTIONS
Sun	Joy, success, happiness, achievement, day to remember.
Mercury	Ideas, things that excite the mind. Pleasure or stress from studying.
Venus	Love, jealousy, heartbreak, happiness, top of the world, or bottom.
Mars	Jealousy, hatred, attack, sexuality, lust, wanting everything now.
Jupiter	Expansiveness, happiness, desire for justice, desire to explore.
Saturn	Depression, loneliness, sadness, fatigue, disappointment.
Uranus	Desire to break out of restriction or boredom, desire for change.
Neptune	Love, kindness, obsession, confusion and loss.
Pluto	Rage, resentment, jealousy, need for security.
Chiron	Seat of pain, sickness, pleasure from arts or combat.

Old astrology books tell us that the Sun represents action and the Moon represents reaction, so the Moon can only offer an emotional reaction to any situation. The reasoning that used to be given for this is that the Moon cannot create any light itself but it can only reflect the light of the Sun. I may not be the biggest brain in the world of astrology, but it strikes me that none of the other planets do their own shining either, and they produce all kinds of effects, so that argument falls rather flat, doesn't it? Certainly the Moon represents a more emotional side of our nature than most of the planets, and it can show how we react in certain situations.

Inner Motivation

To some extent, the Ascendant and the Sun represent the outer manner or obvious nature of a person, but the Moon represents the inner, hidden side. Thus someone who appears soft as butter but is in reality hard as nails, has a Moon that is very much at odds with the outer manner. Alternately, someone who appears happy-go-lucky on the outside can be hurting badly inside. Also, if you want to see what a person really values and feels to be important, take a look at the Moon's sign and house.

Nurturing

Here are some old ideas and several newer ones about the Moon, motherhood and nurturing:

- Old astrology books state that the Moon represents the mother and the Sun the father.
- Most modern astrologers see the Moon as the mother and Saturn as the father.
- Bruno and Louise Huber suggested that Saturn represented the mother, as it was she who disciplined the children and saw to it that they had proper food, clothing, education and good manners, while the indulgent, lunar father turned up from time to time, took them out and spoiled them.

Is that what fathers do? In our world, many fathers vanish over the horizon and disappear into the mist, so one could suggest that fathers can be better represented by Neptune!

Frankly, I see the Moon as the maternal or nurturing influence. It may be the mother that gives the children the attention, love and care that they need, but it could come from the father, or both parents at once or both in turn at different times. Sometimes the main influence in a child's life is another relative, someone outside the family or even different people at different stages of the subject's life.

The Moon sign can sometimes symbolise the experience that the mother herself had during her life. It can show what she is like as person, and it can also demonstrate the influence she had on the subject. However, you can't limit this to the mother herself, as it shows the experience of being mothered – or neglected or maltreated or loved - by whosoever happened to take on this role.

The Moon in some signs shows a deep attachment to the mother or to a mother figure, while in other signs it denotes a friendly but detached relationship, while it others it can symbolise, disappointment, dislike and disapproval.

The following table is a kind of quick rundown of the way in which adults tend to look at their mothers.

Moon Sign	Feelings for Mother
Aries	Fondness, but irritation, and sometimes a burden.
Taurus	Some love, but the mother may be considered a burden.
Gemini	Friendship, shared intellectual interests, but not living out of each other's pockets.
Cancer	These two can cling to one another, or get on each other's nerves.
Leo	The child will try to love the mother, but may eventually give it up as a bad job.
Virgo	The child finds the mother a complete pain.
Libra	A casual and friendly relationship, but some irritation.
Scorpio	Superficially close, but with much resentment and sometimes hidden stores of rage and hatred.
Sagittarius	The child is dutiful, but with little real love on either side.
Capricorn	The closest relationship is to the father, but the mother is also deeply loved.
Aquarius	At best, love and a friendly and respectful relationship. At worst, no real contact.
Pisces	A close relationship with much to talk about, but they often irritate each other.

Family Life

Just as the Moon can show one's feelings about the mother, so can it show one's attitude to family life. Some subjects will make considerable sacrifices for their families and especially for their children, while others only focus on themselves and leaving their relatives and even their children to find nurturing elsewhere.

Women
The Moon represents the feminine principle, so it often refers to women or to dealings with women, especially when it comes to trends and events.

The Home, Property and Land
The Moon rules the home, and in particular the kitchen, cooker, fridge and everything to do with the preparation of food. The Moon sign can indicate a greater or lesser interest in these things. If you are looking into the value of your property, whether to buy, sell move or speculate on property, it's worth checking out the natal Moon and the progressions by the Moon and to it, and the transits to the Moon. Also check the condition of the nodes of the Moon, natally, by progression and by transit at the relevant time. Land is also a lunar interest, although it can connect with other planets depending upon circumstances – such as with Venus for ownership, and with Mars and Pluto if an inheritance is involved.

Providing What the Public Wants
This covers a wide area of operation, but the general idea is of the provision of goods and services that the public makes use of.

Farming and Food Production
Everything related to foodstuffs comes under the realm of the Moon. It can come under other planets too, to an extent. The asteroid, Ceres (among others) also has something to say about harvests, crops and foodstuffs. The Moon is especially concerned with dairies, cows, dairy products and even mad cow disease, foot and mouth and so on.

Shops, Businesses
The Moon rules the kind of small shop that an individual can own and run independently, as a franchise or linked to a buying organisation. So, this might range from your local bookshop, the local shoe-mender/key cutter business, café or grocery shop. The Moon rules as pubs, restaurants, dairies, farm shops and convenience shops. One could ague that the Moon also rules a massive supermarket, because it provides goods that the public need, but the business as a whole - for example, all the supermarkets in the chain, the

shareholders, finance, distribution and much else - are not lunar matters.

The Moon rules small businesses of all kinds, especially those that people run from home, thus astrologers and astrology writers who work from home are at least partially ruled by the Moon – along with other planetary influences.

Attitude to Money

Money is an emotive issue, so the natal Moon sign and progressed Moon can show the attitude towards money and even the financial situation at any time. The need for security is a lunar issue, so this also relates to money.

Travel and the Sea

Before the discovery of Neptune in the middle of the 19th century, the Moon was considered to be a restless planet that was connected to the sea, and by extension, to travel, so it was associated with an inability to settle down. It's interesting that so many aspects of the Moon deal with family life, parents, homes, property and land, farms, shops and businesses, which are all things that tie us to people and places. Old time astrology told us that the Moon changes its shape and even disappears completely from time to time, thus it symbolises a desire for change and for getting away from things. The Moon can represent novelty, changes of scene, days out by the sea, the desire to roam and general foot-looseness. The Moon also rules changeable moods, a need for a new perspective and the urge to get away from it all once in a while. When we are desperate for a change, the Moon can move into just the right position to bring it along.

I haven't noticed the Moon being especially important in the charts of those who work on the sea, but others might know of such a connection. As far as the travel trade goes, there does seem to be a preponderance of people with the Moon in Gemini.

Mind

We forget that older forms of astrology associated the Moon with the mind, so it can show whether a person's thinking is quick, slow, original or traditional. It can show whether the mind is filled with obsessive ideas or flitting from one thing to another.

Career

Although not really associated with work, the Moon shows how we like to spend our days and what we feel is important to us and to the world. It can show talents, and it can point to certain types of interest, careers and hobbies.

Health
This is important. Transits, returns and progressions of the Moon are important indicators of serious health problems, and the Moon's movement can act as a trigger for these. In itself, it rules the chest, breasts, breathing and fluids in body, and being "cold and wet" by tradition, it rules arthritis and fluid in or on the lungs and heart. It can rule mental sickness, due to its unstable nature.

Reflections
The Moon can borrow some of its nature from the sign directly opposite to the sign which it occupies, so here is a table of the signs and their opposites.

SIGN	OPPOSITE SIGN
Aries	Libra
Taurus	Scorpio
Gemini	Sagittarius
Cancer	Capricorn
Leo	Aquarius
Virgo	Pisces
Libra	Aries
Scorpio	Taurus
Sagittarius	Gemini
Capricorn	Cancer
Aquarius	Leo
Pisces	Virgo

The Zodiac

We know that the earth orbits the Sun, taking a year to complete the orbit, but it appears from earth as though the Sun goes around us, and the path that it takes is called the "plane of the ecliptic" or the "ecliptic". It's also called the zodiac.

Genders, Elements and Qualities
Each alternate sign is masculine or feminine, which is a bit like the Chinese idea of yang and yin. There are also three signs in each element of fire, earth, air and water, and there are four signs in each quality, of cardinal, fixed and mutable.

The Gender
This has nothing to do with sexuality. Some astrologers call these signs positive and negative but their energies are perhaps better expressed as extrovert and introvert or yang and yin. All fire and air signs are masculine, while all earth and water signs are feminine.

Sign	Gender	Element	Quality
Aries	1. Masculine	1. Fire	1. Cardinal
Taurus	2. Feminine	2. Earth	2. Fixed
Gemini	1. Masculine	3. Air	3. Mutable
Cancer	2. Feminine	4. Water	1. Cardinal
Leo	1. Masculine	1. Fire	2. Fixed
Virgo	2. Feminine	2. Earth	3. Mutable
Libra	1. Masculine	3. Air	1. Cardinal
Scorpio	2. Feminine	4. Water	2. Fixed
Sagittarius	1. Masculine	1. Fire	3. Mutable
Capricorn	2. Feminine	2. Earth	1. Cardinal
Aquarius	1. Masculine	3. Air	2. Fixed
Pisces	2. Feminine	4. Water	3. Mutable

The Zodiac

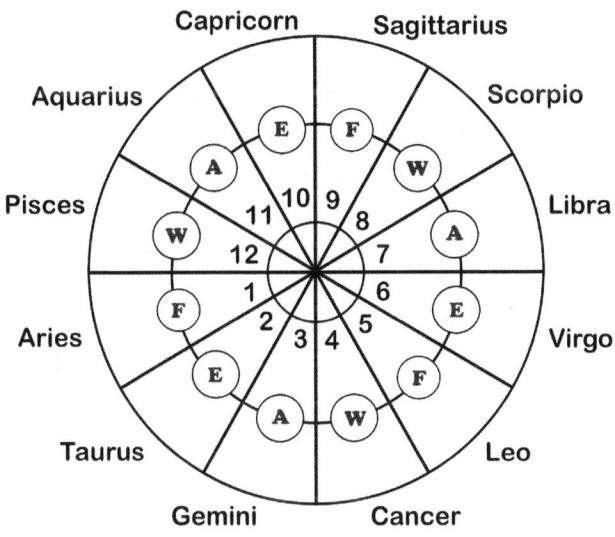

The Elements
Fire= F, Earth= E, Air= A, Water= W

The Fire Group - Masculine
Aries, Leo, Sagittarius

This group is associated with speed, quick thinking and fast responses. People with the Moon in fire signs don't lack initiative and they can get things off the ground quickly when they want to. They may lack patience with slower people, so it doesn't take much to irritate or anger them and they don't stand fools gladly. These subjects can concentrate on a project if it interests them, but they soon become bored if it doesn't. There are times when their self-centred attitude can make them appear arrogant, but they are not as confident as they look and they can be subject to sudden fits of depression. They need a steady partner who they can rely upon.

They are generous and good hearted as long as others don't take advantage of their generosity. As long as there is no heavy emphasis on earth or water signs, these people can be somewhat overgenerous when it comes to their own family. This is partly because they have faith in their ability to earn money in the future, and partly because they want their relatives and friends to like them, admire them and approve of them. They dress well and put on a good appearance generally, with a nice home and a nice car and all the right accoutrements, and they splash money around in order to achieve all these aims. Having said this, the Moon is different from the Sun, and wherever it's placed, it adds a certain amount of thrift or carefulness. Unless the Sun and other planets are also in fire signs, the person is unlikely to be a complete "spendaholic".

The Moon is associated with water signs, so it may not be comfortable when placed in this group. Sudden enthusiasms may not be all that easy to carry through, and the person's changeable emotions may confuse those around him. The subject himself can be confused by his own nature, because fire gives him a fast and logical mind, while the Moon gives him an emotional and intuitive heart.

Childhood experiences may not be all that comfortable or happy and this leads to a certain lack of self-confidence. The subject may cover this up by having the latest and best car, the trendiest designer clothes and the smartest house, or by looking more confident than she feels.

The Earth Group - Feminine
Taurus, Virgo, Capricorn

When the Moon is in an earth sign, there is a certain amount of practicality. These people like domestic life and they enjoy entertaining in the home. They tend to be thorough, careful and capable of dealing with details and there is a certain stubbornness here that helps them to finish what they start. On the other hand this can tie them into a job, relationship or some other situation longer than is good for them. These people fear poverty, so they work hard for their money and they hang on to what they have, to the point of becoming tight-fisted. Some worry unnecessarily over money matters. They are dutiful to their parents and good to their offspring but their work is also important to them. They may define themselves by their successes or failures at work. The Moon is quite comfortable in earth signs, but this element can make it hard for people to adapt to new circumstances.

As a child, this person would have had a reasonable relationship with his father. The mother would have been a powerful figure who either made unreasonable demands upon the child or was very loving. She may have been so contradictory that it confused the subject.

The Air Group - Masculine
Gemini, Libra, Aquarius

Air signs are mainly concerned with logic, a strong mind and intellect. This Moon placement adds intelligence and speedy thinking, but it can make it difficult for these subjects to cope with upsetting issues or with their own feelings. Some of these subjects avoid emotional situations by burying themselves in work or studies, while others find themselves at odds with partners who may be more emotional. A few of these people can be unrealistic, with dreams far above what life can hope to offer.

Saving and spending or giving and taking can be a problem for these people. They are inclined to be extremely self-indulgent, but they can be peculiar when it comes to dealing with others, either being over-generous or unnecessarily tight-fisted. Some give freely to one person while keeping others on a tight leash. Just like their confusing financial ideas, their emotions can be equally confusing, especially to themselves.

Childhood relationships are pretty reasonable and their parents will have done all they could to give these subjects a good education and plenty of intellectual stimuli.

The Water Group - Feminine
Cancer, Scorpio, Pisces

The Moon is supposed to be most at home in water signs, but this can put too much emphasis on the emotional and intuitive nature, making these individuals subject to elation at one time and depression at others – not to mention angry outbursts. Part of the problem is that they are quick to pick up on atmospheres and surrounding emotions. They absorb the feelings of those who are around them and sometimes get upset as a result. These sensitive people love deeply but they also hate with equal passion. Where practicalities such as money are concerned, they fear poverty but they may have to cope with this at some point in their lives. Water signs tend to be thrifty and careful at the best of times, and the watery Moon in a water sign adds to this tendency, so unless there is a preponderance of fire in the chart, this person can become tight-fisted and an advantage-taker.

The childhood can be difficult because these youngsters are not altogether on the same wavelength as those around them. This may put them at odds with their parents, siblings, schoolmates, teachers and so on.

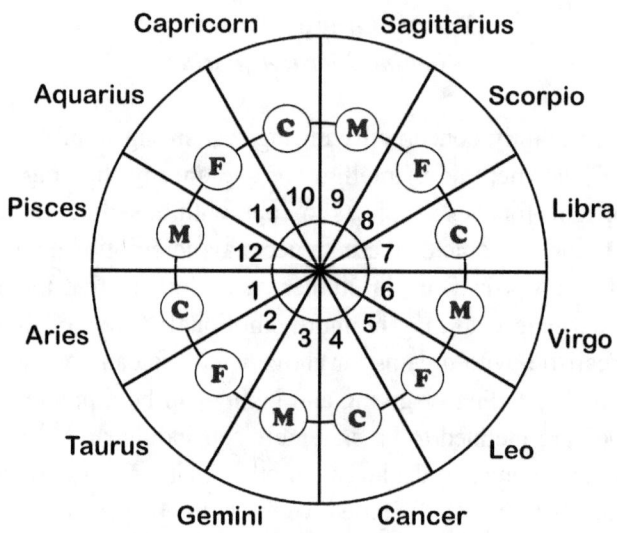

The Qualities of the Signs
Fixed = F Cardinal = C Mutable = M

The Cardinal Group
Aries, Cancer, Libra, Capricorn

These people try to maintain equilibrium in their lives but their destiny tends to force them to cope with quite profound changes in circumstances. They may move house several times, change partners or live through sudden bereavements or sudden career changes. They can think on their feet when they have to, and they can be extremely successful and wealthy at some points in their lives – sometimes due to a lucky marriage or an inheritance. Cardinal sign people cannot live under someone else's rules and they are perfectly capable of ignoring the demands of others. They like to make their own decisions and sometimes live only by their own rules.

The Fixed Group
Taurus, Leo, Scorpio, Aquarius

People with the Moon in fixed signs form their opinions when they are young and they find it hard to change these later. They aren't flexible and they find it hard to see a variety of ways of solving problems, so they become disappointed and depressed if their plans don't work out. They go after what they want in a dogged manner, sometimes by sheer hard work, but sometimes by freeloading. They can be self-absorbed. They are usually reliable and faithful in love relationships, and they are very attached to their families and those who they love. Some of these people are extremely emotional while others find it almost impossible to deal with emotions - even their own.

These people find it hard to let go of pain that is left over from their childhood or their past, so these things can haunt them and affect the way they react to things throughout life. In a more material sense, they find it hard to throw stuff out, and they can end up living in a very small and cluttered space, due to the amount of junk they hang on to.

The Mutable Group
Gemini, Virgo, Sagittarius, Pisces

These people can attract lame ducks, and some of them are lame ducks themselves. They may sacrifice themselves for the sake of loved ones and even for strangers, so they need to be discriminating in their choice of friends and colleagues. They should try to avoid jumping in and offering help too quickly or taking on too much. Their own fluctuating moods make them difficult to understand, and they can suffer from chronic ailments, especially when unhappy or when they feel that their lives are out of control. These individuals make good friends and they are sympathetic, but they can be neurotic, nervy, emotional, stingy and inclined to pick fights over small matters when tired or stressed.

Dignity, Exaltation, Detriment and Fall

You will notice these strange terms cropping up in this book. They come from ancient forms of astrology that considered certain sign and planet groupings to be good and others to be less good. Some of these are easy to understand, such as "dignity", which simply means that the planet is in the sign that it rules. The detriment sign is the one opposite the dignity one. Exaltation and fall don't have any major reason for their existence, but they probably have something to do with the astronomy of the signs and their position at certain times of the year according to ancient astronomers.

The houses act in similar ways to the signs because each house links to a sign, but these concepts are now called 'accidental'. Needless to say, every planet has this same system going for it; but this section is about the Moon, so as far as we are concerned, the table below shows how the system affects the Moon.

Sign	Moon's Condition	House	Moon's Condition
Aries		First	
Taurus	Exaltation	Second	Accidental Exaltation
Gemini		Third	
Cancer	Dignity	Fourth	Accidental Dignity
Leo		Fifth	
Virgo		Sixth	
Libra		Seventh	
Scorpio	Fall	Eighth	Accidental Fall
Sagittarius		Ninth	
Capricorn	Detriment	Tenth	Accidental Detriment
Aquarius		Eleventh	
Pisces		Twelfth	

Moon in Aries

Ruled by Mars

The sun shall not smite thee by day, nor the moon by night.
PSALM 121

The sign of Aries is masculine, positive, fiery and cardinal whilst the Moon, through its association with the sign of Cancer, is feminine, negative, watery and cardinal. This Moon position gives its owner an underlying need for power and a desire for leadership. This may lead you to reach for the top in your career or to become the leader of whichever group you find yourself in. Women with this Moon placement face emotional conflict within their personality due to their highly assertive inner nature, and they frequently resolve this by choosing weak partners so that they can reverse the traditional man/woman roles.

Some choose single life and a demanding career in preference to housework and motherhood.

Both sexes have an inner power pack of energy, forcefulness and courage. The cardinality of this sign means that you rarely allow the grass to grow beneath your feet, and if faced with a problem you would rather sort it out immediately. You may actually get others to do this for you, but help is appreciated when it's given. Your mind is highly original and, given other encouraging factors on your birthchart, you may be able to turn your ideas into moneymaking projects that could give you the means to get yourself up the ladder of success. However you may be so idealistic and enthusiastic as to be unrealistic. You have a tendency to do things on too large a scale on some occasions, while over-optimism can cloud your brain and make you unrealistic in your expectations. You need an element of risk in your life that may be reflected in the job you do or in your personal life.

Being quickly responsive to any situation, you can be relied on in a crisis; the sight of people who are in trouble does not embarrass you –

indeed you will do what you can to help them. Your emotional reactions are fast and instinctive and your behaviour can be over-impulsive, but time and experience of life may soften some of the rough edges. Care should be taken not to be critical and impatient with those who see and do things differently from you, as this can lead you into a narrow-minded and bigoted stance. You quickly become irritated and may have difficulty in keeping your temper due to the combined blanketing effect of the watery Moon and the fiery impulsiveness of the sign of Aries. This tension may be released in sudden outbursts of temper and biting sarcastic remarks. You prefer other people to be forthright and honest in their dealings with you and unless there is a very good reason for secrecy, you prefer to be direct and honest yourself. Your excellent sense of humour gets you out of a lot of trouble and you have the ability to take a joke against yourself.

Your ability to put ideas into action can be an inspiration to others; also you can motivate people by your optimistic outlook and your faith in the future. You know instinctively how to raise the spirits of others. However, you sometimes plunge into action without weighing the consequences, and therefore you need to cultivate a sense of proportion. Be careful not to override the feelings of others when you are in the throes of a new idea, although it's never your intention to hurt anyone. You have little patience with people who withdraw into their shell, sulk and won't tell you what's the matter with them; your own hot temper can make you insensitive at times, but you don't hold a grudge. The lunar Arian heart is warm and you are the first to help and comfort those who are in trouble. You respect the beliefs of others and are happy to preserve their independence; your broad mind makes you able to relate to people of all classes and colours. You really cannot stand neurotic people who whine for nothing. You will help anyone who has practical problems but have little patience with emotional doubts and worries and you tend to avoid having them yourself.

You are more of a city person than a country type, but you like to get away into the fresh air, and love being in the sun. It's a fact that many lunar Arians are excellent sportsmen and sportswomen. The fiery quality of Aries indicates a need for excitement and change. A monotonous job may pay the bills, but won't satisfy you for long. This need for excitement can also make steady relationships appear unappealing, and this may even lead you to choose unreliable partners. Some of you, on the other hand, seek to steady your own inner nature by marrying a much more placid and reliable personality than yourself, while a few of you may even destroy a relationship simply because it has become boring. I have a theory that Moon in Aries subjects of both sexes prefer a younger partner, as this suggests that you would enjoy moulding them to your own design.

Many of you choose a partner who is careful with money because you can't trust yourself not to overspend. You enjoy the pursuit of love and fall in love fairly easily but the flame can also burn out quickly. A relationship based on friendship is more likely to be enduring than a swift passion, but there must be excitement, sex and warmth or it will not work at all. Women with the Moon in Aries have a touch of masculinity at their core; that is not to say that they are all budding lesbians, just that there is dissatisfaction with the traditional feminine role. Whatever your gender, if you have this Moon placement, you may be hard to live with at times, because you can fall into the habit of being picky and fault-finding due to unreasonable fears based on imagined threats to your independence.

You can be quite a good homemaker as long as you have time and money to spare, but if you are short of both, you will ignore your surroundings. You enjoy buying gadgets for the home and you can put up with noisy or messy major alterations going on in the home better than most people can. However, when the atmosphere at home becomes unbearable, either for practical reasons of too many builders around the place or due to relationship stress, you find a good reason to get out of the house for a while.

You are a caring parent, but unfortunately you could belittle any child whom you considered weak and silly. You do your best to see that your children have all that they require and will move heaven and earth to get them a good education. You may not actually wish to spend too much time with your children, and the parent/child relationship works better if you have a fulfilling job and can direct some of your energies away from the home situation. You will never hesitate to spend money on your family's appearance because you consider that good clothes give a good impression.

Sexually, your attitude should be straightforward but you may wish to dominate your partner. Talk of sex excites you but background music during lovemaking may put you off! You enjoy fun and laughter while making love but you need friendship and appreciation from your partner as much as you need sex.

Many of you love the arts, especially music and dancing, some of you will find your way into an artistic career, certainly you need a measure of creativity in your work. Many subjects with the Sun, Moon or Ascendant in Aries have a lifelong desire to study music or art but somehow never quite get around to it; perhaps the fear of failure is too great.

Career
The position of the Moon on a birthchart rarely determines one's actual career, but can show inner motivations. You are happiest in a job where you can make your own decisions and you may prefer to be self-employed. If not too impatient, you can rise to an executive position in a large and well-structured organisation. You enjoy wielding power and should make a sensible and benevolent manager or employer, you have the ability to delegate tasks to others and then leave them to get on with the job. Taking orders from someone you don't respect is impossible for you and you would respond very angrily to anyone who tried to bully you; however you, in turn, must try not to bully or laugh at others.

You need to be able to use your initiative; you would find it impossible to work for a wet blanket type. Work in the military or paramilitary field might appeal to you as might work as an engineer, in the electronics field, teaching or any kind of work that influences the public. You may enjoy working in the media and being in the public eye so that you can receive open adulation. Marketing, promoting and thinking up new ideas comes easily to you. Your Achilles' heel may be that you are susceptible to flattery. Your love of mechanics and vehicles makes you a good driver and even a good pilot, and you are quick to grasp IT concepts. You could make a living from sport or dancing, but some form of construction or property development would be a good choice.

Parents and Background
This Moon position shows a difficult relationship with the father, you may have loved him and hated him at the same time and you may also have tried to emulate him. Whilst growing up, you probably found yourself in a number of nose-to-nose shouting matches with him. There

is a fight for emotional supremacy in this relationship with the father seeing the child as being unrealistic and the child seeing the parent as being overly restrictive or unhelpful. Sometimes the father actually shows contempt towards the child. Your mother may have been cold towards you or just too busy to take much notice of you. The family itself may be attached to a large and very structured organisation such as the armed forces or the civil service. The Aries Moon child may follow his parents into the same organisation but he would only be happy in that environment if he quickly gained a position of rank and decision-making.

Your parents encouraged you to stand on your own feet at an early age. They would have applauded and encouraged any physical activity (sports, swimming, dancing) and wanted you to do well at school. You don't have much attachment to the past or even to your own family, this is especially true if you feel that they don't appreciate you.

Your mother might have had to face some kind of circumstances where she was forced to leave you to cope alone. This was probably due to problems at that time; however it's possible that she was vain, selfish and all too easily bored by the tasks of motherhood. The Moon sign sometimes jumps back a generation, so some of the circumstances given here for your childhood could actually apply to your mother's experience when young. There may even have been jealousy and bitterness between you and your brothers and sisters.

Health
In so far as the Moon sometimes reflects continuous or chronic health conditions, any trouble in this case would be in the area of the head, eyes, nose, ears (upper) teeth and throat. Your impetuosity may lead you to have silly accidents such as cuts, burns and possibly bruises as a result of dropping things on your feet.

Additional Information
I haven't come across as many lunar Arians as other Moon signs. This could mean there are fewer lunar Arians, but on the other hand, it could indicate a lack of interest in astrology.

Sun, Moon or Ascendant in Aries folk have soft speaking voices, and some males with this Moon placement dislike their voices because they are slightly high, but many of them have good singing voices, so perhaps this offers a little consolation.

There is a fondness for culture but this can be hidden under a very ordinary exterior, so a lunar Arian can be a rough, tough engineer or businessman who loves literature, art and music.

You have to take care not to bully or shout down others.

Moon in Aries Celebrities	
Jose Maria Carreras	John Cleese
Divine	Bill Gates
Jennifer Lopez	Martina Navratilova

Moon in Taurus

Ruled by Venus
(The Moon's exaltation)

Ah, Moon of my delight who know'st no wane,
The Moon of Heaven is rising once again:
How oft hereafter rising shall she look
Through this same Garden after me - in vain!
FROM THE RUBAIYAT OF OMAR KHAYYAM.

The sign of Taurus is feminine, negative, earth and fixed, while the Moon, through its connections with the sign of Cancer, is feminine, negative, water and cardinal. The Moon is fairly comfortable in Taurus, adding a measure of stability to the personality and bestowing an uncomplicated response to sensual pleasures. You enjoy eating, drinking, making love and listening to music. The feminine aspect of this placement prevents you from being much of an initiator; indeed you prefer to spend your life sailing along on a steady course than for it to be full of storms and disruption. The fixity of Taurus stabilises the natural restlessness of the Moon and makes you very purposeful and determined, particularly when it comes to getting what you want or hanging on to what you have. You try at all times to maintain the status quo; you may find that the circumstances of your life force you into this position. You might even find yourself putting up with a long-term lifestyle that is not of your choosing.

The Moon is said to be exalted in the sign of Taurus and this gives an inner sense of strength and resilience. Lunar Taureans are noted for their robust health and their ability to obtain practical results in all that they undertake. People who have the Moon in an earth sign love the natural world, which means that you can make a hobby out of botany or animal biology. You could become involved with some scheme that seeks to preserve the countryside. Even if you aren't actively involved with these pursuits, you will love getting out into the fresh air and into your garden. Many lunar Taureans choose to work as representatives or even milkmen, so that they can be out and about and thus keep in tune with the seasons. You have a strong need to build for the future and create things which will be useful and long lasting, this could be reflected in your choice of a career. You like the sea, but not with the same intensity as solar or lunar Cancerians, and you wouldn't have any great urge to run off and join the navy. Your affinity with nature could lead you to take an interest in ancient religions, such as paganism and Wicca.

You don't enter into relationships lightly, because the fixity of Taurus, along with your inner urge to build and preserve, leads you to take any form of emotional commitment very seriously. Most astrology books tell us that this Moon position leads to possessiveness and jealousy and to some extent this is true. Possessiveness is more of a problem than envy or jealousy but this is a rather subtle concept to grasp. You don't envy the things that other people have or the relationships that they enjoy but if your partner were to leave you for another, you would be very upset indeed. A woman with this Moon placement can become taken in by a man who promises to leave his wife at some future date, and then doesn't. In these situations, it's hard for you to give in gracefully and accept defeat, especially in the face of betrayal. As you can see, your tenacity and endurance are both strengths and weaknesses of this particular Moon Sign placement. Your tendency to be stubborn can lead you into psychologically damaging and obsessive relationships.

Your senses are strong, especially touch, smell and hearing. You love the scent of flowers and the feel of velvet. Your musical taste is well developed. One Moon in Taurus lady told me that she hates the sound of a "murdered" song, but loves the sound of laughter. Obviously this sensuality leads to a love of sex with all its scents, textures and passions, although relating is more important to you than sex for its own sake. You love to be cuddled and stroked in both a sexual and an affectionate manner, and ideally all this snuggling should take place within marriage.

You prefer to be faithful to your partner but if for some reason you find this impossible, then you would try hard to wait for your children to grow up before actually leaving the family home, so you try to do your duty for however long it takes. Oddly enough, you are quite a flirt, but this is "social" flirting that is not important. You don't flirt in order to make your partner jealous; you do it just for the fun of it. You can annoy a partner by asking where he or she is going and when they intend to return, but this is not intended to irritate them or to show any lack of trust on your part, you just need to make sure that your family is safe.

You take to parenthood easily, you love your own children and you have patience with those of others. If you marry someone who already has a family, you cope with this very well. You take a responsible attitude towards those who depend upon you without making heavy weather of it. You are very loving and caring and really enjoy looking after those you love but you become understandably resentful if this care is taken for granted and not appreciated. You are good with sick people as long as there is not too much mess to clear up; the one thing you really hate is the sight of blood (especially your own). You are good at attending to practical needs but you may be less keen on attending to your partner's psychological needs, and you may forget to validate a partner or a child. Sometimes you just can't see what others want of you. I remember a friend called Alana, who is an otherwise intelligent and sensitive woman, saying that she could never figure out what her ex-husband really wanted from her.

Your deep attachment to your family, and your occasional misplaced pride in them and desire for them to be the best can make you overcritical and even tyrannical at times, especially when you are in a bad mood. You respect strength in others and you can walk all over those who you consider weak. You aren't over-competitive, so you will help a partner or workmate to get ahead. Above all you need a stimulating partner who has similar interests to yourself. You are emotionally habit-forming, not keen on too much change or excitement, and you must beware that monotony does not seep into your sexual behaviour. You are attracted to beauty and people who have cheerful, pleasant natures. Your pet hates are fatness, ugliness and people who wear dirty, tatty clothing. Both the people around you and your own surroundings must be clean and attractive.

You like your bills to be paid on time, so you are careful with money, and you like to have some savings to fall back on. You can earn good money but you can't make it by get-rich-quick schemes. You aren't particularly lucky with money and a confidence trickster can take you in because there are times when your judgement deserts you.

You control your feelings very well and are adept at hiding them from others probably due to childhood training, but being a feminine and emotional sign this can lead to moodiness. Occasionally your patience deserts you and you can also cut your nose off to spite your face. You may break out in a sudden angry response when something upsets you, but on another day, the same thing wouldn't bother you at all.

Being naturally rather cautious, you prefer to allow new acquaintances to do the talking, it's only when you know people better that you can relax and open up. You aren't above a bit of manipulation in social circumstances but you generally use it in the form of humour to defuse a tense situation. You usually guard your tongue well and rarely run off at the mouth. Once you have formed an opinion it's hard for you to alter it, and you can have the rather unfortunate habit of laying the law down to others. Your worst faults are laziness and a tendency to sit back and let others do the work for you or keep you in style at their expense.

Attitude to Career

You are undoubtedly ambitious for yourself and your family. Women with this placement seem to be given the message by their parents that they should stick to the old-fashioned idea of the feminine role, so they often start out as secretaries, nurses, cooks or children's nannies. All the lunar Taurean women to whom I have spoken tell me that they resented this, and also resented the associated implication that they were not as bright or as important as their brothers. They have all subsequently drifted towards less overtly feminine forms of work.

In common with the other earth signs of Capricorn and Virgo, Taureans of both sexes often have to put aside their dreams and ambitions for the sake of practicalities, and they may never bother to revive those dreams, which is rather a shame. One lady told me that she always dreamed of carrying the Olympic torch. Many of you dream about being a musician, dancer or singer, and with a bit of luck from elsewhere on your birthchart, you may just be able to make it into show business. Your practical side leads you to supply people with the things that they need, therefore you may deal in food, and furniture, household objects or even the things that help people make themselves and their homes attractive. Other typical Taurean trades are building, architecture, farming, market gardening, make-up artist, musician, artist and dancer. Because it's the Moon that we are dealing with here, you will not necessarily follow a Taurean trade at all but the need to be useful, get out and about and help to create something that is both durable and pleasing to the eye is a strong motivating force. You aren't drawn to speculative ventures which is just as well, because you are neither a lucky gambler nor particularly good at handling business crises. You aren't keen on sending memos or making up office reports - for one thing, you hate anything to be too cut and dried – but if you have to produce these, you will do them thoroughly.

You finish practically everything that you start and you can deal with details without becoming bored. Your persistence makes you good in the field of sales, and your creative flair can lead to a career in marketing (especially luxury products). A lot of this depends upon the rest of the chart, as a touch of Pisces, Aquarius or Sagittarius would add the ingredient of imagination. You hate to be rushed, and you can cope with anything when left to work at your own pace.

Parents and Background

According to most astrology books you should have enjoyed a happy and peaceful childhood, but my experience as an astrologer tells me that this is not so. Whenever the Moon is in a fixed sign there is at least one parent who has a bullying or intransigent attitude or who may also take advantage of the subject. This may be due to the fact that the parent has had a hard life and has subsequently developed an unsympathetic outlook. This leads to a hidden fear of parental disapproval then can develop into a fear of authority figures or an approval-seeking attitude.

It seems that one of your parents grew up in deprived circumstances, which may have been due to poverty and lack of opportunities, although a shortage of love might apply too. This parent is left with the feeling that things are safer than people and that one must obtain goods and money in order to survive. Therefore you may have grown up in a home where your practical needs were supplied but where real care, consideration and love was missing. You may have had a strong mother and a weak or ailing father.

Health

Insofar as the Moon influences health on a birthchart, an afflicted Moon in Taurus would bring problems in the area of the lower jaw, ears, throat, voice and tonsils. There may be thyroid problems and possibly diabetes. You may have that famous Taurean tendency to gain weight, but this will be mitigated if there is a lot of air on your chart. Some of you love food too much, while others can live without much food, but tend to drink too much.

Additional Information
Sometimes these people get a bee in their bonnet that makes them focus on one thing at the expense of everything else. I have known women with this placement who fall for a married man and then wait years for him to leave the wife, even though it's patently obvious to everyone else that this is never going to happen. I have known others who are mad keen on some sport or interest, to the point where it absorbs all their money and spare time. There are others who hate a particular race or group of people for no logical reason.

On a lighter note, lunar Taureans are always nicely dressed. Not outrageously, like some solar Taureans, but well turned out on all occasions.

They love going to the sales and picking up a bargain, and females really do know how to look good without breaking the bank. They enjoy gardening, and many grow vegetables and salad for their family.

Moon in Taurus Celebrities	
Joe Biden	Bob Dylan
Elton John	Monica Lewinsky
Meryl Streep	Dionne Warwick

Moon in Gemini

Ruled by Mercury

When they got there, the West Wind asked him if he could tell her the way to the castle that lay East of the Sun and West of the Moon.
FROM A BOOK OF OLD NORSE LEGENDS

The sign of Gemini is masculine, positive, airy and mutable, while the Moon, through its association with Cancer, is feminine, negative, watery and cardinal. The Moon is not really comfortable in this sign, and this may lead to some conflict within the personality. The instability of Gemini plus the fluctuating nature of the Moon could make your emotions a little too changeable and your nerves jumpy. If you have something steady, such as Leo or Taurus as your Sun or Ascendant, then the Gemini nervousness will be confined to bouts of irritability. Your health is not particularly good, but you try to ignore bouts of illness and you hardly ever take time off work to recover or recuperate.

The mutability of this sign makes you interested in new people and places, and this may lead you into the kind of job where you continually come across new people or where you move around. You like to be in the swing of things and you hate to miss anything that is going on. Your private life is probably less changeable than your working life but you certainly have many friends and can often be found on the end of a phone somewhere.

Women with the Moon in Gemini like to go out to work and some have an underlying nature that is ambitious and rather calculating. Both sexes like the home to be clean and orderly, and many can make a nice home with very little money. Both sexes like to look nice, and feel confident if they go out knowing that they are well dressed. You have strong dress sense and a good eye for matching up an outfit, although your taste is formal rather than flashy. Your mind is very active and you like to keep up to date. You may have had very little formal education, but you will educate yourself by reading a great deal and perhaps by taking courses later in life. Your mind (unless Mercury is badly placed) is very quick and acute, and you have a fine, fast sense of humour and a gift for making amusing and witty comments. The reverse of this coin is that you may become sarcastic if irritated.

Lunar Geminians think fairly deeply and they are less likely to be content with surface knowledge than are Sun-in-Gemini subjects. In addition to this depth of thought, you also have a dustbin-like mind full of rag-tag bits of knowledge. Although chatty and superficially friendly, your strongest relationships are with your family and a few close friends. Your moods change quickly but you don't sulk, and you have no patience with those who do. Your attention span is strange, because people who moan about their problems or go on at length about their pet subject bore you, but an interesting book or TV programme will hold you riveted for ages. Your thought processes are logical and you learn in an orderly fashion, but you can blend this logical approach with instinctive or even psychic awareness if there is help from other areas of your birthchart.

There is a kind of Peter Pan aspect to this Moon position, which may also apply to the other air signs, Libra and Aquarius. Somehow, you never quite grow up and you can display quite babyish behaviour when away from the outside world. The reverse side of this coin is that you keep your youthful looks and a young outlook on life far longer than most. You have creative, artistic ability and you may paint, make ornaments or interesting clothes, or you may enjoy model-making or computer-aided design. Many of you are into music and you may play the guitar or even a banjo. Gemini rules the hands, so using them to play music or fix things is a common trait.

You learn to drive a car while you are in your teens, then you explore your own neighbourhood and start to travel the world as soon as you can. Cities appeal to you more than the countryside, and you particularly enjoy visiting interesting foreign cities. You are resourceful and you can usually find a way to solve practical problems.

Although not a social reformer, you hate racism and ill treatment towards those who can't stand up for themselves, and you may become involved in some form of politics, especially the kind that involves getting a fair deal for some underdog group of people. You may be very fond of animals and you may want to do something to help them as well.

As a parent you make quite sure that your own children are well treated, but you don't want to spend all your time looking after them, because you must do something to keep your brain active. Your worst fault is a certain inner coldness and a sharp and hurtful tongue, or a habit of switching off and even of disappearing for hours when others get you down. While you can work for the community or give practical help to those in need, in a personal sense, you can't cope with those who wish to lean on you or use you as a victim, so you can give the appearance of having very little depth of concern for others.

The Moon in Gemini doesn't make you flippant where relationships are concerned, so once you have made your choice of partner, you stick to them pretty well. Having said this, I have come across one or two folk with this Moon placement who stay free so that they can play the field. You rarely fall head over heels in love or become so obsessed with someone that you end up getting hurt – indeed, you go to great lengths to avoid getting yourself into an emotional mess. In some cases, lunar Geminians can appear to be caring and loving, while actually not feeling very much of anything. Most do have a heart and you try your best to make relationships work; this is particularly admirable, as you tend to choose difficult people to care about. You might be tempted to marry for money, but this wouldn't last, any more than marrying someone for their looks. It's intelligence that you value more than anything because you are a communicator, and if you can't bounce ideas off a partner and help them with theirs, there isn't much to glue you together.

Some of you delay marriage or parenthood until you feel that you are sufficiently mature, but when you do take the plunge, you are quite serious about it. You make a delightful parent; you never quite grow up yourself, so you relate easily to children. You will break the bank to provide them with a good education, and your children will never be short of books, materials or any other kind of mental stimulation. You try to remain close to your grandchildren too, because you value family life.

Oddly enough, you can suffer from depression at times, and you can become very downhearted. This is most likely due to overwork and exhaustion, because you have few reserves of energy to call on, and you have the habit of going beyond your limit if something needs doing. Prolonged stress, overwork and worry will make you ill. You might keep busy in order to hide a deep well of unspoken unhappiness.

You could attract (or choose) a weak, dependent partner, who would be drawn to your inner strength – remember Gemini is a positive masculine sign – but you are better off with one who can stand on his or her own feet. You may need to get in touch with your own feelings before being able to handle those of others. You could be a theoriser and, as far as emotions are concerned, you may prefer to read about, and to rationalise emotional matters, than to feel them. To some extent, this derives from a mistrust of the opposite sex and possibly a lack of sexual self-confidence. You don't like to be emotionally fenced in.

You don't suffer from jealousy if you see other people making a success of themselves and, like most of the lunar masculine signs, you measure your own successes against your achievements. Not being jealous or possessive yourself, you resent being on the receiving end of this behaviour by others. You are proud of your achievements and also proud of your family; you will encourage (perhaps push) your children educationally, and you will make sacrifices for them.

Sex has to start in your mind and if you aren't careful, it can stay there too, as you may be happier fantasising about sex than actually indulging in it. If you find a compatible partner who encourages you to relax, you can bring all that sexuality down from your mind, and then you could become the lover you always wanted to be. You are easily put off by coarseness. Your nerves are sensitive, therefore a quiet atmosphere, an amusing lover and a couple of drinks will work wonders. Oddly enough ,both solar and lunar Geminians are tactile. They enjoy hugging, touching and being touched as long as they are not smothered or held too close. The main Gemini problem is a tendency to moan, groan and grizzle!

Attitude to Career

The position of the Moon will not indicate a specific career, but will show inner motivations. People, mental activity, words and travel are essential to your working life. You may work in telephone communications, marketing or sales. Writing, especially journalism, may appeal; also all forms of teaching, possibly job training, sports or dancing. You are generally respected, both for what you know and for your pleasant way of handling people. You may work for the public good in general, as in banking or in the political arena.

Travel appeals to you, especially air travel, and many lunar Geminians work in the air force or the travel industry. You love driving and may be able to fly a plane as well. You have a quick grasp of new ideas and you communicate them well to others, so you are very good at handling people and you make a wonderful manager. You can be canny and crafty in business, and you love wheeling and dealing, but some of you may not always be a hundred per cent honest. You are at your best when teamed up

Moon in Gemini

with a practical partner. As this sign rules the hands and arms, you could be a super craftsman, printer, manicurist or even a palmist.

Oddly enough, religion and mysticism may interest you, but in a kind of one-step-removed fashion, as you are unlikely to take up a religious lifestyle yourself. You may enjoy the social side of a religious group rather more than the deeper elements of its philosophy. Another slightly odd thing about this Moon sign is an interest in military life or in history, and especially in military history. Some of you also like to read fairly bloodthirsty books as well.

Parents and Background

The chances are that you had one parent, probably your father, who tended to lay down the law or who was held up to you as a paragon of virtue. Your childhood home was probably filled with books and educational aids, and your parents will have been quite happy for you to have tuition in practically anything. There would have been stimulating conversation and interesting visitors in your home. You should have been born fairly easily and you may have been the youngest child in a small family or the only one of one sex among a family of the opposite one. There is some evidence of deep unhappiness in childhood and a sense of not fitting in, and this may have been within the family or at school. You may have been suffered racial or religious prejudice! You may have been compared to some other brother or sister or even to a dead parent and made to feel that you didn't measure up to them.

An unusual mother is indicated for you. She may be a career woman, highly intellectual or just plain eccentric! Your mother would have shown you, either by direct reference or by example, that women must be able to stand on their own two feet in life. This will influence females to follow a career and males to choose a career woman for your partner. Your mother may have been involved in charity work if she didn't have a career as such.

Health

Your lungs may be weak also there could be problems with your hands and arms. Some lunar Geminians suffer really horrendous accidents that affect their arms, hands, teeth and faces, leading to bones and features needing to be rebuilt! You can suffer allergies and may have asthma, eczema, rheumatism, migraine, psoriasis, ulcers, colitis or some other autoimmune ailment. Your nerves may be your worst enemy. You need to find an outlet for your nervous energy, such as sports and fresh air pursuits, along with doing anything that makes you relax. People with the Moon in Gemini shouldn't smoke cigarettes or take too many over-the-counter pills.

Additional Information
Traditionally speaking, Gemini rules siblings, so you probably have brothers, sisters, cousins, step or half brothers and sisters, other relatives of around your own age, or friends about whom you care very much. You make the effort to keep in touch.

According to tradition, you probably work fairly near to where you live, so you make lots of short journeys back and forth. You like to have goods delivered to your home, so you shop online quite a bit, and you love receiving mail. You also prefer to live near shops, perhaps in the centre of a city so that you are at the heart of everything that is going on. Although not a great drinker, you like to visit the pub to meet up with your friends and catch up on the local news.

Lunar Geminis are not stupid about money, so you probably have a savings plan in place and you don't get into debt the way that solar Geminis can. You like nice things, but you will wait until you can afford them.

The worst problem with Geminians is that they can moan, whine and go on and on about something that has annoyed or upset them.

You like to dress well and always look good, but you aren't extravagant when it comes to spending money on clothes.

You may travel a lot and have good friendships with foreigners. You may even marry a foreigner and have strong connections with your partner's home country and family; you may even emigrate after marrying a foreigner.

Moon in Gemini Celebrities	
Noel Coward	Edwina Currie
Kirk Douglas	Goldie Hawn
Barack Obama	Claudia Schiffer

Moon in Cancer

Ruled by the Moon
(The Moon's dignity)

It was the lovely moon - she lifted
Slowly her white brow among
Bronze cloud-waves that ebbed and drifted
Faintly, faintlier afar.
IT WAS THE LOVELY MOON, BY JOHN FREEMAN (1880-1929)

The sign of Cancer is feminine, negative, watery and cardinal. The Moon rules this sign, so it's quite at home here. Like those with the Sun in Cancer, your reactions to people and places are very strong, and this is taken into account in any decisions that you make. Your feelings are very sensitive, which means that you link very quickly to other people's feelings, to the point where you can feel if they are unhappy or in pain. You can sense the atmosphere as soon as you walk into a room.

Unless there are conflicting forces on your chart, you should have the Cancerian ability to listen sympathetically. In business, your intuition usually gives you an instinctive feel when a deal is about to go wrong - or go right!

The negative side of this coin is over-sensitivity. Like the other feminine water signs of Pisces and Scorpio, you can take things too personally, brood, sulk, lose your temper and shut yourself off. Some of you appear very even-tempered, but hurts and worries tend to go inwards and these can make you ill. They say that Cancerian moods change with each tide, and in some cases this is true. Moodiness, sulking and sometimes sheer nastiness from being in the wrong frame of mind are your worst faults.

Women with the Moon in any of the water signs are susceptible to period problems and hormone-related mood swings. The very worst aspect of this placement is that you may indulge in emotional blackmail by shutting off from others and sending out disapproving vibes. On a very bad day, you can be critical and faultfinding. This kind of behaviour is rare because you are much too kind and thoughtful a person, far too receptive to the needs of others to be this unpleasant for long. You are one of the most generous people in the zodiac, and you put yourself out to help others even when you are hardly in a position to help yourself. You don't feel threatened by the success of others, although you would like to have a bit of it for yourself as well.

You are able to adjust yourself to your surroundings and fit in fairly well with other people. You may complain about the situation you find yourself in but you will make the best of it, and will often find a way of changing and manipulating the circumstances to suit yourself. Your instinctive reaction is to put things right and create a better atmosphere. The ability to initiate projects and to see them through depends upon a variety of factors in your birthchart, but your instinctive reaction is to set things in motion and then encourage others (or find someone else) to see them through. If you are really stuck for an answer to your problems you can always look a bit pathetic in the hope that someone will take pity on you and help you.

You are considerate towards others, especially your family, and it would be almost impossible for you to desert them, and you would only do so under extreme duress. I think that you would try several times to put things right before giving up on them for good. You have patience with children and young people and you are probably very fond of animals. You aren't entirely selfless, it's only when you are settled and satisfied that you can relax and give sustenance to others. Your greatest requirements are for emotional security, such as a partner you can rely upon, harmony in the home and friends who help build up your confidence. Lack of confidence in your own abilities and feelings of relative worthlessness are your worst enemy and it's these that can make you feel jealous and resentful towards others, often without justification.

You like children and enjoy having them around you, not only being good to your own children but kind to other people's as well. However, you greatly resent having other people's children being dumped on you. Your gentle inner nature responds to the vulnerability and honesty of children.

You may remain close to your own children after they have grown up, but in some cases, lunar Cancerians want them to be independent but can't get rid of them! Alternatively, your own mother may cling to you after you have grown up! It may be difficult for you to forget your own childhood as you have a slight tendency to live in the past.

There is a tendency for you to attract parasitic people who hang themselves on to you and make demands. This is most evident among those of you who have your Sun or ascendant in a steady earth sign or an enthusiastic fire sign. Fortunately for you, you are astute enough to be able to spot these people before they get their claws into you, and to off-load them quickly. When you care for someone, you do all you can for them and you can become worked up on their behalf if you think that someone else is hurting them. Unfortunately, unless there is a lot of strength elsewhere on the chart, you won't actually do anything practical to help.

You might be sensual but you aren't greedy. You don't have a large appetite for food; you prefer small amounts that are well cooked and presented. Your sensitive stomach may reject spicy foods. (One Moon in Cancer friend tells me that he cannot eat raw onions.) You probably enjoy good wines but there is no evidence of this Moon placement leading to overindulgence. You may be a good cook yourself but this will depend upon other factors in your birthchart, along with your lifestyle. You can put up with any amount of chaos around you at work but you need peace and harmony in the home. Your senses are all strong, especially that of hearing, you really hate discordant noises. The senses of smell, touch and taste are well developed and you could be long-sighted. Sexually, you absolutely come into your own. The whole concept of an experience that involves all the senses plus love and affection is just too much for you to miss. Being basically kind and thoughtful, you should be a considerate - even a practised - lover. The fact that you are the faithful type works against variety in sexual experiences.

You may have the Cancerian trait of collecting things, ranging from valuable antiques to junk. You enjoy the company of new people and visiting new places but also you have an attachment to old ones. You have a habit of observing the behaviour of others, and in a way this is a form of self-protection. Being emotionally cautious, you are slow to fall in love and open yourself to the prospect of hurt and rejection. Others may fall in love with you because you listen to them and you understand their problems. If the one who falls for your sympathetic attitude expects you to continue to be an unpaid psychotherapist for them, they will be disappointed.

Being cautious, you may react in a slightly hostile manner towards new people. If you have something very outgoing, such as Sagittarius, on your Ascendant, there will be an open, confident attitude, however the caution will still be there hidden away underneath. You are basically honest and you can be trusted in any kind of confidential situation and with any kind of information. However, one less pleasant attribute is that you can occasionally display a touch of smarminess, flattering those whom you wish to get round or to make capital out of. This is a successful ploy in most cases, but it won't wash when dealing with people who are particularly perceptive.

You can be slightly mean in small matters, as is the case with all who have the Moon in water signs. Both solar and lunar Cancerians find it hard to get rid of anything. Once in a while you decide to turn out the cupboards, only to put almost everything back again, because there is too much sentiment attached to your junk for you to be able to throw it out. You need a base to operate from, therefore, not only your home but also your office are important to you and you don't want these to be disturbed or cleaned-up too much. You aren't over-fussy about the appearance of your home, and you can make a home anywhere.

You have courage in odd places where others lack it. For instance, you are adept at asking questions, probing, finding out what makes people tick and keeping up to date with the local gossip. You aren't above giving a gentle form of third degree. Lunar Cancerians have a long memory, therefore, you can hold a grudge if you are hurt, but you also remember those who have helped you. Being rather sentimental, you remember birthdays and anniversaries and you feel peeved if yours are forgotten. Your intuition is very strong and this may just be a helpful tool in everyday life, but you can also be drawn towards psychic work. Because you can be trusted with secrets, you could work as a psychic consultant of some kind.

You like the countryside and really love the sea. If a Cancerian Moon is very prominent in your birthchart, you could choose a job on or near the sea. Another of your interests is the past, so you may study history or collect things that have been around for a long time.

Attitude to Career

The Moon will show how you approach the idea of work rather than give specific career guidance. Unless there are other factors on the chart, you will be an efficient and conscientious worker but you need variety in your work or you will become bored and walk away from a job. Your inner nature leads you towards the kind of job where you can be helpful. Many lunar Cancerians work in hospitals, schools and with the elderly, while others are attracted to the world of business. Some of you are drawn towards the field of antiques, rare coins, stately homes or genealogy. Insurance may attract you because of its protective image, and some may work in estate agencies. Many of you retrain later in life if your original career ceases to be viable or if you find that you lack certain qualifications that would help you to get up the career ladder. Many of you run small businesses, shops and small agencies. Being good with your hands, you could work as a plumber, carpenter etc. Lunar Cancerians also make excellent teachers.

Your sensitivity means that you could make a good salesman or business executive, personnel manager or counsellor. Politics may appeal, as could accountancy, and you have a theatrical side to your nature and might be drawn to the world of entertainment or sports. The drawback to this is the irregularity of work and the general uncertainty of this field; being a worrier, you would probably be happier in a secure job while singing and dancing during your time off. You would be a good partner for a very go-ahead person, as you don't seek to hold others back.

Parents and Background

The Moon in this position suggests that your mother gave birth to you easily. The parental home will have been comfortable and the relationships there will have been reasonable, at least on the surface. The chances are that you are the eldest child in your family (although this is much more likely if the Ascendant were in Cancer). The background and history of your family is important to you and you may try to trace your family tree. The family may travel a bit and you would have travelled with them, but you wouldn't have moved house a lot during childhood.

Your mother may have been traditional and ordinary rather than eccentric. You would be close to your mother throughout life, you may love her very deeply and be really close to her. You could be best friends as well as mother and child.

Health

This Moon position suggests strong health with good recovery from illness and operations. The weak areas are the chest, lungs, breasts and stomach. There is no reason to suppose that you are any more susceptible to the dreaded disease of cancer itself than any other sign.

Additional Information

There may be a flare for foreign languages, or a connection to those who spoke different languages. Religion or mysticism can play a part, either because the subject becomes interested in these things or because they marry someone of a different religion or due to the family background. They may decide to be different from their parents, espousing a different religion to theirs.

MOON IN CANCER CELEBRITIES	
Janis Joplin	Liza Minelli
Sharon Osbourne	Franklin D Roosevelt
Paul Simon	Tatum O'Neal

Moon in Leo

Ruled by the Sun
*Or when the moon was overhead,
Came two young lovers lately wed;
I am half sick of shadows said
The lady of Shallot*
BY ALFRED LORD TENNYSON

The sign of Leo is masculine, positive, fiery and fixed, while the Moon, through its associations with the sign of Cancer, is feminine, negative, watery and cardinal. At first sight, it doesn't look as if the Moon would be very comfortable in Leo, but in many ways it is. For the sake of convenience, astrologers call all the bodies in the Solar system planets, but the Sun is a small star whilst the Moon is a satellite of the Earth. These two objects dominate our view of the sky and their movements dominate the lives of every being on the face of the Earth.

The main differences between the Sun and the Moon from an astrologer's point of view are in the attitudes to relationships, especially inter-generational relationships. The power of the Sun seems to dominate the Moon, permeating the deepest layers of the personality with Leonine characteristics that bubble their way up to the surface. If you have this Moon placement you are basically kind, generous and honourable with an instinctive need to encourage others. There is a real touch of Leo nobility deep down inside of you. It's worth remembering that many members of the royal family have the Moon in Leo. Being naturally dignified, you are far too proud to scrounge off others. Your need to appear honest and honourable may not reflect reality; but if you are caught out in a cowardly or underhanded act or if it becomes obvious that you harbour jealous feelings, you can react in an angry and aggressive manner. You can get on your high horse if your dignity is pricked. The fixity of the sign gives you the determination to see things through and to finish everything that you start. It's possible that you may dig your heels in too much and try to lay the law down to others. You could be stubborn and unbending at times.

You sometimes appear to behave in a distant and superior manner, this is your shield when you are in unfamiliar situations. When hurt, you retreat into something that you see as dignified silence and others see as the sulks; however, under normal circumstances you are cheerful, friendly and open. You occasionally have doubts about your own self-worth, but also occasional feelings of intense superiority. The emotions are always held under control when the Moon is in a fixed sign, but they may break out strongly from time to time. You could become quite aggressive if pushed, or if you are on the receiving end of aggression from others. If others hurt you, it makes you suffer from jealousy, anger and resentment.

Lunar Leos can be surprisingly self-sacrificing towards loved ones but heaven help them if the loved one doesn't appreciate their sacrifices. You place the objects of your love on a pedestal and feel hurt when you discover that they are only human. Your intense feelings give you a longing for excitement, drama, romance and passion, and with a bit of luck you will find this within a steady relationship; but if not, you will look for romance, passion etc. elsewhere. You may even create tension within a relationship to keep it alive. You also need an exciting career, as you can put up with an insecure one but not a boring one. Too much contentment bores you.

Your mind is broad and you are unlikely to follow any of the more fanatical religious or political beliefs. You may have a religious and philosophical outlook that is different from that of your parents but this should not be a big problem in your life. Although not in any way bigoted, your opinions are formed early in life and you may find it hard to change your mind later.

The Moon is associated with the home, so yours will be attractive with an interesting sort of decor. You are very fussy about your own appearance and may even be vain (men with this Moon placement are actually worse than women). The one thing that is the bane of your life is your hair. You may consider this to be too thick, thin, wiry, curly or if male, too bald! You may be vain about your body and even your sexual performance. One lady who is married to a very nice Moon in Leo guy tells me that he doles out sex as if it were a treat! As a lover you could be bossy and demanding but you could equally be comfortable, relaxed and kind. Being romantic, you enjoy dining out, giving and receiving presents and remembering birthdays. You are fussy about your choice of partner, nothing less than the best will do for you. You have a strong sex drive but couldn't cope for long with a relationship based on sex alone. You need romance; passion and above all, you need love. Life without love, in all its applications would be too cold to contemplate.

You may feel a need to attach yourself to some source of power. You may work with powerful and successful people or even with large and powerful animals, but you might also be fascinated by the power of magic and the spiritual world. This would enable you to enjoy risk-taking at second hand. Your courage, fire and enthusiasm could lead you to learn how to wield power by copying powerful people who are around you.

You will do anything for those whom you love but you need your generosity of spirit to be appreciated. Being a fixed sign, you resist change and find it hard to admit defeat in any situation, therefore, you would find it difficult to cut your losses and start again. You can put up with the wrong job for far too long and also hang on to a rotten relationship long after the time has come to end it. You are possibly a little too good at maintaining the status quo, especially in emotional situations. You may be self-centred emotionally and possibly inclined to hang on to those you love - this applies to your children as well.

Unless there are very different characteristics in your Sun and Ascendant you are sociable and enjoy being entertained but being much shyer than the solar Leo, you can only entertain others in a quiet way. Sports and the company of young people appeal to you. You might become involved in some organisation like the Boy Scouts, Girl Guides, the Territorial Army or the Red Cross. Your fondness for looking and feeling good means that you don't only join a gym, you actually use it.

There is no need for you to be the centre of attention in the world outside, but you like to be in the centre of things within your own home. If you found yourself in the spotlight, you could cope with it but you don't seek it consciously. You like to know where the various members of your family are and to make sure that they are all right, you have an inner need to organise them and keep them on the right lines.

Your inner nature, unless you are feeling hurt, is playful, sunny and friendly which makes you popular in a quiet kind of way. You appreciate beauty, creativity and art and have an instinctive sense of style. You are proud of your loved ones and even of your friends, and you prefer not to be surrounded by dirty down-at-heel types. You never forget a hurt but your strong loyalty means that you remember those who help you too. You need to belong somewhere and you may be attached to a particular set of bricks and mortar or to an area of the country with which you feel a particular affinity. Needing space, you hate cramped surroundings; you love to get away into the countryside and to take your holidays in a warm and pleasant place. You need holidays and breaks because you tend to put a lot of effort into your job and into life itself. Your vitality is never drained for long as you have inner reserves of strength.

You make an excellent parent, often treating your children as young adults and always preserving their dignity. You don't seek to hang on to them when they grow up. You are able to teach and encourage them through play, but you may not be too patient with them at times; nevertheless, you can be relied on to give them a cuddle whenever they are down-hearted or ill.

Attitude to Career
The position of the Moon does not indicate any specific career, but will show your inner leanings and drives. Both solar and lunar Leo subjects learn more after leaving school than before, and you may become qualified for something long after leaving school. You lack confidence in your abilities, so achieving something of this kind can only help you. Even if you don't have much formal education, you understand people and learn well from life. You have an inner need to be in an executive position, and if your circumstances are against this, you could be self-employed, so that you are the king or queen of your own world.

You make a good employer, as you understand the need to preserve the dignity of others. You are career-minded and with your good concentration and good organisational skills, can climb the career ladder in a steady manner. Your ability to make the right impression could lead you to the fields of marketing, personnel work, the display of works of art or antiques. You could have big dreams but you may be too lazy to make them come true. You want to be at the top of your field but are strangely uncompetitive, being too self-centred to worry about the status of others; your own high standards give you enough to compete against.

You are good at calming people down and dealing with touchy situations. You may choose to work with troubled youngsters. Your attraction to glamour might interest you in some form of show business. Being drawn towards children and young people, you could be a teacher but you might prefer to be a nursery nurse or probation officer. Your love of the good things in life could make you a good restaurateur or hotelier but you might be best employed out in the front as the maitre-de, as under no circumstances would you want to be the one to do the cleaning and cooking. You are competent, efficient and capable as long as you are allowed to work at your own pace but you detest being hassled and put under pressure.

Parents and Background
There is probably something wrong here, and there are many possible scenarios. One possibility is that your father (or father figure) was autocratic, authoritarian or just unable to relate to children, so you probably got on much better with your mother. Your parents may have expected more from you than you were able to produce, especially if you happen to be shy and not outwardly successful or pushy. At the worst end of this spectrum you may have been afraid of your father or made to feel that you couldn't live up to some impossible image of perfection. He may have been a very successful man himself or he may have achieved a great deal while he was still young. You need parental love, encouragement and appreciation from at least one parent or from brothers and sisters. The background may have been traditional, even religious, involving rituals and certain kinds of behaviour.

Health
The Moon is not the only indicator of health problems on a chart, but it might point out any underlying chronic condition. There doesn't seem to be a real problem with this Moon placement, but Leo rules the spine and heart, so keeping your intake of food and drink down and taking exercise can only help, as would keeping the stress level down.

Additional Information
Childhood hurts linger in your mind and can never really be forgotten.

You dress in a formal but highly fashionable style, and you may spend a lot of money on designer clothes. Males with this Moon sign fuss and worry about losing their hair.

You might fall out with some members of your family and lose touch with them. It's possible for you to lose complete touch with your children due to a divorce situation.

You like high-status people, places and things, and you would find poverty a real drag.

Moon in Leo Celebrities	
Barbra Streisand	Clint Eastwood
Ringo Starr	Seve Ballesteros
Margaret Thatcher	Winston Churchill

Moon in Virgo

Ruled by Mercury
*Pale moon doth rain, red moon doth blow
White moon doth neither rain nor snow*
PROVERB

The sign of Virgo is feminine, negative, earthy and mutable, while the Moon (through its association with Cancer) is feminine, negative, watery and cardinal, so there is an uneasy alliance between the sign of Virgo and the energy of the Moon. You may find it very difficult to shape your world the way that you would like, it seems that the cardinality of the Moon (cardinality implies action) is halted in mutable, negative Virgo.

If you cannot make your job work for you, create the right kind of environment or find the right partner, you could retreat into fiddling about and fidgeting. You may never quite finish decorating your home, you may try out one partner after another or you could become your own worst enemy at work. If thwarted, you will develop a tendency to meddle, criticise, ruin, lose or destroy the very things that you most need. You could over-analyse yourself and everything around you then hide your fears and phobias under a layer of fussiness. Be careful not to fall prey to a psychological need to organise every detail, prepare for every eventuality so that you programme out not only life's unexpected problems and but also its pleasant surprises.

Virgo brings an inner need to serve people in a practical way, so you prefer to work in a field where you can be useful to others. You feel more comfortable in the workplace than in a social setting, especially if your talents are being used to the limit. Being dutiful and caring towards your family, you show your love for them by helping them in a practical way or by giving them material things, rather than by open displays of affection or even of verbal love. You are especially helpful and understanding if your loved ones or your friends are ill. You are reliable, businesslike and efficient in all that you do, and being loyal and trustworthy, you would never betray a confidence. Most lunar Virgoans are more alert in the morning than in the evening, and this also gives an impression of dutiful energy.

Your mind is very clear and logical, your thinking is usually realistic and you prefer to think before acting. Your imagination works best when harnessed to some kind of structure, such as, writing poetry, making a garden or computer-aided design. You enjoy debating when you are among people with whom you can relax, and you never swallow what you are told without verification. Be careful not to spend too much energy on details and miss the main point. Also, you should try not to let problems revolve round in your head growing out of all proportion. Some lunar Virgoans are vigorous social reformers, but others just talk about what should be done without doing much about it. You can take practical decisions almost instantly and will go anywhere at the drop of a hat; when decisions have an emotional content, this is not so easy. Oddly enough, although the mind is quick, your bodily movements may be slow. Female lunar Virgoans are good homemakers, often loving their homes, but they need an intellectual outlet and to work in an interesting job. Although your thought processes are logical, you can also be very psychic. There is an acceptable logic to psychic matters that you seem to grasp more easily than many other people. Religion may not interest you overmuch and blind faith is never acceptable to you.

Virgo being a mutable sign suggests that you can fit yourself in to almost any type of company. You are unlikely to be prejudiced about race, religion etc. because all people interest you. You are shy at first but very sociable when you feel that you can relax. Although hardly likely to be the life and soul of the party, and even less likely to get drunk and make a fool of yourself, you enjoy socialising, especially in the company of witty and interesting people.

I very much doubt whether you see money in terms of the power it may give you, and you have little desire to waste your hard-earned pennies on flashy things. Virgo as a sign is supposed to be careful with money, but it seems to polarise either way, with some of you being very careful indeed and others being happy to max out their credit cards.

Being an earth sign, gardening appeals to you, especially growing your own fruit and vegetables, along with filling the house and garden with sweet-smelling flowers. Your senses of taste and smell (and your stomach) are easily upset; therefore good, homegrown produce is a favourite with you. Reading and listening to music provide you with a passive form of escapism. One active form of escapism that is very popular among both solar and lunar Virgoans is acting, because this is where you can forget yourself for a while and take on a completely different personality. This gives you the opportunity of behaving outrageously without having to risk being taken seriously.

Relationships can be a minefield for you, because you tend to make yourself useful to your partner and then wonder why you are being used. In a way, the most successful relationship is with those who have important and interesting careers, where you can help to smooth their path for them. There must be a mental rapport between you and your partner, so shared interests or work in common will help. You are prepared to make an effort in a relationship. Some of you attach yourselves to a glamourous, glittering personality and enjoy being a part of their life while not having to suffer the embarrassment of taking centre stage yourself. Any relationship based solely on sex wouldn't hold you for long. You are easily embarrassed by the apparent ludicrousness of the sex act, and you find it hard to relinquish your dignity and make the necessary adjustment that enables you to surrender to your feelings.

A second problem is that you may be ashamed of your own capacity for passion, possibly due to early childhood influences and incidents. You may fill up your time with work in order to avoid dealing with the whole relating and sexual scene. Shyness doesn't help here, but most of this can be overcome if you find yourself a kind and encouraging partner. Coarseness puts you off immediately and criticism will squash you. However, Virgo is a very critical sign, so you must endeavour to avoid criticising others, even when you are angry.

If a relationship goes wrong, you can become desperate. You can be so insecure that you actually decide in advance that a relationship won't work out, and this becomes a self-fulfilling prophecy. On the other hand, you may go too far the other way - keeping your emotions on such a tight rein that you never allow yourself the luxury of love and romance, and this is a shame because you need a partner and a family.

You may find it hard to relate to your own children, so you may pay too much attention to their practical and educational needs and not enough to their need for love and affection. On the other hand, children maybe the ideal outlet for your love, giving you the opportunity to give and receive affection unreservedly. Teaching comes naturally to you, so you enjoy opening your children's minds to the world of books, museums, nature.

Given a secure and loving partnership, you will gain confidence and really begin to blossom. You have an acute sense of humour that so often is able to save you from much unhappiness. If you can find an intelligent partner to laugh with, then you are really made. You are loyal and you have high standards of behaviour, so with a bit of luck, you can be very happy. You need to be hugged and comforted, especially if things are not going well for you. You need validation that you are a worthy person, and a feeling of solidarity in your relationships that shows you that your family circle will stick together and stick up for each other against the world.

Attitude to Career

You have a creative side that can be expressed in sewing, carpentry, cooking or writing because you like problem solving and bringing together separate parts in order to make a whole. Skills such as typing, driving and accounting come easily to you. You make an exemplary office worker, being neat, efficient, quiet, clean, practical and helpful. If your Sun and Ascendant are in an outgoing sign, you may enjoy a life in a skilled branch of the armed forces because technical matters would hold no terrors for you. The downside is that you become bored once you have worked out how to do the job, and you can't cope with repetitive work. You need variety.

Lunar Virgoans make good nurses, doctors and dieticians, while some work in the field of disease prevention or medical research. You may be drawn to a career in teaching. Maths, scientific subjects or business studies suit you but languages may be a problem, because while you can learn and teach the grammar but you may be too inhibited to throw yourself into speaking.

It may be difficult for you to be a manager, because delegating requires confidence both in your own leadership qualities, along with confidence in others to do a good job. Your tendency to become critical may not do you any favours. You get angry when you see others displaying an attitude of uncaring inefficiency. You may not be overly ambitious, but you like to do things well and to be appreciated for it.

Parents and Background

At best, your childhood would have been a fairly cool affair, at worst, it may have had nightmarish qualities. "Nightmarish is just about right," said Pamela, an elegant, divorced systems analyst. "I used to study my father to judge which rules I should be playing by and just when I got the hang of the game, he changed the rules. I could never win, my place was always in the wrong".

There may have been a great emphasis on being on time for meals, washing behind your ears and doing your homework. You may have been compared to other children in the family or even at school and criticised for not being clever, pretty, tall, sporty etc. as them, or perhaps you were not born into the preferred gender. If you were a diligent child who was naturally tidy, quiet, organised and clever at school, you would have pleased your parents and therefore have had an easier time of it. You may have only been able to win their approval by achieving success in exams or winning medals at sports or dancing. Some of your self-esteem problems result from being afraid of your parents and finding them impossible to please. You may even have been a timid child whose boisterous parents valued boldness. You didn't need harsh discipline at home or at school as you were easily ashamed and embarrassed at the very thought of doing something wrong and you strove not to make mistakes.

There is always the possibility that the Moon's position reflects the mother's youth, so the interpretation could be an indication that your mother had a hard time while young, rather reflecting your own experiences.

Health

Both solar and lunar Virgoans are strong and healthy, but the nervous system is delicate. Ailments include migraine and asthma, allergies, skin conditions and stomach ulcers. Tension and overwork is your enemy, so you must take exercise in order to relax.

Additional Information

Virgo is an earth sign, and therefore both obstinate and determined, so you have an inner level of toughness that is not often obvious on the outside.

Some of you are very tidy while others are quite messy, but you know where to find things, and you resent other people trying to tidy up your stuff.

You have a good head for details, which could lead you into work that requires analysis and a good memory as well as being able to discriminate.

Many lunar Virgoans have secret love affairs that go on for years, or they have lovers who refuse to commit.

Moon in Virgo Celebrities	
Dustin Hoffman	John F Kennedy
Madonna	Joanna K Rowling
Gordon Ramsay	Robert Redford

Moon in Libra

Ruled by Venus
*The tide is full, the moon lies fair
Upon the straits; on the French coast the light
Gleams and is gone; the cliffs of England stand.*
DOVER BEACH
MATTHEW ARNOLD

The sign of Libra is masculine, positive, airy and cardinal, but that most feminine of planets, Venus, is its ruler, so Libra is already a mixed up sign, without adding the lunar equation to the pot! The Moon, through its association with the sign of Cancer, is feminine, negative, watery and also cardinal. The cardinality is the most important factor here because even if the Moon is not really at home in such a strong sign as Libra, its cardinality will give you the inner dynamism to put things into action, albeit slowly. Being an air sign, your thought processes are logical, and provided you have a fairly active Sun sign, you could achieve a high position in life.

Libra is a cardinal sign, which means that when you decide on a course of action or when you decide that you want something, very little stops you from getting there, so you never lose sight of your objectives, and you never give up on a goal. You are more ambitious than your outer manner may suggest. Your mind is fair and balanced and you hate any form of injustice, so some of you will take up a cause that champion the underdog. You object strongly to any form of racism. When others argue, you seek to be the peacemaker but you can argue like a Jesuit when the mood takes you. You're always open to new ideas but will not swallow what others tell you without proof.

Whenever the Moon is in a masculine sign, the subject is naturally competitive and a high climber, but is only really impressed by his own measurements of success. With the Moon in Libra, you could have a similar "what right do they think they have to tell me what to do!" attitude as you would expect from Moon in Aries. Although charming most of the time, you can be extremely sarcastic and hurtful when provoked.

You seem to need a touch of glamour in your life and could be drawn to work in some kind of glamourous or luxurious trade. You make sure that both your home and your working environment are comfortable and attractive with a pleasant peaceful atmosphere. You have no patience with ugliness in any form, and you loathe ugly or dirty people. Being fussy about your personal appearance you are also rather inclined to be vain about your own looks, and while you are young, your partners may be chosen for their looks rather than talent or personality.

Your nerves can sometimes let you down; therefore you need peace in the home environment. Both sexes of this Moon placement are good homemakers you're both attached to your own plot of land and house. You enjoy doing things around the home, but a life made up purely of housework would stifle you. Your good taste will ensure that your surroundings are always comfortable and elegant. Some subjects are musical or artistic, and you may have a nice speaking and singing voice. You certainly enjoy listening to music and you hate discordant noises. All your senses are strong but sight could probably be the strongest, because if something doesn't look right, you couldn't live with it.

Being an air sign, you need the stimulation of meeting new people and you are usually welcoming towards newcomers. Travel is liked, as long as you can do it in comfort, so you feel perfectly at home in the world's nicest hotels and watering places. Although you enjoy your own company from time to time, you really don't really want to live or work alone for long. There is a need to keep in touch with the world and to keep your mind stimulated with new people and up-to-date experiences. You enjoy being part of a group, and seem to need the approval of your peers but you wouldn't necessarily wish to lead the group. You prefer to be fairly near the top so that you can delegate the more distasteful chores to others.

You are excellent in a crisis, but unable to give sustained help, because you quickly become bored with other people's problems. You have no patience with fools, although you often hide your irritation under a layer of urbanity. Your mental responses are surprisingly fast and you can be quite calculating when necessary.

Your pet hates are loud discordant noises and, according to my lunar Libra friends, being travel-sick! Perhaps this is because you have delicate eyesight and hearing (through the reflected association with Aries). You like the sea and the countryside but are really a city person at heart, because you like to be where it's all going on. You may travel a lot for business and you certainly will do so for pleasure. With luck, you may have a holiday home in some exotic location.

You aren't always easy to live with, as you can be critical, fussy, demanding and occasionally downright childish. However, you need to love and be loved; you also need friendship with people of both sexes. Some of you are strong in business but weak and henpecked at home. You can be capable of using, even of manipulating others, but you need to be needed, therefore you also allow yourself to be used by those whom you love. As a young person you can be inconsistent in emotional relationships, wanting the challenge and excitement of new faces practically each week. You enjoy the opening phase of a romance more than the later stage of commitment, because you don't like to be emotionally fenced in.

You love children and you want emotional security, so sooner or later, you will settle down into domesticity. Even so you will always be a flirt! Apart from the need for an attractive partner, you need one you can take anywhere. Your partner should be the kind of person who can be relied upon to be the genial host or gracious hostess who will help out with the social side of your career. I have actually seen Moon in Libra subjects become ill because they were unhappy at work or home. Men with the Moon in Libra have a curious split in their personality which, on the one hand, gives them a somewhat macho image, while at the same time endowing them with an almost feminine gentleness, especially when it comes to caring for young children. There is no evidence of you being an animal lover, but you couldn't hurt an animal or see one hurt by others. Your gentle manner with those who are weaker than you adds to the attractiveness of your personality.

Lunar Librans are very clever with intricate machinery, and like the other air signs, they all seem to have a love affair with vehicles and with speed. You respect the dignity of others and treat them with tact and charm. Those of you who have a strong Sun sign may hide strong feelings and opinions under this charming exterior, but those who have an unassertive Sun sign may need to develop your own point of view and learn how to make a stand.

You could turn out to be one of the best lovers in the Zodiac! This, of course, depends upon other factors in your birthchart. Your sensual nature cannot be denied, and with a bit of luck you will find fulfilment within marriage, but if it doesn't work for you, you will move on and seek fulfilment elsewhere. You could actually relate well to a difficult partner who keeps you on your toes, so you may choose to live with someone unpredictable enough to give you a few lively arguments and passionate enough to satisfy your strong sexual needs.

Knowing instinctively when your partner is ill or unhappy, you rise to the occasion and do all that you can to make them feel better; you don't really like to see anyone downhearted. You are good at providing little treats but you can't always be relied on to remember anniversaries etc. this is because your giving is spontaneous rather than organised. Lunar Librans need to give and to receive affection, tenderness and sympathy. If you have the Sun or ascendant in fire signs, you could be a little too dependent on the approval of others. Some lunar Librans can be easily influenced and swayed by others but most of you have a mature outlook and can make up your own mind about life, most of you try to keep your emotions under control. You consider yourself to be cool and logical, but this may be something of an act, because your emotions and fears can be powerful, but you don't want to be controlled by them or for them to become obvious to others.

Attitude to Career

The position of the Moon alone is unlikely to suggest any specific type of career but it can show one's inner motivations. Firstly you will want a job which gives you scope to express your creativity and this may be in an artistic genre such as architecture or fashion. You are persuasive enough to make a good salesman, but unless there are strong factors elsewhere on the birthchart, you would not have the kind of sustained energy which selling requires. Public relations and marketing would be better as would being a buyer, due to you talent for selecting the right goods for the job.

The world of catering might appeal; certainly glamourous hotels and restaurants are your natural habitat. Being good at calming others and even better in a crisis, you could make a good negotiator. You have a talent for arbitration and your quick mind and sense of humour can be used to defuse potentially dangerous situations, therefore you might succeed as a union negotiator or as a particularly urbane politician. Personnel and recruitment are also possible career ideas.

You can appear to be lackadaisical while working furiously behind the scenes. You are a good listener, so long as the person who is doing the talking doesn't go on too long. You enjoy money for what it brings, and while you don't need to have power, you do need a largish income to really enjoy life; therefore you will aim for the top anyway. The only thing you really cannot do is rough and dirty work among coarse people. You get on well with workmates and colleagues. With your logical mind, you would make a good engineer. Driving and even flying come easily to you. Finally, you could earn a few pennies as a spare-time musician if needs be, and more than a few pennies as a professional sports person. You are naturally sporty and competitive, so you are probably good at a number of sports and games. You certainly enjoy watching these.

Parents and Background

There is some evidence from this Moon position that you were born easily. You may have had a father who pushed you educationally. This does not mean to say that you were unhappy as a child, you seem to have been loved and understood by your parents and even overindulged a little. Your charm, even as a baby, will have got you everywhere. Your mother was probably ambitious, clever or even eccentric, she may have forgotten to feed you or wash you on occasion but she never forgot to love you. The home was a stimulating place full of books, conversation and interesting visitors. This means you grew up without having to develop a suspicious attitude or a strong shell to hide behind. Nevertheless you are happier to be an adult – possibly because your schooldays were not a very happy time for you, maybe because schools and exams test what you know rather than the power of your personality.

Health

You are generally strong but may develop diabetes, cystitis or skin problems. You need to take exercise and keep your weight down as you gain it very quickly. You may eat too much rich food and you could definitely drink too much. Smoking is dangerous for you, as is working in a dusty environment, as you could develop chest problems, such as hay fever and farmer's lung. You may eventually suffer from arterial or arthritic problems.

Additional Material

You are lazy until something grips your interest, then you become self-motivated, which leads you to a high position in life. Your strange mix of laziness and hard work is due to the Moon's restless nature. You can be moody and sulky at times.

You will live and work in more than one country and while you love travel for business or pleasure, it has to be in comfort, so no camping for you!

You are independent and you solve your own problems. You can't stand clingy or self-pitying types.

Some Moon in Libra subjects make enormous sacrifices for their children, and even a divorced father will do his best to maintain a close relationship with his children.

Moon in Libra Celebrities	
George Bush Senior	Leonardo DiCaprio
Mel Gibson	Patti Hearst
Derek Jacobi	Sylvester Stallone

Moon in Scorpio

Ruled by Pluto and Mars
(The Moon's Fall)

*It's a very sobering feeling to be up in space
and realise that one's safety factor
was determined by the lowest bidder
on a government contract.*
ALAN SHEPARD

The sign of Scorpio is feminine, negative, watery and fixed whilst the Moon, through its association with the sign of Cancer, is feminine, negative, watery and cardinal. This would suggest that the Moon is comfortable in Scorpio but it must be remembered that this is the sign of the Moon's fall and therefore, it projects some of the most difficult aspects of both the sign and the planet. Scorpio's influence on the Moon adds intensity to the nature, also tenacity, capability and strong resistance to disease. It endows its natives with a strong instinct for survival along with an attraction to the more dangerous aspects of life. If this is your Moon placement, you have a tremendous ability to bounce back from illness, disappointment and even the door of death itself.

There are two quite separate needs within your personality and, bearing in mind that these needs hide under the more outward and obvious aspects of your nature, so this can make you very hard for others to understand. You seem to require challenge and excitement on one hand plus constancy and security on the other. You prefer to stay in a job with which you are familiar, occupy the same house for years and remain with the same partner even when the partnership is no longer viable, but the other side of you cries out for the brink, the edge, the place where you can test your strength. Some lunar Scorpions become involved with risky or even illegal business interests while others involve themselves in risky romances or strange sexual encounters. You seem to have the feeling that you are invincible, bombproof: and you are probably right! A constructive way of dealing with this might be to have an interesting and risky hobby, such as a part-time attachment to a paramedical or paramilitary organisation, so you can find yourself up against difficult situations without actually going out and looking for trouble. One lunar Scorpio friend of mine has a daughter who, after twice becoming involved with the shady side of the law, turned up at her house one day eight-and-half months pregnant!

Emotionally speaking, you have the ability to go at two speeds at once. When you meet a new attraction, you are cautious, watchful and apt to sit back and see what transpires, despite the fact that you are perfectly able to sum up anyone who is likely to become important to you within minutes of meeting them. You can be manipulative towards others, but often only for their own benefit. Like all Moon in water people, you can occasionally be emotionally wearing, but you hate others being emotionally demanding towards you. You are perfectly willing to come to the aid of someone who is in a state of crisis, but if they continue to demand help and support after the immediate problem is solved, you become bored with the whole thing. Moon in Scorpio subjects all have a built-in bullshit detector and therefore are quicker than most at spotting a phoney. Sometimes the emotional sufferings of others make you feel helpless and powerless. Your worst fault emotionally is a tendency to become jealous and possessive towards others.

Your home must be peaceful, clean and attractive. Your taste runs towards the antique rather than the modern and you will spend a considerable amount of time and money on furniture and fitments. You probably spend even more time and money on your garden because your love of beauty and strong sensuality draws you towards the beauty and scent of flowers. You enjoy the countryside and outdoor pursuits. The sea is attractive to you and you love to feel both its power and its peace. You are probably a good swimmer.

You keep a tight grip on your own emotions and you tend to bottle up anger and allow your feelings to seep inwards. This can result in angry outbursts that may affect your health. On those occasions when you become ill or suffer from some setback in life, your first reaction is anger. If you can't do something right away to solve the problem, you become silent, withdrawn and depressed. An athletic hobby would make a good outlet for your considerable energies. You can usually spot the feelings and motives of others quickly; you're able to find their weak spots and then use this information to help and encourage them or to wind them up and throw them off balance. You conceal your own feelings from others so that they don't get a chance to make use of you. Many of you hide your true feelings under an outwardly jolly manner.

Neither solar nor lunar Scorpios like officialdom, but you seem to have an uncanny knack of "working the system" when you need to. You are persistent in pursuit of a goal, and when faced with opposition you will either find a way around it or as a last resort, force your way through assertively. You rarely consider asking others for help, seeing that as an admission of weakness.

You enjoy family life and make a reliable parent as long as you can step back a little from your children and let them be themselves. Many of you seem to have difficult or sickly children to care for, but you handle these problems better than most. You must be careful neither to smother your children nor try to mould them too forcefully, and you should allow them to develop their own individual personalities. Many of you are wonderful with animals and you love them more than people, so you may be a vegetarian as a result of this. Alternatively, you may just be funny about food, possibly due to a weight problem, but possibly because there are only a few things that you really like to eat. You may also prefer to eat alone than in company.

If you find something that interests you, you can be a hard worker. You try to finish everything that you start, and you dislike being interrupted. Preferring to work slowly and thoroughly, you hate being rushed or placed under a lot of pressure. If there is a little help from the rest of the birthchart, you can be surprisingly artistic. Both solar and lunar Scorpios have a strong sense of structure, an eye for detail and a well-developed sense of touch. This leads to a natural ability to handle materials in a creative manner. You could make an excellent sculptor, potter, design engineer or design dressmaker. Other structured interests such as dancing and sport appeal to you.

Your sexual feelings are intense and, if not fully gratified, you can become extremely irritable. Your deepest need is for a stable relationship with a reliable person who has as high and interesting sexual drive as you have. If you do not find satisfaction within your marriage, you will look for it on the outside. Your compelling nature makes you a pretty exciting lover but you are also sensitive enough to tune in to the needs of your partner and give as much pleasure as you like to receive. Depending upon your mood at the time, you can be extremely receptive to the needs of those around you or surprisingly dense. This depends upon your mood and the state of your health at any one time. You mustn't try to reform your partners but learn to accept them as they are. It would be better if you could pour your energies and reforming drive into the outside world if you can.

You have strong intuitive and even psychic gifts and may be drawn to discover more about these aspects of life. Being mediumistic and clairvoyant, you may take a further interest by studying the occult in all its forms. You seek deeper meanings in everyday events and may consider them to be omens of some kind. Many of you feel that other people block your progress or even cause you to have bad luck instead of accepting that things do just go wrong from time to time. You may be superstitious and inwardly fearful when faced with new circumstances and unknown factors in your life. Many of you are drawn to the arts of witchcraft and magic that give you the opportunity of linking into group energies and earth energies. The Qabala is another potential interest. The healing and caring aspect of psychic work attracts you. You have the potential to change the world, by politics, science or even by means of war.

Attitude to Career
The position of the Moon in a birthchart does not show one's actual career but the inner motivations that may affect one's choice of job. You are a slow, methodical worker preferring to stick to a job that you are accustomed to. You have an exceptionally pleasant voice and manner which makes you a natural for dealing with people, and your enjoyment of new and interesting people both at work and in a social setting, gives you the potential to be a good salesman or woman. You can inspire others to get things moving, but you should strive for success yourself as you can become resentful of the success of others if you don't. You can learn from others and can encourage them and guide them, but you don't have enough patience to become a teacher. Medical matters appeal to you and the sight of blood does not easily upset you, your patience and eye for detail would make you a fine

surgeon, but psychiatry would also come naturally to you. Any work that brings you to the heart of matters is right for you, so you could become involved in the legal, forensic or political fields. In business you can make spectacular gains and even more spectacular losses. Many lunar Scorpios love the sea and can make their living on it as sailors, fishermen or swimming and diving experts and also, of course, in the navy. A life in the armed services appeals to many of you, as it requires the kind of skills and dedication that come so easily to you.

Parents and Background

Many lunar Scorpios are born into an inconvenient situation and are adopted soon after birth. On the other hand, some of you are born to families who already have a number of children and don't want any more. There is no doubt that you are on a different wavelength (possibly even a different planet) to that of your parents, and you will have been constantly misunderstood as a child. Your experience may have been poor because you were not really the type of child that they were hoping for or because you were compared unfavourably to another child in the family. I've come across two lunar Scorpios who had clever older brothers who were the favoured ones. There doesn't seem to be any real problem at school.

Many lunar Scorpios love their somewhat inadequate parents very much and take a really caring if rather dutiful attitude to them later in their lives.

One peculiarity associated with either the Sun or the Moon in Scorpio is there could be a death in the family at the time of the subject's birth ,or soon after.

Health

Although usually very fit you can worry over your health. Your weak spots are your arteries and veins and you could suffer from high blood pressure later in life. You may suffer from headaches and migraine, or allergies such as hay fever. The main problem seems to be in the reproductive organs.

Additional Material

You are highly intelligent but you are probably happiest when helping people or caring for animals. You could make a living as a psychic medium or healer.

Many of you care for a partner whose health is poor or relatives or children who are mentally or physically handicapped.

You are outraged by injustice.

Moon in Scorpio Celebrities	
Dwight D Eisenhower	Bette Midler
Bob Monkhouse	Katie Price (Jordan)
Steven Spielberg	Elizabeth Taylor

Moon in Sagittarius

Ruled by Jupiter

*I have never met a man so ignorant
that I couldn't learn something from him.*
GALILEO GALILEI

The sign of Sagittarius is masculine, positive, fiery and mutable, while the Moon, through its association with the sign of Cancer, is feminine, negative, watery and cardinal. Neither the planet nor the sign have anything in common with one another, therefore each will work against the other in some way. Problems that result from this will be felt in the area of your emotions and in your relationships with others.

You probably didn't receive much physical affection from your parents, especially your mother, perhaps because they weren't the kind who went in for touching and cuddling, or because you yourself pushed them away. It's possible that your parents had to work hard and didn't have much time to spare for you. Being unaccustomed to touching or being touched by others, may make you in turn shrink back from being touched by others when you become an adult. However, any physical problems that you may experience are more than made up for by the excellence of your mind. Everything interests you but you accept nothing at face value. You enjoy reading and you enjoy television programmes that have something to say. Some of you are deeply philosophical in your manner of thinking. You may have been brought up in a religious family, rejected the ideas and found others later that suited you better.

You need personal freedom and independence, as you need to be in charge of your own life rather than being under someone else's thumb, and you must be able to come and go as you please. You cannot be cooped up anywhere, and you may even suffer from claustrophobia when travelling in a lift or in the back seat of a two-door car. New faces fascinate you and you need plenty of friends because you become bored if you have to spend every day in the same company. Sagittarius being a mutable sign means you can adapt to most situations and enjoy all kinds of people. You are broad-minded and never racist or bigoted.

Like most mutable sign subjects, you need to get away on your own from time to time in order to think and to recharge your emotional batteries. You have exceptionally clear vision and can see to the heart of a problem when others can only see muddle, and you are resourceful enough to solve most problems both for yourself and for others, although you do appreciate a helping hand when it's offered. You will help anybody who is in trouble but you can end up being used. You are sensitive to atmospheres and you can walk into a room and know right away if there has been an argument going on in there. You may over-react to people who show hostility towards you. Your temper is explosive and your tongue sharp and articulate; therefore you could make an unpleasant adversary. However, you don't hold a grudge and prefer to forget bad feelings and look towards the future with optimism.

The Moon is associated with the home and Sagittarius is a dextrous sign, therefore you should be good at do-it-yourself jobs and cooking. You don't like mess and dirt and cannot stand living in chaotic surroundings, as you need peace and calm in the home in order to rest your delicate nervous system. Your most important traits are your absolute honesty and your sense of humour. You can diffuse difficult situations with humour when necessary. You don't use honesty to hurt others, so you are perfectly happy to use little white lies for the sake of diplomacy, but you aren't a crook and you can be relied upon to do what you say you will.

You enjoy sports and you may be a good swimmer, and you are too active to spend your spare time sitting about so any form of sports or dancing would appeal to you, as this also brings out your competitive spirit. Although you may be a little on the shy side, you enjoy singing, music or artistic hobbies. Your active nature makes you choose work where you have the chance to move around and meet people and also where you are up on your feet rather than sitting about. Your pattern of working may alternate between manic activity and apparent laziness, because you aren't good at keeping to a regular routine.

If you have to leave your home for any reason, you would set about making another attractive place for yourself as soon as possible. Being attractive and rather vain about your appearance, you enjoy buying nice clothes and you may tend to spoil yourself while conveniently forgetting that there are bills to be paid. Your appearance and your body are very important to you, as activity is so much a part of your nature.

As with most of the mutable signs, there is a strange duality about you. You want something passionately and then go off it once you have got it. You need security but you also need freedom. This can make you appear irresponsible to others, but somehow you always find an answer and seem to be able to pull the irons out of the fire when things go wrong. You are no stranger to debts but you hate to be in debt. You can soon put other people's problems in perspective for them but you may be hopeless at sorting out your own muddles.

There is another split in your attitude to personal relationships, because you need and want to love and be loved, but you may find it hard to be faithful because there are so many interesting people out there. You could appear to promise much and not really deliver anything at all! You may actually prefer friendship to affairs anyway, and you certainly are an excellent and most reliable friend. You cannot cope with someone who lays the law down to you and under those circumstances, you assert your independence and probably walk away.

You are two sided in the world of work too. You are highly ambitious but not necessarily money-minded. You need money to pay the bills and to have money for fun, but not for power or to impress others. Women of this lunation like to control their own finances. You need to work at something that you enjoy and which keeps you in touch with people. You can appear lazy because you have a habit of preparing your work at home either before or after your normal working hours, thus hiding the actual amount of effort that you put in. Even if you love your job, you need to relax and socialise, and you aren't a workaholic. You are a well-rounded person.

Women of this particular sign can become wrapped up in causes, and this can bring problems on the domestic front as there will sometimes be too little time left for the family. Being slightly bossy, a woman with the Moon in Sagittarius would need a very understanding husband. She is normally wise enough to find the right one for herself, and if she doesn't do so the first time, she will try again later. Both sexes love children, but spending your days looking after small children wouldn't stimulate you enough mentally. Many of you are brilliant with older children and may involve yourself with the scout or guide movement or something similar. Lunar Sagittarians make excellent teachers.

Your sense of adventure means that you could take up anything from hang-gliding to mountain climbing and you enjoy every experience that comes along. This is the sign of the traveller, and the Moon being associated with travel (especially on or over water) means that you take every opportunity to travel at the drop of a hat. Desert and mountainous areas where you can stand tall and see for miles fascinate you.

Anyone choosing to live with you would find you a happy and optimistic partner, as long as you have the freedom to do your own thing. You cannot stand people who try to dominate you or control your actions, and neither could you live with a partner who whines and nags. You hate those who criticise you while considering themselves perfect.

Your intense need for freedom and independence means that you spend time away from the home, possibly travelling in connection with your work. You would be happy to be married to someone rather like yourself, as you wouldn't seek to tie your partner down. If you have an ambitious partner, you will help them to get ahead in their career. You are generous and kind, but your unpredictability can be hard to live with. You may choose a partner who is out of the traditional mould, for instance someone older or younger than yourself or of a different racial or religious background.

You may attract repellent people, drinkers or drug addicts and you can put up with their behaviour because somehow, you aren't as repelled by them as others are. It's hard to find someone who is right for you mentally, physically and spiritually, so friends tend to fill some of the gaps. I discovered while researching this book that lunar Sagittarians have many connections with mental illness, either through senile parents, a schizophrenic child or a depressive spouse. There are times when you are so busy trying to adapt to their unrealistic behaviour that you begin to wonder just who is the dotty one!

An alternative to choosing difficult people as lovers and partners is to take up humanitarian work on behalf of those who drink, take drugs, live on the streets and so on. This makes sense, as there is an inner need to help others and to do God's work. Another alternative is helping sick, injured or unwanted animals, and if there is at least one animal in need of a good home, it will find its way to you somehow or other.

As a parent you are proud of your offspring and will do all you can to help them get on in life. You respect their need for space and a separate identity and also their need for dignity. There is a possibility that you could live apart from them for some part of their childhood, either due to work that takes you away from home or as a result of divorce.

Many of you will have parents who were born in a different country from the one in which you live. This may, to some extent, explain some of the splits in your personality, as you may have been educated in a different manner from those around you. Your parents may have a different religion from those of their neighbours or they may have spoken a different language at home. One such person told me that her parents moved around Europe when she was a child, so she was always the new girl at a school where she either didn't speak the language, or spoke it with the wrong accent.

Attitude to Career

The position of the Moon on a birthchart does not show which career you choose but it can show your inner motivation. In the case of Sagittarius, your greatest need is for freedom of action and the ability to communicate with others, possibly on a rather large scale. You are a natural teacher and if you don't work directly in education you would still enjoy helping and guiding others and passing on the knowledge that you have accumulated over the years. Most of you are surprisingly modest about your work and your achievements and tend not to promote yourselves very well, therefore, it's only when one gets to know you better that we learn just how knowledgeable you actually are.

You would enjoy a job in broadcasting, publishing or even as an entertainer. Many of you are good actors and singers, but shyness may hold you back. You are adaptable enough to get on with anyone and to work anywhere, but you may start too many projects and then become worn out from trying to do them all at once. Your amazing memory and your sense of humour and timing could give you a successful career in comedy.

The travel trade would attract you, as you love to expand your horizons in a practical sense as well as in a mental one. Some of you can work on dicey projects that involve intuition and the ability to guess right. This could be something like the futures market on the stock exchange or some business connected with gambling. Being over-optimistic at times, this could occasionally run you into trouble. Whatever you do, and even if your own confidence deserts you at the wrong moment in your career, your great sense of humour will always see you through. Lunar Sagittarians are excellent salespeople as long as they believe in the product they are handling.

Parents and Background
In many cases, the relationship with your parents was good but distant, possibly because they were busy or because they didn't encourage closeness. "I just couldn't keep my parents' attention," says Joe. "My father led a busy life that took him travelling and my mother was always preoccupied with cronies at the church." You may replicate your parents' lack of closeness when it comes to your own children.

Health
You could suffer from some of the Sagittarian ailments of leg and hip problems, varicose veins, phlebitis, rheumatism and blood disorders.

Additional Information
Your pleasant appearance and friendly, open attitude makes you popular, as does your sense of humour.

You ensure that you have a nice home that is not built on a pile of debt. You may appear to have values that are more spiritual than material, but that isn't really true, as you appreciate the good things of life and want them for yourself, but you aren't afraid to work for them. Sadly, some of you can be stingy and penny pinching.

Not all of you travel that much in reality, so it may be your mind that does the travelling by being full of interesting bits of knowledge. You are bound to get a good education one way or another, either by doing well at school, going on to further or higher education later, and always by reading a great deal and by studying the many things that interest you.

A downside is that you can be self-indulgent, which means that you may escape into the world of drink and drugs or overeating perhaps, when you feel pressured.

You will very likely have luck in property dealings when buying, selling or inheriting property

Moon in Sagittarius Celebrities	
Simon Cowell	Danny DeVito
Charlie Sheen	Mary Shelley
Justin Timberlake	Oprah Winfrey

Moon in Capricorn

Ruled by Saturn
(The Moon's detriment)

*There are no secrets to success.
It is the result of preparation,
hard work and learning from failure.*
Colin Powell

The sign of Capricorn is feminine, negative, earthy and cardinal, while the Moon, through its association with the sign of Cancer, is feminine, negative, watery and cardinal. The planet and the sign are fairly compatible, but the Moon is said to be in its detriment in Capricorn because the sign is opposite the sign of Cancer, which is the Moon's natural home. This means that the emotional side of your life could be a little suppressed.

Whatever you appear to be on the outside, inwardly you are sensitive, vulnerable and shy, especially where your personal feelings are concerned. The earthiness of Capricorn endows practicality, so if you find that an idea works for you, you will use it, otherwise you will reject it. You are very shy when you are young but later in life you hide your lack of social confidence with a layer of polish. Nevertheless, inwardly you are rather deep and somewhat unfathomable. You resist serious illness and have, in addition to bodily strength, considerable strength of character. These strengths enable you to survive almost anything, plus giving you the kind of tenacity and determination that allows you to finish whatever you start. You rarely take time off from work, even when you're ill.

Many of you go into business for yourselves thereby giving yourself the opportunity to create something of your own which will stand the test of time. You learn self-discipline early in life and feel inwardly that life is a serious business. You have the feeling that you should work to build up your finances while you are young so that you can relax and enjoy the result later on. You will probably live to a ripe old age, so you are right to think like this. Another reason for self-employment is the fact that you enjoy being in a position of responsibility and you carry authority well without throwing your weight around.

Your careful attitude to money may simply ensure that you have a roof over your head and money in the bank, but it can also lead to stinginess or constant unnecessary worry about money. You aren't a great candidate for self-employment, as the income is too up and down for comfort, but you like doing your own thing, so you often end up with your own business, despite worrying about it all the time. One sensible thing that you do is to invest in property, and this can both be the property that you live in and property that you buy as an investment. At the very least, you probably have some bolthole that you can retreat to if a relationship fails.

You need security, because your idea of hell would be to be dependent upon others, and you hate the idea of being a burden or having to suffer the embarrassment of having to ask for help. You are resourceful and hard working but you could be a little scheming and just a touch dishonest when chasing a goal. Your serious nature is relieved by a delightfully dry and witty sense of humour. You don't make hurtful jokes about others but just see the world in an offbeat way, and those who share your sense of humour will find you very funny. You enjoy the company of humourous people too.

You learn well and may be academic but practical subjects really suit you best. You can think and plan on a large scale and in a structured manner, rules and methods come easily to you, whether they are mathematical, engineering, or the pattern made by a series of dance steps. You prefer not to gamble on life but to plan your course, moving forward and then consolidating your position. Although your values are material rather than spiritual, the most important aspect of your life is probably your relationship with your family. You are very caring and you take your responsibilities towards them very seriously. You are dependable and faithful in marriage and you will try to make almost any kind of situation work. Your work may occasionally come between you and your family but if they are ill, they get all of your attention immediately. Oddly enough you really enjoy hearing all the local gossip, and not just family gossip either, and you can really get your teeth into a nice juicy piece of scandal but you yourself would hate to be in the middle of it yourself!

As a parent, you are gentle and caring, and although you would be unlikely to join in rough games with your children, you would do your best to teach them and to open their eyes to the possibilities that life has to offer. You may be a little old-fashioned in your approach when they reach their teens but you will try to see things from their point of view. At least you would always be aware of your children's need to be treated with dignity.

You exert considerable control over your own inner nature in order to prevent your feelings from getting the better of you. Your somewhat formal manner protects your vulnerability; for example, it would be impossible to imagine you getting drunk and making an ass of yourself. It takes a lot to make you lose your temper but when you do so you can go over the top and cut your nose off to spite your face. You may expect too much from your friends, relatives and partners, and this means that you inevitably get let down and hurt. All those who have the Moon in cardinal signs like to get their own way, and you can be bossy; although you would argue that you only boss others around for their own good. The Moon in earth signs can make you stubborn and blinkered, which makes it hard for you to see someone else's point of view. If you allow your attitudes to become too entrenched, it will ruin your relationships and friendships and destroy your chances of happiness.

Making friends is a slow process, but you keep your friends for years. In a way, you are better able to adapt to new places than to new people and can fit in almost anywhere. Your pet hate is to be embarrassed and humiliated. For example, a spell in a hospital that is staffed by insensitive people would be dreadful for you. Another pet hate is coarseness or vulgarity of any kind. You have a love of beauty and grace in all things and a hatred of any kind of ugliness, from an ugly appearance to ugly behaviour. Being reserved, you don't readily reach out to touch people but you love to be held and touched by your partner and you love to cuddle children. Earth signs are sensuous, and this could show up in your case as a love of flowers, music or the seasons of the year. You may love art, music, design or literature but you can also be very heavily into spiritual matters. Many lunar Capricorns derive much benefit from meditations and from joining New Age interest groups, including those concerned with astrology.

You are kindly and helpful towards other people, especially in a work situation and you would make a good financial adviser or a good teacher on a small group basis. You need a strong and independent partner who can, to some extent, protect you. Your hidden sensitivity can give you nervous ailments and you can be a hypochondriac. You listen to any advice that is offered to you but in the end you prefer to make up your own mind.

Where sex is concerned you improve with age, and also with the overcoming of your shyness and inhibitions. You are fastidious and very particular both in your choice of partner and in your behaviour. One-night stands are not for you! The feeling of closeness while making love is as important to you as the act itself. You may choose to marry someone who is older than yourself but whoever you choose, whatever their age or appearance, you will feel protective and caring towards them. You even like to work with a partner so that you can share the same problems. One problem is that you either choose difficult people as partners or you nit-pick and cause arguments, so relationships may be a major problem area for you. You don't always realise what a strong personality you are or how much you seek to control others.

One relationship that you will always keep going if at all possible is the one you have with your parents. If a parent needs financial or practical help, they have only to call on you and you will be there, even if the parent is feckless or a loser, you will do all you can to help, and you will never stop doing so. You may resent this a little at times but your love for your parents is strong, so you don't really mind.

You need to get away from time to time, and you really appreciate a holiday. You may not be a footloose traveller, but you may travel quite a bit in connection with business. You aren't very experimental with foods, you don't have a large appetite, and. you may be a vegetarian. You enjoy eating well-cooked and presented foods in pleasant surroundings. You aren't much of a drinker, but you enjoy the little that you do drink. Comfort is a necessity for you when travelling, and you aren't likely to be found on a camping site.

Attitude to Career
The position of the Moon on a birthchart does not necessarily indicate your choice of career, but it can show your inner motivations. Lunar Capricorns

prefer to do something useful; this could be anything from structural engineering to making medical supplies. You may be happy to work in a large, international organisation that moves goods around the world. You have a good head for maths, and money matters come easily to you, so you could work in banking, the stock exchange, accountancy or insurance. The civil service and government departments are also good areas for you. You prefer being in a position of management. Computers hold no fears for you.

Travel and transport or working for a chain of shops are possibilities too. You can get everything done, but you need to do so at your own pace, and you get upset and disconcerted if someone starts to push or hassle you. Being thorough and efficient in all that you do, you become annoyed by petty inefficiencies in others, and you can get worked up when the bus is late or paperwork has not been properly done. You may be an early riser. Whatever you do, you are ambitious and will climb slowly towards the top of your career.

Parents and Background
There could have been some conflict between you and your father, and this may account for your slight air of watchfulness when around new people. A very frequent scenario with this Moon is poverty. There may have been too many other children in the family, or a parent may have had to struggle alone to bring you up. Your parents may have been slightly insensitive or critical of your schoolwork, or you may have had critical teachers who made you feel small. However, you were a quiet and obedient child, so you did well at school and gave the teachers no problems. Health problems may have made sports difficult. Many of you go on to further education, especially of a practical nature.

Health
Your weak spots are the bones, especially the knees; therefore you could have rheumatism later in life. Hearing problems are a possibility, especially tinnitus. You may have skin problems and you may be shortsighted. If life gets difficult, you will suffer from nerves. Generally speaking you should live a long and healthy, if rather hard-working life.

Additional Information
You are ambitious and you don't mind putting in the hours to achieve your goal. You like status and status symbols. You like to live in a nice area and

drive a nice car. You may join some prestigious club or group such as a golf club, but you probably won't become a committee busybody.

You may marry someone much older or younger than you are.

You have a good head for details, and when you add this to your good memory, you could become an expert in something like hallmarks, numismatics or antiques.

Moon in Capricorn Celebrities	
Johnny Depp	Michael Douglas
Elizabeth Montgomery	Julian Clary
Ozzy Osbourne	Jimmy Perry

Moon in Aquarius

Ruled by Uranus

*A Brand for a company is like
a reputation for a person.
You earn reputation by trying to
do hard things well.*

JEFF BEZOS

The sign of Aquarius is masculine, positive, airy and fixed, while the Moon, through its association with the sign of Cancer is feminine, negative, watery and cardinal. The power of the Moon is rather muted in this sign, the greatest effect being to reduce the feeling element from the emotions. Inwardly, you are detached, independent and rather cool. Although controlled and possibly a little bottled up at times, you like other people to show that they need and want you.

When meeting people for the first time, socially or at work, you are pleasant and affable if a little shy; meanwhile, you weigh people up in a slightly watchful manner.

You have a strong inner sense of self that allows you to take a calculated risk in a career or even in a relationship.

Although sensible, you aren't over-cautious; therefore you accept most of life's challenges, whether they put your finances or your feelings at risk.

This ability to inwardly weigh and measure confuses those who fall in love with you, because although you can discuss feelings in an articulate manner, one wonders just how much you really care.

Your inner nature is offbeat and you could find yourself travelling in a different direction to everyone else. Like your solar Aquarian cousins, you are educationally minded and will choose a career where you can stretch your mind and broaden the minds of others.

You are kind, helpful and humanitarian, but this goodness may be directed more towards the world in general than to those who are closest to you. Although helpful in practical ways, there could be an element of embarrassment and helplessness when faced by the sight of other people's emotional pain.

You fear that if you allow weak people to latch themselves on to you that they will drain your energies or worse still, bore the daylights out of you! Your general outlook is balanced, optimistic and cheerful, and to all except the most neurotic you would be a good friend.

Your mind is excellent, and whether you are educated and academic or shrewd and streetwise, your thinking processes are fast and your intuition is strong. You possess a dry and intelligent sense of humour. Your ideas are often excellent and you have the ability to put them into practice.

Being strongly independent, you prefer to cope alone with your own problems, however harrowing they may be, and you may reject outside help in case it makes you appear weak and incapable. One Moon in Aquarius friend of mind wouldn't allow anyone to go with him when he went into hospital for a major heart operation, and he only allowed his family to see him once he was better.

You don't like people who try to own you or manipulate you, although you can be adept at manipulating others. Another pet dislike is of being falsely accused - you are willing to admit to your own errors, but will not carry the can for others.

Your friendliness is universal and you wouldn't reject anyone due to colour, age, race or religion. Many lunar Aquarians belong to clubs and societies, and many of you enjoy sociable and charitable hobbies.

You can take any amount of chaos going on around you at work, but you need peace in your home, where you can be in control of your own environment. You enjoy visitors but you don't appreciate people who dump themselves upon you.

Many of you are clever at do-it-yourself, enjoying the challenge of working on your home and garden and often finding imaginative and original ways of solving practical problems, and you may be a very good cook. There is evidence that you wouldn't be so happy if the hobby was a particularly noisy one because you hate loud discordant noises.

Your memory may be strangely selective, easily recalling things you find interesting, but tuning out things that you consider irrelevant. You don't duck really important issues, as you have high standards of honesty and integrity.

You don't go in for petty jealousy and neither do you make mountains out of molehills. If your pride is hurt, you can be quite spiteful and very sarcastic, and you really do need a creative or useful outlet or you can become bored, gossipy or aloof. Some of you are lazy and easygoing while others can be truly very eccentric. Indeed, you consider that everyone is entitled to his or her own opinion but you don't have to take any notice of it, and anyway, you are never going to change your ways in the face of criticism.

In close personal relationships you are kind, pleasant, thoughtful and passionate, and you could even be rather romantic. Aquarius being a fixed sign suggests that you don't easily walk away from situations, so you may stay in the same house, the same job or the same relationship, even when it becomes clear that you should really move on.

However, if the day comes when you do move on, you can do so in a decisive manner, looking mentally forward rather than backward. You can wait years for the right person to come along, but if this paragon does not appear, you are happy just to have lots of friends. If you become bored with a partner, you may look outside the relationship for change and excitement.

If you fall in love with someone new while you are still married, and especially if you have children, then you will be terribly torn between the need to be loyal and the need to be with the one you want. However, your famous Aquarian detachment comes to your aid here and allows you to work out logically what would be for the best.

There is no doubt that you need an interesting and stimulating partner, along with shared interests and mutual respect, as without shared interests, the marriage can drift into failure and loss. Either sex can be strangely blind to the needs of your lover, and you may never really get to know your lover on a deep level. This lunation does produce amazingly sexy people, as your combination of action, imagination and stamina seems to bring something special to the act of love.

Your partners are chosen to some extent because they have the right appearance. Obesity turns you right off, as does dirt and mess.

The relationship between lunar Aquarian parents and their children is pretty good, as long as the child isn't the clingy, needy type. There is a natural sensitivity to young people and you offer help without making undue demands upon your children or smothering them. It's just possible that you could expect too much of a very timid child but for the most part you make a successful parent.

You are always ready to stump up cash for education or hobbies, but you might be a little absent-minded about some of the practical details, such as making sure that they have a clean shirt for school.

Needing a pleasant home and a nice garden, you have no special preference for the town or the country. I think you would make the best of it wherever you were, as long as you aren't isolated from people or fenced into a very small space.

Money is not your god, but you need to feel comfortable and you aren't afraid to work, so you put your back into ensuring a decent standard of living for yourself and your family.

Attitude to Career

The position of the Moon on a birthchart rarely determines one's actual career but can show one s inner motivations. You take work seriously and don't like chopping and changing jobs, preferring to find a career that you can settle into. You are interested in ideas and willing to learn; therefore you do well at school and continue to learn later on. Certainly, your parents encouraged you to progress.

Working with children might appeal to you and you have the patience to deal with difficult ones, so you might take up youth work. You take well to challenges and can ride out most problems without falling apart, therefore the armed services or police may appeal to you.

Your incisive mind may lead you into the legal sphere, or medicine, psychiatry or even astrology. You usually learn from your own mistakes and are fairly forgiving towards others for theirs, as long as the mistakes do not occur too frequently or are not too obviously stupid. You solve problems in an original way, but you must learn to keep lists, because your memory is actually a forgettery!

You seem to be happiest when working in large enterprises, so you may wind up in the civil service, a large commercial firm, a bank, the teaching profession or government.

Computers, maths and science are your forte, so you may find a job in some specialised area of programming. Some aspect of astronomy or space may interest you and it's possible that you will travel and work in space some time in the future. You are capable and inventive and will give the whole of your attention to the task in hand, therefore you can create some highly original and very workable methods of production, so designing comes easily to you.

You don't like being pressurised by others, preferring to work things out in your own way and to do things slowly and thoroughly.

Some of you enjoy being attached to some kind of glamourous or powerful enterprise where your own dynamism can come to the fore. Although ambitious while young, you are prepared to settle for something comfortable later in life. Most solar and lunar Aquarians have a need to do something worthwhile and to put something back into life.

Parents and Background
On the face of it, you had a good childhood, certainly your practical needs were attended to, and if you came from a background where there was little money to spare, your parents would have made sure that you had enough to eat and were dressed and equipped in a clean and decent manner.

Your mother may have been a busy career woman or she may have poured her energies into some personal interest. One lunar Aquarian friend of mine had parents who were actively involved in the church, but they didn't foist their beliefs onto the children.

Your parents discouraged you from making scenes or allowing your emotions to become a nuisance to others. It's possible that you were never really close to your parents or that you loved one and ignored the other.

Your parents probably took a reasonable view of your educational needs; they encouraged you to learn but didn't push you unduly. They may not have been so accommodating when it came to hobbies and interests, possible due to lack of money.

Health
You are basically very strong. Blood pressure could be a problem especially for women during pregnancy. Allergies such as hay fever, asthma, eczema, psoriasis and hives can occur, also migraine, menstrual problems in women, rheumatism and diabetes are possibilities. The weakest part of the body is the lower legs and ankles, which could

involve problems with veins, phlebitis and thrombosis, also leg ulcers later in life.

Additional Information

You can have a bee in your bonnet or some fixed idea of how things should be. For instance, some of you may be animal lovers who become incensed at those who hunt, while others may be so into green issues that you oppose road building and so on.

Some may have particular political views that take them well to the right or left, and they may sit-in at military bases and so on. Indeed, others may be so right wing that they are able to actually run the military base!

I have even known people of this Moon sign who are deeply into playing chess or bridge, so that all their spare time is taken up with this, to the detriment of other more practical matters.

You could be extremely good looking or unusual looking in some nice way. You certainly like to look nice and you spend a fair bit of money on your appearance, and you can be quite vain.

Many lunar Aquarians are sporty in a quiet way that doesn't involve heavy teamwork. Some enjoy fly-fishing, badminton, tennis, horse riding, ten-pin bowls or outdoor bowling and some play snooker.

Your love of independence means that many of you are self-employed and self-motivated; happily, you are also dexterous and clever in your line of work.

These people are unusual and interesting to be around, but despite their apparently kookiness. They have contrary natures, being sociable and having many friends, but also being independent loners who can take off at a moment's notice. They may appear quiet and even shy, but they have strong egos and determined and ambitious natures, and they can make a success of their wildest ideas. They enjoy being a bit different and want to be seen as unique. When hurt or criticised, they become detached, cool and distant and they hide their surprisingly sensitive natures from all but those friends or relatives who they trust absolutely. Some dampen feelings they dislike with alcohol.

I have noticed that these people enjoy the sound of their own voices, so they are talkers rather than listeners, and they take very little notice of what others have to say, unless it is useful to them. They have an idealistic streak and can be humanitarian, because relating with people at a distant in a semi-detached manner can be less frightening to them than close personal relationships.

Moon in Aquarius Celebrities	
Cary Grant	Larry Hagman
Sarah Palin	Princess Diana
Britney Spears	Denzel Washington

Moon in Pisces

Ruled by Neptune
I am the star that rises from the sea
The twilight sea.
I bring men dreams that rule their destiny.
I bring the dream-tides to the souls of men
From The Worship of Isis

The sign of Pisces is feminine, negative, watery and mutable while the Moon, through its association with the sign of Cancer, is feminine, negative, watery and cardinal. This would make the Moon appear comfortable in Pisces but to some extent the mutability of Pisces weakens the active, cardinal nature of the Moon. Pisces is an emotional water sign, so this person's feelings run deeply.

If this is your Moon position, you will spend some part of your life searching for answers to deep and indefinable questions. You will contemplate the meaning of life and the possibility of an after-life and you could even be drawn to a religious or quasi-religious way of living. Your energies to some extent will be directed towards trying to improve the quality of life for others and to introducing people around you to a gentle and healthy understanding of their minds, bodies and spirits. Life may disappoint you, as it may never match up to your idealistic dreams and indefinable yearnings. Yet, somehow, life must go on and you will probably wish to live it to the very full. Therefore a particularly Piscean form of practicality often seems to combine with your desire for perfection, and the requirements of the hereafter.

You can be surprisingly ambitious. This ambition may take the normal route of upward mobility in the working and the suburban community or it may take a totally private form. You could push yourself to improve your performance in a creative capacity. Either way, you have the long-term patience to achieve your goals. You also have the gift of creative visualisation. The only real drawback to you reaching your goals is your lack of confidence and your fear of making other people angry with you for competing with them. A sarcastic remark can wound deeply and it's never forgotten.

On a more mundane level, you can be sensitive to the needs of others and some of you are extremely kind and considerate. Some of you have to stop and analyse your feelings from time to time to ensure that they are your feelings and not those of the people around you. You should also note that it doesn't always do to rush in and smooth the path of others, as it might be better to allow them to solve their own problems from time to time. Not everybody will want your intervention - although, human nature being what it is, most people will take advantage of free help when given the chance. If you become a permanent listening ear for neurotic friends and relatives, you will become worn out, depressed and even physically ill. There are people who don't actually want their problems solved because this would stop them from attracting the attention and sympathy of others. You must make a special effort to avoid the truly mad, bad and sad, even if it means abandoning some of those who call themselves friends.

You have an inner streak of resilience and you can usually find a way round your own problems. If absolutely pressed, you can stand up for yourself very well and dish out a surprisingly devastating dose of criticism. People tend to forget that just because you are so ready to sympathise and to understand their needs, that you also see their faults and inner motivations. If you are wounded you withdraw into your shell but if the problem is too great, you can be very spiteful and destructive.

An unpleasant trait is stinginess and penny pinching in small ways, moaning about small expenses and some subjects are penny-wise and pound-foolish. You may be broke, but you usually manage to do the things you like doing.

Some lunar Pisceans are kind to everyone and generous to a silly degree, even to the point of taking in lame ducks and having the house full of relatives who take advantage of your good nature – and of the contents of your fridge! If you belong to this type, you won't tolerate injustice in any form, you value loyalty above all things and hate to let anyone down. Friendship is terribly important to you and you can be far too caring and giving towards those who you consider friends.

You are creative, many are artistic and you need to express this creativity somewhere in your daily life. You work at your own rather strange pace, often going at it like a dervish for a month at a time and then switching off for a week to recharge your batteries. Most of you enjoy some kind of sport. Swimming is probably high on your list, also dancing, tennis and walking the dog. Every lunar Piscean that I have come across is a naturally good dancer, and some become champion ballroom dancers.

Some will become serious athletes if there are competitive elements elsewhere on their chart. Those of you who have a very ordinary job will probably have a creative interest on the side. Some work in the psychic field or become involved in Wicca or traditional witchcraft and it's likely that the people at your normal place of work have no idea of this other interest. You may be superstitious and fearful of unexplainable dark forces that sometimes seem to gather around you. Even the most practical among you can feel patterns in events.

You aren't as changeable in your moods as most astrology books would suppose and when you get upset, the feelings go deep. You are able to hold a grudge forever but you are equally apt to remember those who stand by you in times of trouble. If someone hurts you gratuitously even in a minor way, you will never quite be able to trust or like them again. In some ways your apparent moodiness stems from your inability to get the whole of your life together at any one time. It seems that if your work is going well, your love life will be in a state of collapse and vice versa. If everything is going well, you can be discontented due to boredom!

Many of you work wholly or partly from home, and this can involve people coming to your home. The place is also permanently full of friends and neighbourhood children. Lunar and solar Pisceans are supposed to be loners but I have yet to see any evidence of that, as your phone and your doorbell are always ringing. Your home is attractive and comfortable but not over-decorated or cleaned to the point of sterility. You love warm colours, interesting textures, pictures, music and loads of books. There will be novels, books about the occult, history, psychology, health and magic on your shelves.

You can be so adept at hiding your inner nature that your kind heart might be buried under a shield of efficiency, toughness or even sarcasm. You are slow to reveal your own inner feelings and it takes some time for you to get to know and trust someone. Some lunar Pisceans even go through many years of marriage without their partner ever really being let into their innermost hearts. You can be a little manipulative at times, either to prevent yourself from hurt or in order to benefit those around you. When you are entirely comfortable with someone you can be surprisingly bossy in a rather mother hen way.

You probably make a mistake with the first marriage, but when you find the right partner, you are supportive and loving. You can live alone, but you far prefer to have someone to love. Not receiving the love and understanding that you need in childhood, you actively chase after it in adulthood. Some of you are so shy and repressed that you never get the love you want and then you retreat into a life of daydreams and illusions. Your powerful imagination is both your most valuable asset and your greatest weakness. If you can channel this into creative pursuits, spiritual development or work in the counselling field, you will be happier. Your greatest fault is of over-sensitivity to criticism and attacking those who you think might take it upon themselves to hurt you. This probably results from your low self-esteem.

You make an excellent parent because you understand the needs of children and are happy to spend time playing with them, and you respect the dignity of children. You could be so busy teaching them about the universe, the world around them and giving them all the love that they need that you overlook their need for clean shirts and breakfast cereal. Don't worry, they will survive your dottiness and love you all the more for it.

Although you are friendly and non-hostile in your approach to new people, if you really fancy someone, your first reaction may be to run in the opposite direction, because you fear rejection, ridicule and loss. You are afraid to become close to people, in case you learn to rely on them and then lose them again for some reason or other. Love relationships make you nervous because you are aware of your great need for emotional sustenance and of your vulnerability. Adolescent relating can be very painful, and although you eventually learn some protective techniques, you still fear rejection. Being incredibly romantic, you appreciate little presents, birthday cards, and candle-lit dinners and shared memories. You have a stock of romantic melodies and catch phrases that you link to your lover.

Your nerves are delicate and often over-stretched, so sex gives you a tremendous release of tension. There must be affection and fondness, if not outright adoration, for you to be able to really relax and enjoy yourself. You need affection and cuddles even more than you need sex, and you need to be able to have a laugh with your partner. Oddly enough, you don't much like to be touched by strangers, so you need to keep a little distance from them to protect your sensitive aura. Some of you escape into alcoholism or drug addiction or both, while others of you attract addicted partners who you try to reform. You can be too serious at times and you should let your friends encourage you to let your hair down and have some fun.

You like fresh air and the countryside, but not in cold weather. Finally, you need good clothes and you may be fussy about the shoes you wear.

Attitude to Career

The position of the Moon does not suggest any specific career but can show one's underlying motivations. You are creative, inventive and easily bored, therefore a routine job will not satisfy. Not having endless reserves of strength, you tend to work in fits and starts, so you need a job where you can work at your own pace. Many of you have an urge to do something useful, so you find work in hospitals or even in prisons. You can be found in the world of music, acting, dancing and art. Creative work obviously appeals; floristry and cookery are typical interests. glamourous work such as fashion interests you, as does the more up-market kind of public relations work. Many of you are skilled engineers, electricians, telephone engineers and precision sheet-metal workers, because the work is detailed, creative, requires problem-solving techniques and involves drawings.

I belong to an organisation called the British Astrological and Psychic Society and we have always had more than our fair share of lunar Pisceans involved in the society and particularly on the committee. Among the collective skills are astrologers, palmists, tarot readers, numerologists, clairvoyants, healers, complementary therapists, trance mediums, aura-readers, graphologists, sand-readers and much more. All lunar Pisceans are natural psychics and healers, and many are drawn to work in the field.

Parents and Background

You may have been born with difficulty and could have been the youngest child in the family or perhaps an only child. At least one of your parents was not particularly interested in having a child at that moment in time, possible due to having other problems to cope with. One way or another your childhood was rather lonely. Some of you felt yourself to be "different" in some way, possibly being the only artistic and sensitive child in a household full of rugged and practical people. Even with nothing tragic or "out of gear" in the childhood, there was a need to withdraw into your imagination, to get away and spend time on your own, reading, drawing and thinking.

You may have been badly bullied at school or badly treated by your family. Some of you will have grown up in a home or boarding school of some kind. You may have felt embarrassed by your appearance, thinking yourself too tall, short, fat, thin, etc. You found it hard to relate to your parents and may have been afraid of them or afraid of other people around you. There may have been an over-emphasis on a particular kind of moral or religious observance, or too much emphasis on passing exams. Your natural inclination was to please your parents and teachers but you may have found this impossible to achieve.

You developed a watchful approach to adults and learned how to gauge their moods and how best to please them. This could be carried into adult life making you adept at finding out just how to please people. You learned to turn yourself into a whole variety of things that you aren't in order to please others or to keep them off your back.

Adolescence is likely to have been a minefield as you learned to adapt to one person after another. Pisces is a sign associated with illusion, but you eventually learn to channel your illusions into artistic or creative work and you learn to find people to love and who love you back. Eventually, you become settled and less of a victim.

Health

You could have been weak as a child and you may have spent a good deal of time alone or in hospital due to illness. Later in life the legacies of your childhood have a habit of lingering on. Your energies are quickly depleted and your nerves are delicate. The traditional problem area for Pisces is the feet, also the lungs. Heart trouble is a possibility; also skin allergies, migraine or asthmatic problems. You may retain water or have blood disorders. You may need counselling and comforting at some point in your life if you are to stay balanced.

Additional Information

Both the Moon and Pisces are associated with the sea, rivers and lakes, so you may prefer to live by water. I have the Moon in Pisces, and at one point in my life, I lived on an island in the Thames; I now live a few hundred yards from a river and two miles from the sea. Pisceans also travel quite a lot, possibly due to having relatives in other countries, but also due to their work or just for the fun of it. You enjoy travelling.

Moon in Pisces Celebrities	
Hillary Clinton	Catherine Zeta Jones
Piers Morgan	Robert De Niro
Michelle Obama	Elvis Presley

Find Your Ascendant

Here are some useful ideas for finding your Ascendant (Rising Sign).

- Make a note of the exact place and time of your birth – or as near as you can get to the right time.
- Ask an astrologer to make up a birthchart for you, and note down a list of the planets' positions and houses for you. As long as the astrologer doesn't have to interpret the chart, the charge should be small.
- Get an astrology app for your phone or tablet.
- Currently, www.astrodienst.com is one example of a very good, all-round site that also offers basic free chart services.

Meanwhile, here is an easy Ascendant Finder to help you to find your Rising Sign, and even discover the houses that your natal Sun and Moon occupy. It isn't as accurate as a fully drawn natal chart, but it does cover most situations.

Speedy Ascendant Finder
Place your Sun in the house corresponding to your time of birth, and then add the sign of the Zodiac that lies on the cusp line (house division).

For example, if you were born at 2.30 am on the 14 April - which is during the sign of Aries - place your Sun in the 2 am to 4 am space, then write "Aries" on the 4 am line.

Place the remaining eleven signs of the Zodiac on the cusp lines around the chart in an anti-clockwise direction.

Place your Moon in the appropriate sign. This will give you your Rising sign and the house placements for your Sun and your Moon.

Find your Ascendant

1	Aries	♈
2	Taurus	♉
3	Gemini	♊
4	Cancer	♋
5	Leo	♌
6	Virgo	♍
7	Libra	♎
8	Scorpio	♏
9	Sagittarius	♐
10	Capricorn	♑
11	Aquarius	♒
12	Pisces	♓

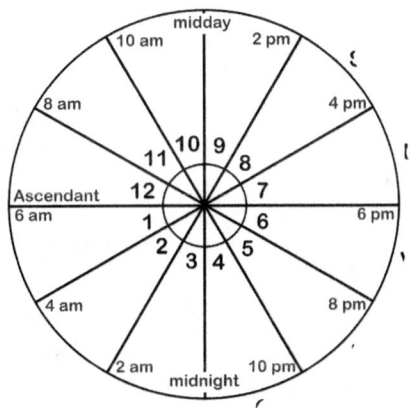

The Sun and Ascendant in your Horoscope

The Astrological Houses

House Systems

A house system is a way of dividing up the chart into twelve segments. There are various house systems that astrologers use, with Placidus being the most common in the UK. All but the Equal House system divide the chart into unequal segments. These systems are not easy for a beginner to use, so I always recommend the Equal House system to beginners.

N.B. Angular Houses are those that come immediately after the lines made by the Asc, IC, Dsc, and MC. Succedent Houses follow those, and the houses after those are called Cadent Houses.

First House

Angular
Similar to Aries
Ruled by Mars

This shows how you appear to others, how you present yourself and your normal manner of expressing yourself among people who are new to you, so this can be your outermost personality. Obviously, this shows the first impressions that you give, but also the first impressions that you receive, so it can show what initially attracts you in other people. This house represents your childhood experiences, the parental home and the attitudes to be found in it along with early school experiences, early actions and reactions. It shows how you tackle new ventures. As this also contains information about your physical body and health, it might have a bearing on your appearance but other factors, especially the Sun sign, must be taken into account here. Any planets found here are very important, especially in respect of one's early experience of life.

Second House
Succedent
Similar to Taurus
Ruled by Venus

This house concerns your own possessions and anything of value, also investments and the ability to earn money, along with personal funds and personal debts. Personal and moral values can show up here, also personal requirements such as freedom versus security or the need for personal fulfilment. To some extent, this concerns partners and relationships, especially where money and goods are involved. It symbolises, matters related to property, farming, building, gardening and the land, along with artistic and musical abilities or interests, if any. To some extent this rules the way you give and receive love, and your attitude to beauty. Along with the first house, this can relate to your image.

Third House
Cadent
Similar to Gemini
Ruled by Mercury

This rules the local environment, matters under negotiation and in some cases, papers to be signed. Messages, phone calls, correspondence of both a business and private nature. Local journeys, methods of transport. Brothers and sisters, neighbours, colleagues, sometimes nephews, nieces and friends. Business matters related to buying and selling. Education, training and retraining, foreign languages and writing of all kinds. Some sports and games. It shows the way you think.

Fourth House
Angular
Similar to Cancer
Ruled by the Moon

The home, property and premises of all kinds. Small businesses. Domestic life, roots and background, the basis from which you grew up into adulthood. The mother or any other person of either sex who nurtured you while you were young. The beginning and ending of life, also how you are viewed after your death. Your attitude towards family commitments. Security.

Fifth House
Succedent
Similar to Leo
Ruled by the Sun

Children, young people and their education, even pregnancy. Fun, holidays and leisure pursuits of all kinds. Games of chance, sports, dancing, singing, writing, entertainments and any aspirations to glamour or show business. Creativity and personal projects, even a business of one's own, as long as it offers the possibility of making a personal statement. Also publication, politics and social life - especially if influential. Traditional and religious attitudes, along with lovers, love affairs, fun and leisure pursuits.

Sixth House
Cadent
Similar to Virgo
Ruled by Mercury

Duties and day-to-day service to others; usually related to work, but includes those chores taking place in the home. Employers and employees, superiors and subordinates. Everything related to health, doctors, hospitals and hygiene. This could apply to the types of health problems you will encounter yourself or among your family. Your clothes and how you wear them. Details and analytical methods, meticulous work, analytical thinking and even changes in your way of thinking. Aunts and uncles. Healthy eating habits. Food and nutrition.

Seventh House
Angular
Similar to Libra
Ruled by Venus

Open partnerships and relationships, husband, wife, live-in lover. Open enemies. The giving and receiving of co-operation. Colleagues one is closely involved with, business partners. Work in a glamourous or attractive field. Creative and artistic endeavours that are done in partnership or a small group. Attraction to places, things and people, therefore, to some extent even sexual attitudes and exploration. The kind of person one looks for to work or live alongside who fill in the gaps in your character. To some extent documents related to partnerships are indicated here. Land, farming and gardening involving co-operation with others. Legal matters and justice.

Eighth House
Succedent
Similar to Scorpio
Ruled by Pluto and Mars

Beginnings and endings. Birth and death. Sexual matters. Money involving other people, e.g. spouse's income, mortgages; taxes, wills, legacies, banking and insurance. Above all, partner's assets or lack of them. Shared feelings, feedback of other people's feelings (especially if they are intense). Crime and investigations and the police. Surgeons and surgery, also some illnesses. Hidden assets, secrets. The occult. A sense of commitment to anything or anyone. The things we really need from other people. The ability to regenerate or recycle anything. Deep feelings, deep thinking and such things as deep resentment and anger are to be found here. Also, psychology and psychiatry.

Ninth House
Cadent
Similar to Sagittarius
Ruled by Jupiter

Expansion of one's horizons e.g. travel, higher education, new environments. Foreigners, foreign goods and foreign dealings. Legal matters, important legal documents and court cases. Religious and mystical matters, including the philosophical and spiritual side of psychic matters. On the one hand, science, and on the other hand, intuition, dreams and visions. The church and the clergy. Sports and games that are taken fairly seriously. Outdoor pursuits. Gambling (especially on horses). Interest in or work with large animals. Need for personal freedom. Teaching and learning of a high standard also ethics and some aspects of public and political opinion. In-laws and grandchildren.

Tenth House
Angular
Similar to Capricorn
Ruled by Saturn

Aims and aspirations, your goal in life, your professional reputation and standing in the community. This may represent one's career, but also political ambitions, creative aspirations and future success - or lack of it. The ego and its chances of being satisfied. Your employer if you work for a large organisation. Authority figures of all kinds, including governmental and public authorities. Achievements, fame and personal promotion. The organisation of the church or any large organisation. The parents, especially father, or father figures. Status, your standing in the world. Responsibilities and visible commitments. Self-promotion. Limitation, hardship, shyness and hard work.

Eleventh House
Succedent
Similar to Aquarius
Ruled by Uranus and Saturn

Social life, friends and capacity for friendship, clubs and societies. Detached relationships but also love received, even the affection of friends. Intellectual pursuits and hobbies. Hopes, wishes, desires and goals and the chances of achieving them. Conversation, learning for pleasure. Teaching and learning of the usual kind, also instruction at work, political or philosophical training of a specialised kind. Money from one's job, especially if there has been training involved. Eccentricities, unexpected changes and circumstances. Stepchildren and adopted children.

Twelfth House
Cadent
Similar to Pisces
Ruled by Neptune and Jupiter

One's inner thoughts, feelings, secrets and secret worries. Suffering, sorrows, limitations, frustration and handicaps. This house can show whether you are your own worst enemy or not, it also shows inner resources and inner weaknesses or anything which is too painful to face up to. Hidden talents, hidden thoughts, hidden love, hidden angers. Also inhibitions, restraints, secret enemies and hidden danger. Any association with hospitals, mental institutions, prisons and other places of confinement, even exile. Any tendency to escapism, or things that we seek to hide from others. Your subconscious mind, plus karmic or spiritual debts. Self-sacrifice, love and help freely given (and possibly received). Also public charity and kindness, given and received. Inspiration and insights. Illusions, meditations and daydreams. Hidden friends and enemies. Here is where one could reach the stars - or mess one's life up completely. Oddly enough, also strategy, such as the kind that politicians and military people need to understand.

The Moon through the Houses

Moon in the First House

You love your home and family and you don't want to live alone. Your nature may appear quiet and introverted but you have an inner desire to be recognised. You will do much to help others but you're not prepared to make too many sacrifices on their behalf. Your mother was a strong influence on you and she may have been an exceptional woman in her own right, so you could find yourself walking in her shadow. You may choose a motherly type of person as a partner or perhaps a childlike one who you can mother. The sea calls you so strongly that you may choose to live and work by or on it. You may be physically restless, finding it hard to sit still, or you may love travel, preferably with your family along for the ride. You may be drawn to hobbies or even work in the field of food and nutrition and could be a vegetarian possibly due to your love of animals. It comes naturally to you to support the underdog wherever you can. This placement suggests a need to work for the public in some way, either before them as some kind of celebrity or, more likely in a humanitarian or welfare capacity. Being finely tuned in to your own body you usually know if you are going down with some illness. You must try not to allow your moods to dominate your personality.

Moon in the Second House
(The Moon's accidental exaltation)

Material things matter to you, because you need the security of money and possessions. There is a suggestion that these may be hard to obtain or to keep hold of. You need emotional security, possibly as a result of a materially or emotionally deprived childhood. There is a shrewd and slightly calculating business head on your shoulders but your pleasant approach to others hides this well. Women will be involved in your personal finances in some way and women could help you, possibly by inheritance or through family connections. You will probably take an interest in Taurean pursuits such as cooking, dancing, building, music, the arts, gardening and the creation of beauty.

Moon in the Third House
You need to communicate which could lead you towards a career in travel, the media or education. You are restless and curious but possibly lacking in concentration and easily bored. You pick up knowledge casually from those who you brush up against, and your parents might be clever and bookish. Throughout life you will keep learning and then passing on information to others. You have a natural affinity to the telephone and also to vehicles.

Moon in the Fourth House
(The Moon's accidental dignity)
This is the natural house of the Moon due to its association with the sign of Cancer that is ruled by the Moon. You prefer to work at home or at least to do your own thing, preferably in your own business. You may be nervous of the big wide world and have a habit of scuttling back home when the going gets rough. You are sympathetic towards those who are weak and helpless and you are especially fond of animals. You could be strongly attached to your parents or separated from them by circumstances beyond your control. It's possible that you lack confidence or feel insecure due to childhood problems. You need love and affection and should try to avoid hurting yourself further by forming relationships with destructive types. The past attracts you and this might lead you to work in the field of antiques or history. You are patriotic. You enjoy being by the sea.

Moon in the Fifth House
You like children so you might work as an infant school teacher or become involved with young people's sporting activities. Your emotions are strong and you seek fulfilment on both a practical and a romantic level in relationships. You could have a number of affairs if marriage does not work out for you. You have a good deal of charm, you are good to look at and you keep a youthful appearance throughout life. You could work for or in a theatre or in marketing and public relations. A creative outlet is an emotional necessity for you. You would make a good teacher, writer or publisher. Be careful not to cling to your children

Moon in the Sixth House

You have a strong urge to serve the needs of others, so you may work in some kind of caring profession, especially medicine. You could be drawn to a career that involves the production of food or something that helps the public to stay in good health. Your career will have to appeal to you on an emotional level, and you can even walk out of a job if the atmosphere or the people there didn't suit you. You need variety, so you could be better suited to having a couple of part-time jobs rather than one full-time one. You are considerate to others and would be a caring employer.

Moon in the Seventh House

You get on with most people because you need company and companionship. Where relationships are concerned, you will bend over backwards to make them work even at the expense of giving in to others for the sake of peace. There is a feeling that while young, you aren't quite sure who you are, so you may look to others to validate you. You prefer to work in co-operation with a partner or in a small group, and you may be drawn to work in an agency of some kind. You are politically minded and you have a good grasp of office politics. Glamour appeals to you, drawing you towards the world of fashion and music and this could become part of an interesting hobby. Your partner may be moody and difficult, but it's possible that you could understand them where others don't.

Moon in the Eighth House
(The Moon's accidental fall)

Women will be instrumental in helping you to gain money or prestige. You could work in trades that cater to women's needs or work mainly among women. You have an interest in psychic matters and you will be drawn to the mediumistic and spiritual side of these things. Your clairvoyance could be prodigious, but it will depend upon other factors on the chart as to how this is directed. There is a feeling that love, affection, sensuality and sex are important factors, and you could have your greatest successes in life in partnership with someone who inspires you both mentally and sexually. You can be devious, hurtful and destructive to others and even to yourself, even to the point of destroying your career or your future chances of success if you feel thwarted. The Moon and the house are both involved with instinctive and reactive behaviour, so you need to try and keep your feet on the ground.

Moon in the Ninth House

Religion and philosophy will be an important part of your life, and you will go on some kind of inward journey in order to find your way forward. You think deeply and will turn to a consideration of the deeper things of life. You are a natural psychic with the ability to see and feel beyond the boundaries of this Earth. Travel will be an important part of your life, as will any dealings with foreigners or foreign goods, and you may marry a foreigner. You are a natural teacher. You could find yourself attached to unconventional people, because they are more interesting than ordinary ones.

Moon in the Tenth House
(The Moon's accidental detriment)

This gives you an inner urge to shine before the public in some way, or to help humanity on a grand scale. There is evidence of an emotionally impoverished childhood during which something went wrong. Your parents (especially your mother) could have been super-achievers whom you seek to emulate. You will change jobs a few times until you find the right road for you. Your achievements will lead to acclaim, or if the Moon is badly aspected, to public scandal and ruin. You are drawn to a career that seeks to supply the needs of women or one that is traditionally carried out by women. Sales, marketing, domestic goods and women's literature are a few possibilities. Your standing in the community, especially your career standing, is of paramount importance to you and to others around you. You will be known and remembered by many before your life is done. To some extent this is a compensation for insecurity deriving from your difficult childhood, and a somewhat arid personal life.

Moon in the Eleventh House

You enjoy the company of others and could be heavily involved in some kind of club or society. Being extremely independent, you hate to be told what to do. Your family are sometimes left in the dark as to your plans and feelings but there is a possibility that you may find it hard to understand yourself. Your aims in life may change dramatically from time to time due to circumstances. Friends, especially female ones, are very helpful to you, and you have a strange kind of luck that brings them to you in times of trouble. You are well organised and able to manage others, but you can on occasion misjudge people and be taken advantage of by more astute and crafty types.

Moon in the Twelfth House

You seek to hide away from the world from time to time and to work in seclusion. Certainly you are happiest doing your own thing and working from your own home. Women will be an important part of any achievement, while men tend to interfere with your life, particularly with your career. You need to get away from time to time to recharge your batteries because too much stress will make you ill. You could be very creative as you have a rich imagination but you find it hard to bring your ideas into being. Your instinctive need to care for others may lead you to work in the field of nursing, childcare or working with animals. You may be too ready to sacrifice yourself for others. There is a secret side to your life and you may have to keep the secrets of others.

The Progressed Moon

The progressed moon is an invaluable tool for predicting the future.

To find your progressed moon position at any time, you either need to visit an astrologer or consult one online or by phone. If you wish to take your astrological studies further, then buying a decent astrological program is worthwhile. A couple of professional programs are: Solar Fire and Winstar. Whatever your choice, ensure before you buy that the program does progressions.

When you have established the position of the Moon for the year in question, check out the progressed Moon information in this book to see what kind of year you are going to have. If you have sufficient astrological knowledge to know what house your progressed Moon is traversing, then use the house information too. Remember, the sign will show the kind of mood or circumstances surrounding you, the house will show how to apply these for the best results.

Progressed Moon in Aries or the First House

Aries and the first house are symbolically associated with birth and with all that is new and fresh. When this progression is in operation you will find that your emotions seem to take on a life of their own, you feel more passionate in every way, and even the most placid among you will become excited and enthusiastic. Being more moody than usual, you could find yourself involved in a series of family arguments; in fact your home could become something of a battleground that starts to resemble a nest full of egomaniacs. There will be problems with regard to your mother or other older females, and you will have to take extra responsibility for them in some way.

Your energy level is high and you are ready to take advantage of the new opportunities that will begin to present themselves to you now. Even without your intervention, you will find that events move quickly. This is the time when you could find yourself a new and more challenging job or make a start in a business of your own. You will take chances with your money and may borrow money without thinking too deeply about how you will be able to pay it back.

The Moon in astrology often refers to the home, therefore you may move house, relocate yourself in another part of the country, or even move right out of the country and spend a few years in another part of the world. There will be new family groupings resulting from marriage, childbirth or divorce, and if you have been sitting in a marriage that has long been worn out, you will find the courage to do something about leaving. The familiar patterns of your life will change quickly now perhaps of their own volition or with your help. If you have been assessing your potential and making plans while the Moon was in Pisces or in the twelfth house, you will put those plans into action now. You have to guard against losing your temper in the wrong place at this time. Also guard against letting all the new contacts go to waste, or allowing your new enthusiasms to fizzle out. Short-term projects will suit you better than long-term ones, but you will need to find a way of expressing yourself rather than just following other people's leads.

You may realise that your moods are more changeable and your behaviour more impulsive. The Moon, of course, rules the emotional response, therefore, while it travels through Aries or the first house, the Moon's power will be at a peak. Women may be able to blame their sudden attacks of over-sensitiveness on an increase of pre-menstrual tension, men will have to look for another excuse! You may eat and drink more in order to cope with your extra energies. There is a feeling of Arian greediness for all that life has to offer.

The lunar influence could bring you into a closer connection with the sea or with work that involves liquids, there could also be an interest in mechanical and engineering projects. Women will feature in your life now and they may inspire you or encourage you to reach for the stars. Women who have spent years as housewives may go back to work under this influence, while others will give up work and have baby. You will take the initiative, find new methods and forge ahead with your life. Many of you will make an effort to identify and then to satisfy your own needs. Your sexual energies will increase and you may change your outlook and your requirements with regard to sex under this influence. If you meet a new love there will be a strong chemistry between you. If there is a child conceived at this time, it should by all astrological theories be a boy. Another unproven astrological possibility is that Aries-type people may figure strongly in your life at this time.

Progressed Moon in Taurus or the Second House

When the Moon moves into Taurus or the second house your emotions become more settled and comfortable. The projects that were begun in a blaze of enthusiasm while the Moon was in Aries or the first house should be well under way by now. This is a time of consolidation in all things and of steady and controlled growth. Material matters move to the top of your priority list now, so your attention will be firmly focused upon your personal income and your financial base. This would be a good time to buy a decent property, especially if it has some land or a garden. If you aren't buying a new property, you might refurbish the one you're in.

If you have been in the habit of living for the moment you will begin to think ahead, no longer allowing your credit card debts to grow. You will be reluctant to lend your money to just anybody, only making loans to those whom you can trust to pay you back in a prompt and orderly manner. If you are challenged about your newly materialistic attitude you will become defensive and awkward, while at the same time demanding a ten per cent discount! You feel instinctively that this is a good time to put personal savings schemes into operation but a bad time to risk money on nebulous or speculative ventures. If you buy anything expensive it must be durable, and the same goes for projects that are started at this time. When the Moon is travels through an earth sign, the prospects are good for long-term projects. Goods, especially luxurious or artistic ones that are bought at this time, will increase in value and business transactions will be carried out in a spirit of pragmatism rather than of overexcited speculation. You will find yourself dealing with businesswomen, and they could become an important part of your financial or working life. There is a danger that there could be too much emphasis on materialism at the expense of other aspects of your life.

This is a good time to form durable business partnerships, especially with women. You could soon find yourself signing leases on premises or land related to your work, and there will be a strong connection to people in the building trades. Emotional partnerships may be formed now but they will not have the explosive chemistry that they did when the Moon was in Aries or the first house. Relationships that have been recently formed will become deeper and more reliable, while new ones will be based on emotional security and possibly also financial security. Your sexual drive will be strong and all your senses will be heightened because Taurus and the second house are both earthy and sensual in character. You will be far less changeable emotionally and will be possibly less inclined towards sexual experimentation at this time. You will be more interested in settling down than in voyages of exploration. Be careful not to become too set in your ways, as you don't want to bore your partner to death. You will set the patterns for your future life now; certainly you will be reappraising your values and priorities. If you form a new relationship, your partner will be attractive, quiet and reliable.

You might find yourself involved with the production of food, and you will certainly do more shopping. This will be a highly developmental time for all artistic or musical interests and you could learn to appreciate art, dancing or music for the first time. All in all, this should be a peaceful and settled period that you can relax into and enjoy.

Progressed Moon in Gemini or the Third House

This will be a very busy and rather restless year for you. You will be moving around your neighbourhood more than you did in the last progression, and if you haven't learned to drive, this is the time to do so, because you are going to need the freedom of your own transport.

This will also be a year for mental exploration, so you could take courses at your local college or at evening classes. The best subjects might be connected with language, communication or computer studies. All studies, whether they are taken for a specific purpose or just for fun will be successful, and you shouldn't have much trouble in passing examinations. You may need to give more attention to your children's education or to their out-of-school hobbies and interests. You need all your communication skills as your work will involve you in activities such as typing, telephone and customer liaison, probably also in selling and advertising. There will be more than the usual amount of meetings and discussions with colleagues and there could be some kind of brochure or catalogue to be made up. You will travel around visiting different departments at your place of work and you will deal directly with clients either at your location or at theirs. You might take a series of temporary jobs or travel around your area carrying your skills with you. This will be an especially interesting time in your life because you will be meeting new people and will begin to become known outside your immediate circle. One simple example of getting around for commercial purposes would be that of a youngster taking a job delivering newspapers or groceries on a bicycle for a local firm.

You will become more than usually involved with neighbours and also with local issues. Although you might want to redecorate or otherwise change the appearance of your home and your garden, this would not be a particularly good time to make major changes or to make a move of house. There will be more visitors to your home than is normal and you will also spend more time visiting friends and family. Party-plan selling with friends and neighbours is a possibility. Gossip and trivial conversations on the phone are all an important part of your life now and you might find other people affecting your thinking in some fairly profound way.

Your own thought processes are more intuitive and instinctive than usual, and in some cases you could find yourself feeling more nervous and jumpy; however when you focus your mind on work or on studies your concentration will be good. There will be letters and parcels to be sent in the post, also possible are rental agreements and other minor documents to be signed. There will be more than the usual amount of dealings with females, and it's possible that products or services that cater to female requirements or that capture the imagination of women could be important in some way. You will be involved with mechanical and inventive ideas and you will have to learn new methods, so your dexterity will increase now. If you have been away from work for some time, you will return now.

This is not a particularly romantic time, but if you become involved with someone new, you will find that conversation and greater understanding are the keynotes to the relationship. If you are experimenting socially or sexually at this time it would be best if you didn't commit yourself too firmly to one person as your heart will be a little fickle. Romance will involve outings to restaurants, theatres and other local events, and even to sporting events. You should become involved in some kind of sport or hobby, which gives you an outlet that helps you to contend with your restlessness. You will tend to over-analyse and intellectualise your feelings.

Progressed Moon in Cancer or the Fourth House

The Moon rules the sign of Cancer, therefore when it travels through this sign or through the fourth house, one's lunar characteristics will make themselves strongly felt. This may make you more moody, emotional and "Cancerian" or it may emphasise your own natal lunar position. Regardless of your basic nature and outlook on life, you will act and react in a far more emotional manner and will become more interested in the private and personal aspects of your life.

Your home circumstances are going to play a major part in your life this year, and this may include a move of house, building work to be done, decorating or buying new furniture and fittings. The definite domestic slant to this progression will temporarily anchor you firmly to your home and family. You will take on more responsibility for relatives, and this could be a source of irritation or a great comfort to you depending upon the prevailing circumstances. There will be more dealings with your mother and with other female friends and relatives, especially those who are older than yourself. Feelings of family loyalty will strengthen, and you might spend some time researching your family history and background. There will be a need to identify with a specific group on the basis of family, race, religion or nationality and you will experience some kind of patriotic or group identity.

You may need to retreat from the outside world and to sink back into comfort and security, having little desire to meet new people and preferring to stay close to reliable old friends. You will want some novelty in your life, but this will come in the form of new domestic interests or learning how to use new gadgets in and around the house. You could work from home at this time or even start a small business from your own back room. The sign of Cancer is associated with shops; therefore you may take a job in one or even open a shop of your own. Whatever sex you are, you will be more concerned with daily chores than you have been in recent years, and the reason for this could range from retirement to setting up a family. Antiques are associated with the sign of Cancer, also history and genealogy, therefore you could find yourself delving into the past for a while or even searching for your roots. You will be over-sensitive, especially over family issues and you could even become unaccountably possessive towards those around you. You may feel alienated, neglected and superfluous, so your moods could vacillate between wanting to be alone and fearing loneliness.

Friends could cling to you now or you could cling to them, and old friends that you haven't seen for years could suddenly come back into your life now. Some of you could start to work with liquids. The sea could prove to be a pull, urging you to live and work on or near it. Travel on or over water will be especially pleasant at this time. Cancerian-type people may influence you at this time and, due to the active femininity of the sign, a child conceived now should, by all accounts, be female.

This time is a time of gradual change where you spend time looking inside yourself and revising your needs and attitudes. Old habits could now be seen as being inappropriate to your present and future way of life.

Progressed Moon in Leo or the Fifth House

During this progression you will be dealing with children and young people. This is often the time when a mother is at the height of her involvement with a growing family. Whoever you are, you will enjoy a more youthful attitude possibly joining in sporting activities and youthful pastimes. Interestingly, when my daughter's progressed Moon moved into Leo, she got a job in a firm that makes jigsaw puzzles and children's board games!

The sign of Leo (and the fifth house) is concerned with creativity; therefore you will embark upon projects that are close to your heart. You should develop the ideas and the determination at this time to make something of yourself and to create something which will stand the test of time, but you might have to wait until the Moon progresses into Virgo before you gain the ability to focus your attention and to get on with the job.

Travel will be important now but it might prove something of a trial to you, as you may have to cart restless and difficult children around with you. Another possibility is that of business travel, which is often less glamourous than it seems. However, this sign is associated with leisure, pleasure and time off, so travel for fun and relaxation is also possible.

There might be some connection with work in a glamourous field, so you may join some branch of show business. You might take up attractive or amusing hobbies now, skating and dancing are possibilities, also light and interesting sports. This is a good time to give attention to your personal appearance, to keep your figure trim and be prepared to go out and knock 'em in the aisles, because it's going to be important for you to look good. This may be the time when you emerge from your shell and find yourself in the limelight; it's even possible that after years of being held back you find yourself breaking out with a vengeance. You may even become the stronger partner in a relationship after years of having been kept down. This is definitely not going to be the time to keep your light under a bushel but to discover the power of your own personality and to enjoy expressing it.

Your feelings will rise to the surface and will be hard to hide and they may even be difficult to control. All your relationships and friendships will be re-evaluated and some changes may be made soon. You could become more aware of and more wrapped up with your own feelings. Sexual feelings will also be high and there might be an affair of the heart (or body) now. None of this may last too long but you will learn a lot about yourself, other people and life generally. You may sometimes appear to be wasting time and energy on frivolities, but this will all be part of the learning process.

The sign of Leo (and the fifth house) is associated with children and you will find yourself dealing with and enjoying the company of children. You might help out the local boy scouts or girl guides, become involved in the activities of the local dancing school or in some other way find yourself in charge of children. You may start your own family now or you may find yourself responsible for someone else's children. All dealings with women will be good, your mood will be generous and happy a good deal of the time and you might gamble a little, either literally or figuratively as this can be a time of great gains, but also there may be surprising losses.

Progressed Moon in Virgo or the Sixth House

Work will be important to you now, and you could find that either your normal job becomes more interesting or that you begin to do something new and highly satisfying. You will have to cope with paperwork, bookkeeping, correspondence and record keeping; computers and word processors might become an important feature of your life now. You will perform precise and delicate tasks whilst analysing and checking your own work carefully, and these jobs could include do-it-yourself work, home dressmaking or gardening. You might take a course at your local evening classes. If you do take lessons, these would be in useful and practical subjects such as car maintenance or cookery. Whoever you are, you will be dealing with household chores and, if you aren't skilled at these types of job, you will soon learn the ropes. If gardening becomes important now, you will concentrate on producing fruit and vegetables.

You will fall into a sensible routine of work this year and may find yourself following a strict set of directions. This is the time to establish good work habits and you will find reliable and efficient colleagues to work alongside at this time. Women may pose problems on the one hand but they can turn out to be of great benefit as well, perhaps one group of women will give you trouble while another will help enormously. All this talk of duty and effort may seem a bit dull, but the resulting rewards will make it all worthwhile. This is not, strictly speaking, a great time for creative pursuits but writing would work out well, especially if it involves specialised research and analysis.

You may become involved with hospitals now, either because you yourself need treatment or people close to you may be sick. It's possible that you could work in a hospital at this time, but either way, you will take more notice of your own state of health and will try to improve it in any way that you can. You may become interested in alternative or complementary therapies now. You will concentrate on your diet and appearance and could even go a bit overboard by becoming too clean and tidy or by developing hypochondria. There will be some irritating nervous ailments to put up with which, although not dangerous, could make life difficult at times.

Your behaviour under this progression might irritate others, as you will try to over-rationalise or over-analyse everything. You must guard against playing the martyr, taking on unnecessary chores and then moaning to everyone about this. Guilty feelings will plague you even though you really have nothing to feel guilty about. You must make time to rest and enjoy life because you will be ill if you don't.

This is hardly the best progression for romance but it's possible that you could meet someone special through your work. Relationships that are formed under this progression should be steady and relatively trouble free, if rather dull. On a brighter note, this is a great time to buy new clothes; perhaps this is a consolation prize result of all that hard work.

Progressed Moon in Libra or the Seventh House

Partnerships and relationships are going to be of paramount importance to you this year. Whether you are at the dating stage or even contemplating the end of your present partnership, new relationships made will have an air of freshness and a strangely experimental feel about them. It appears that you will be searching around for the right person rather than making a serious commitment. This doesn't mean that you won't settle down with your current date, just that you need to keep your options open now. Not all your relationships will be pleasant as there could be some major confrontations especially with women at this time. The seventh house (and the sign of Libra) are supposed to represent one's first marriage, but I have found this progression to be more concerned with forming and breaking relationships of all kinds.

Your emotions will be strong at this time that will cause you to overreact, so you will find it particularly hard to be detached and objective. You may require both security and freedom at the same time, wanting your partner to be faithful while you yourself slip off the leash. There will be an element of sexual exploration and experimentation.

You should become drawn into the world of business, and if you have no business knowledge, you will have to acquire it quickly. The communications side of business will be important, and you will need to keep in touch with current ideas and methods. Although you will not necessarily be directly responsible for the sale of goods and services, you will have to deal with marketing and public relations, which means finding ways to advertise and to present your organisation's image in an attractive and modern manner. There will be a good deal of interaction with other business people and also with the general public. Libra is a cardinal sign (the seventh house is an angular house) therefore, you will be much more decisive and dynamic now than ever before. You will have to present yourself in a stylish way in front of others, therefore your appearance and manner of dress will become more modern and interesting now.

There will be interesting new beginnings and new working relationships in which you meet inspiring and dynamic people. You will spend far more time in cities than in the countryside but you will probably see something of the countryside as you travel through it on business. Your self-esteem will take a few knocks, mainly due to the fact that you will be working in an unfamiliar field and you will inevitably make errors.

There is some evidence that you will find others trying to manipulate you and you may react angrily when you discover what is going on. On the other hand, people could validate and value you, thus boosting your self-esteem. In the areas of both your work and in your domestic life you could find that your finances and your financial decisions are inevitably wrapped up with your emotions.

Progressed Moon in Scorpio or the Eighth House

You will make the changes that will set the pattern of your life for many years to come. If you have been experimenting with friendships and relationships during the past couple of years, you may settle into marriage now. However, on the other hand, if you have been travelling towards a potential divorce, this is when you might bring it about. There will be major beginnings and endings that might include setting up a home or dismantling one. You could start a family now or find yourself at the stage when your children are leaving the nest. Your children may soon start their own families, or there may be births around you in other branches of your family or among your friends. Unfortunately, there could well be a funeral or two to attend as well.

You will either make a fresh commitment to your present job or make a change for one that will stand you in good stead in the future. A young woman may give up work for a couple of years in order to stay at home with children. Whichever way this progression works for you it will mean transformation, rebirth and a redefinition of your goals both within and outside the home. You may become interested in conservation and recycling. You will spend money on your surroundings now.

Work changes could take you into the farming or food production industries. Another possibility is some kind of professional contact with the police, private detectives or hospitals. Health or legal matters might enter your private life too. You will be more aware of the mystical and psychic elements of life and you might have some kind of psychic experience, possibly for the first time in your life. This progression will make your intuition and hunches strong and you might even go as far as to develop mediumistic qualities.

Financial matters that involve other people's money will become important now also their attitude to financial matters. This could include alimony, legacies, mortgages, taxes, joint accounts and business finances. You must guard against too great an emotional response to legal and financial matters. Joint properties and joint possessions can be sorted out at this time, but you must guard against feelings of greed and covetousness. There may be family or business wrangles, especially over property. These problems would be typical of a divorce, the ending of a business partnership or after a death in the family. The structure of your life will be transformed in some way.

Some activities will be deeply satisfying, and these could fulfil a variety of instinctual needs. These could include almost anything that makes you happy but I would have to put sex pretty high on the list, along with settling into a happy home or a more comfortable way of life. New habits will be formed, probably resulting from a new understanding of your inner needs. Your instinctive side will overshadow your logical mind and you could experience an almost compulsive pursuit of your objectives.

There are some mighty awful problems that could emerge under this progression, and the intensity of your intense feelings could spill over into jealousy and passion of a particularly lustful or obsessive kind. You could become trapped or manipulated into a situation that under normal circumstances you would avoid, or conversely you may seek to possess or manipulate another. The abnormal over-emotional response will take some living with and it could cause you to act in a manner that is totally out of character. This would be the right time to delve into the bottom of a long-standing mess and finally sort out the reasons for it, even if it means bringing a few skeletons out of the cupboard. You might feel as if you are in an emotional mincing machine now but you will emerge at the end of it as if reborn, salvaged from destruction.

Progressed Moon in Sagittarius or the Ninth House

The key idea behind this progression is the expansion of your personal horizons. You might travel overseas for the first time or you could take the time to really investigate a particular part of the world that you have always fancied visiting. Your work could take you away and you might enter into a business venture that involves overseas goods, services or property. You may have to sell to foreigners, thereby learning about them and their way of living. Your family may move to another country or there may be people entering the family who are from a different cultural background and this could be the cause of some of your long distance journeys. Some of you will fall in love with a person who comes from a different country or a different cultural background now and this may cause you to review your own religious or philosophical outlook.

You may be subjected to economic or cultural changes in conditions around you that affect your private or your business life. There is even a chance that you will have to deal with people whose views are biased or even bigoted regarding race and religion.

There might be increased dealings with institutions such as schools, colleges and churches either personally or as a matter of business. You could go back into training or just study for fun at this time. The subjects you choose will be philosophical or mind broadening rather than purely practical, but you may learn a foreign language as a means of meeting a larger range of interesting people or in order to progress in your career. You will find ways to overcome mental stagnation and boredom at this time. School connections may take you into teaching or training others and you may have to give lectures on a special subject. You may go into publishing or you may use the Internet to broadcast information. You could soon create brochures or trade journals for your company.

There is a feeling that the end of a phase in your working life is on the way now and you could finish this progression with a determination to do something quite different. This may be a high point, a culmination of all that you have worked for; alternatively, you may reach the bottom of a pit of unhappiness with regard to your work and decide to change direction for good and all.

You should be able to enjoy life and have some fun. The chances are that you will become enthusiastic about a number of new ideas, hobbies and pastimes, and sports could be high on the list. There will be more chance for you to get out into the fresh air, and you may become interested in the world of large animals, especially horses. Gambling on horses is a possibility, or just taking a chance or two on life. This should be a time of increased fun and a sense of adventure. Your level of confidence will be high, maybe too high, but this might just begin to wane as the progression moves towards the cusp of the tenth house.

Sometimes there is an increase of activity concerning legal matters under this progression, but it's usually the tail end of outstanding problems rather than new ones rearing their heads. This may be a detail or two that is still hanging on from a recent divorce settlement, or some kind of family or business matter that has still to be put to rest. Sagittarius and the ninth house is concerned with second marriages, therefore this may be the time when you meet a second partner or when you decide to marry for the second time.

Progressed Moon in Capricorn or the Tenth House

This is a time of hard work but also of ultimate achievement. This progression may start with a monumental setback in your life or just a feeling that you cannot go on any longer in the same old way. The chances are that the frustrations and the problems that are affecting your working life will spill over into your personal life as well. You will receive a great deal of useful help from others at work now. Those who help you may be in positions of seniority or they may be equipped with some kind of specialised knowledge that they are willing to pass on to you. If you are selling a product or a service, buyers will be more receptive now, and one interesting point is that women are likely to be particularly helpful to you.

You will want to make improvements in your techniques and methods, and if you aren't used to working in a structured organisation, you will learn how to do so. Alternatively, you might go from one sort of structure to a completely different one that runs by a different set of rules. It's important that you are honest in all your dealings, whether they are in your working or your private life and you should find yourself among decent and honest people. You will need to be seen as being respectable both in your public and family life as this is a time when secrets and deceptions might emerge in an uncomfortably embarrassing way.

Your work will bring you into contact with the public and you will perform services for people both individually and in large groups. You will need to dress the part of a successful and competent person, as both you and your work will be highly visible at this time. Sales and promotional work will be important and you will have to make public appearances, possibly even give lectures or make speeches from time to time.

Colleagues will be more sympathetic to your aims than before and you, in turn, will be more responsive to the needs of others. It's possible that you could be temporarily short of money, maybe because you are investing fairly heavily in a project or because your job offers training and future possibilities rather than present financial rewards.

You will take a sensitive attitude towards those you work with and will be careful not to tread on their egos. There will be responsibility now attached to the work that you do and you may well also be responsible for the efforts of others. This is the time to build a team of juniors or a sensible framework of method and experience that will follow you into the future. Delays and setbacks in your career will be followed by success, and good things will come out of bad ones. Your work will need a conventional attitude and old-fashioned skills and there will be the need for a structured and practical outlook. You may find yourself reviving the spirits of a flagging company or institution, which will require you to be responsive to the moods and feelings of groups around you, possibly in the form of union negotiations. Time keeping will be important, either in the form of working hours, timetables or deadlines of one sort or another.

Your professional and personal relationships may become a bit blurred as you could turn towards someone who you work closely with or alternatively, you could begin a work project with someone you love. This is not, truthfully speaking, a romantic time. Your feelings may be dampened or you may be forced to keep them on a tight rein. However, if you do meet someone, it's likely that this will happen through your work.

In personal relationships you will be shyer than usual and also very slow to commit yourself. There may be some strangely public displays of emotion either directed towards you or coming from you. Angry scenes could take place where others can see and hear or feelings of loving and caring which you have been keeping dark might also emerge in a somewhat public manner. Domestic life will have to take a back seat now but the work that you are doing will go to make the domestic scene nicer and more comfortable later on.

Progressed Moon in Aquarius or the Eleventh House

This is a time when friends will be extremely important to you, you will have to rely on them to help you and you will in turn, be a good friend to others. There will be an involvement with clubs and societies, and you will definitely feel the need to become part of a group. This group identity may be political or work related. There may be spare time activities with a sports team, people who are interested in artistic pursuits or some kind of intellectual grouping. You will make achievements as part of a group or a team. At work, you will have to work in co-operation with, and possibly in charge of, others; you cannot achieve much on your own now.

Friendships with women will be important and you will become slightly less attached to your family, finding that your time and attention is diverted by outside considerations. Even in the realm of friendships there will be changes as you move on to newer, more dynamic or influential people. Both you and your associates could try to achieve something that would be of benefit to humanity. Your attitude will be idealistic but possibly rather impractical at times. It would be wise to guard against being drawn into specific and fixed ideologies that don't leave room for differences of opinion.

It will be necessary for you to learn new methods that arise from your work or as a result of a change in your way of life. For instance, if you were to move house at this time, you would have to get to grips with decorating or making a garden even if you have never done these things before. You may learn to sew, drive a car or bring your work skills up to date. If you have school-aged children, you will be dealing with educational matters on their behalf and you may be drawn into some of their school activities. It's possible that you could return to college or even become a teacher yourself. Retirement at this time would give you an opportunity to learn new skills or take up new hobbies. You may have to deal with very modern methods and computer techniques.

You will redefine your personal goals and ask yourself what you want out of life in general terms. By investigating your own hopes and wishes you will change the direction of your thinking in some radical way. One instance may be a person who has thus far, never wanted children deciding that he or she wants them after all, another person who had always been lazy might suddenly become ambitious. New goals and values will replace outworn ones now.

There can be a surprisingly disruptive element in this progression that could change your outlook or your life completely. You might re-emerge soon with a new career. You will almost certainly have a new home soon, possibly even with a new set of personal relationships. This is the time when you revolutionise your own life or that you find that it's being revolutionised for you by bringing a complete breakdown in your present status quo.

If someone else wants to move on and leave you behind, you will learn about feelings of rage, jealousy and rejection. You may react by becoming possessive in an attempt to hang on too tightly. What happens depends upon your circumstances at the time of entering the progression and your particular way of handling change.

If you went through difficult times during the previous progression through this house or sign, you will find this a surprisingly good progression this time round. Money will come your way, gambles come off and your dreams begin to come true. There is no doubt that this is a phase where anything could happen - and it frequently does. Try to keep a strong grip on reality as events around you might become tinged with fantasy or even a subtle form of lunacy. Remember to keep in touch with friends, as they will help you through both good times and bad ones.

Progressed Moon in Pisces or the Twelfth House

This will be a time of reflection, possibly even a time of retreat from the hurly-burly of life. Events seem to be in the hands of fate, and there doesn't seem to be much you can do about it. You may have to suppress your own personality for a while, possibly until your progressed Moon crosses over the Ascendant into Aries. In addition to having to keep a good many of your feelings under wraps, there could be work projects carried on in secret. One example might be of preparing to set up a small business of your own while still carrying on at your usual job. There may, of course, be a secret relationship going on, such as keeping in touch with a "black sheep" relative that the rest of the family ignores. This progression may mark a sad and depressing time, as you seem to be working through some kind of karmic programme. The outcome will be a change in your consciousness leading to a renewal of life and hope, plus a completely new direction.

It's important to keep some kind of hold on reality during this progression, as it would be only too easy to slip into a strange state of mental limbo. Some aspect of your life will be insecure, probably on the emotional level, and you may find it hard to face the facts that confront you. It would be easy to slide into a state of disillusion or even despair worse still; you could try to chase illusion, exacerbating the situation by the use of drugs and drink. It would be best to keep away from opiates at this time, especially sleeping pills.

There is a much more positive side to all this and it's the opportunity for you to learn how to relax, meditate and travel on a series of inward journeys. One way or another, you will be spending much more time alone than you have before and while you are looking inwards, you may discover talents and abilities which you never knew you possessed. The benefits of this progression tend to be recognised only in retrospect. Artistic and creative abilities will come to the fore, but you should be able to enjoy quiet pleasures like reading, listening to the radio and gardening. Photography, filmmaking and art or music is possible too.

If you are naturally rather moody, this aspect of your personality will be accentuated but you may find yourself on the receiving end of someone else's moodiness at this time. Your intuitive abilities will develop and you should follow any instincts that you feel. Being more sensitive and shyer than usual, you may find others strangely difficult or even unsympathetic to your needs and wants. It's possible that psychic or mediumistic abilities will become noticeable now and you might begin to take a serious interest in these subjects. There could even be a revelation, a kind of gateway that thrusts you forward into spirituality.

Typical Piscean or twelfth house circumstances would be that of a young woman finding herself at home with small children at the very time when her husband is having to make the maximum effort at his job and therefore being less supportive than before. Another reason might be the beginning of retirement with its inevitable change of perspective. One unfortunate reason for this situation might be a period of illness, or possibly of having to take care of somebody else who becomes ill or incapacitated. There may well be a connection with hospitals, even mental institutions or prisons at this time, either because you yourself are directly involved or through those close to you. You could even find yourself working in one of these places. You will have an uncanny ability to link with the moods of others and to give real help and understanding to those who need it.

One of the nicer possibilities is of travel. There maybe a move or a drift towards water for you now and, depending upon circumstances you could buy property by the sea, rent a holiday villa on the coast or become involved in the world of boats. Some people go cruising when the Moon is in Pisces.

If you are working, you will be better off as a backroom person than out in front. You may find it hard to trust others either in your private or your working life. Relations with women could be particularly difficult or even peculiar now, and you may have to face a change in perspective regarding the women in your life at this time, probably due to factors that are outside your control. An easy way to grasp the idea behind this progression is to think of a seed spending the winter lying in the soil waiting to come to life in the spring.

Strange and subconscious forces affect your moods as the axis of your previous way of life subtly shifts. This is truly a time to recharge your inner forces by retreat and reflection in readiness for the "first house breakout" which will surely, surely come.

Other Predictive Techniques

Transits

The first predictive technique that anybody who gets into even the most basic forms of astrology learns is transits. This method is used in newspaper astrology and in every normal type of astrological reading. While progressions uses a day-for-a-year technique, transits mean finding the current location of any planet, noting the sign and house it occupies and seeing whether it's making an aspect to any other planet. Although astrologers do this by looking at charts on our computer screens or on paper or in an ephemeris (book of tables) you can actually go outside and do this by looking at the sky This is because we are dealing with the actual planets in the actual sky, rather than just a mathematical calculation.

The following illustration shows a natal chart on the inner ring and the transits on the outer ring.

It's always worth seeing whether a planet is making a transit to the Moon, as it has such a powerful effect on so many areas of one's life. For instance, I recently spent a few weeks feeling quite depressed for no reason that I could account for, and I eventually took the sensible step of looking at the transits. I saw immediately that Saturn was sitting opposite my Moon and that it had been doing so for several weeks. Nothing terrible was happening, but life was dull, the weather was awful, I had too much work to do and I was tired.

The Moon moves so quickly that its transits are not normally worth bothering with, but there are times when they are. If you have some important date or event looming, it's worth looking at the transits, and especially the position of the Moon beforehand, as that can give you some idea as to the likely outcome.

There is a closely related form of astrology, called "electional astrology" because it involves electing (selecting) the best time to do something.

Other Predictive Techniques

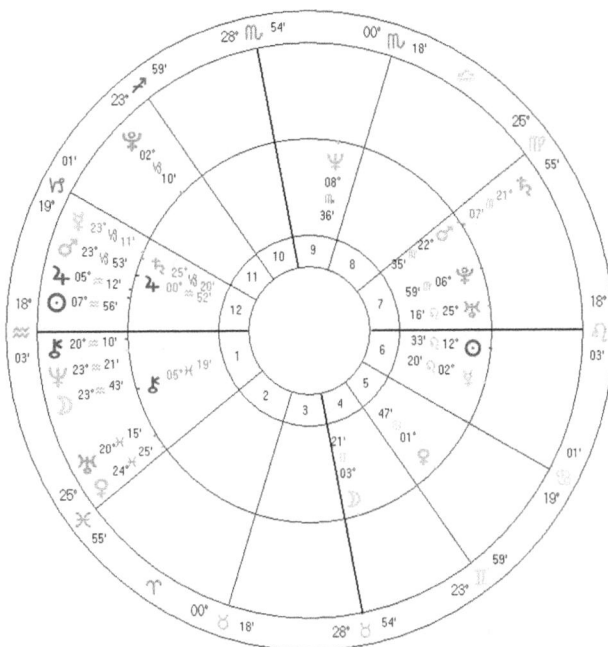

Natal & Transit chart of former USA President Barack Obama, just after his Inauguration

Combining Methods

Professional quality astrology software enables the astrologer to make up a dual chart that has the natal chart in the centre, and the transit or progressed chart surrounding it. This way, an astrologer can compare two charts at one time.

Void of Course Moon

The word "Void" in this situation means empty, and the word "Course" refers to the track or orbit of the Moon.

A "Void of Course" Moon means that the Moon cannot make an aspect to another planet (using zero orbs) before leaving the sign that it's moving through. The following example shows all the planets, apart from the Moon, below 25 degrees. Thus, the Moon will be Void of Course in this example. Many astrologers won't do anything important until the Void of Course period has passed.

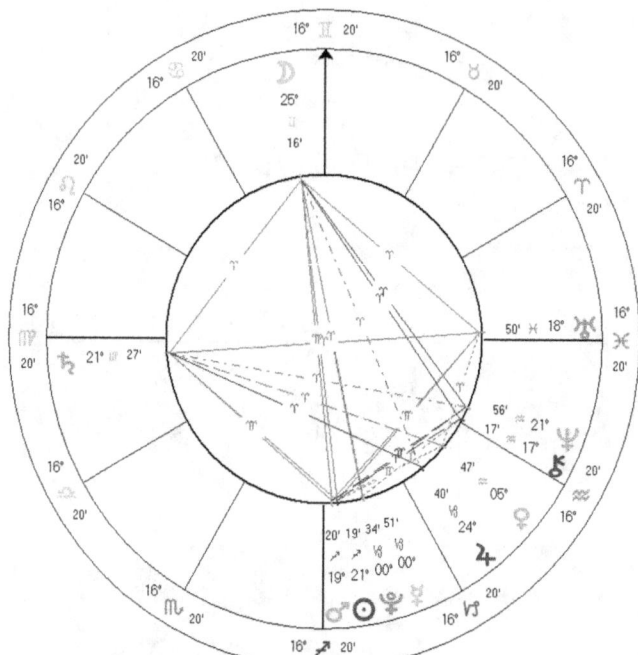

Void of Course Moon

Solar and Lunar Returns

A solar return chart is made up for the moment when the Sun returns to the exact point that it was in when a person was born, which happens once a year. Every time we wish someone "many happy returns" on their birthday, it's the solar return to which we are unwittingly referring!

Naturally, a solar return can refer to any kind of anniversary.

Not all astrologers use solar returns, and even fewer use lunar returns, after all they are nothing more than a picture of the transits at the particular moment in time. I find that they give a sense of the atmosphere at the time in question, and that can sometimes be useful. I don't usually look too deeply into these return charts, but a quick glance will show the rising sign, and thus the emphasis of the year or month in question. For instance, if the Ascendant was in Aries, with Mars rising in the first house, I would surmise that the subject of the chart would have a fight on his or her hands during the coming period.

Even a quick scan will show the house that the Sun or Moon or other significant planets occupy and whether they are being afflicted by challenging aspects or helped by positive ones. It's worth checking out the position and aspects to and from the planet that is associated with the Ascendant. For instance, if the solar or lunar return rising sign is Taurus, it's worth seeing what Venus is up to.

My friend Jon Dee (now sadly passed over) used to say that in his experience, the events shown in a lunar return chart won't necessarily kick in at the start of the lunar month, but often only when the month is three-quarters of the way through.

Moon and Planet Conjunctions

A lunar transit will only last a day or so, but a lunar progression will last for a few weeks. The effects will be felt before the Moon reaches the planet and perhaps for a little while after it has passed by. When the Moon approaches a planet or object, it makes an "applying" aspect, then it becomes "exact" and finally a "separating" aspect. Professional software expresses these as "A", "X" and "S".

Moon/Sun Conjunction
There may be events concerning children, also this is a time of increased self-confidence or even of personal triumph. Fun, holidays, speculation, games, sports, will become part of your life now. You could fall in love with an exciting person and have an affair to remember. There is a possibility that you may buy yourself a holiday home or a house in the sun. There should be some good times with older relatives now. You might find yourself dealing with more than the usual number of Leo type people at this time.

Moon/Moon Conjunction
Domestic matters come to the fore, there could even be a move of house or you may take out a lease on business premises. Travel is a possibility especially over or near water and you may revisit the place of your birth. There will be some special dealings with females, especially mother figures. Your emotions will be stronger now. There could be a connection with the provision of food or domestic goods. Things that have been kept secret may suddenly be revealed. You may have more dealings with Cancerian people now.

Moon/Mercury Conjunction
Communications with the family characterise this progression. There may be documents to be dealt with in connection with property and premises. There could be a new vehicle for you now or you may simply

change your method of daily commuting. Paperwork will be important. Any educational courses undertaken now will go well, exams can be passed at this time, as can the driving test. There should be friendly dealings with neighbours, friends and relatives of your own generation or a bit younger. You could take up a new sporting interest in company with others. Groups of friends may begin to meet in your home. You will begin to think about diet and food values and could make plans to alter the appearance of your home. There may also be a rethink about your methods of working and improvements in the methods you use. You may begin to write for publication. You may have more than the usual amount of dealings with Gemini or Virgo people now.

Moon/Venus Conjunction
Family affairs come to the fore; you will get on well with the women of the family. There could be public relations involving women, or even a business partnership with a woman. This is a good time to decorate the house or to have a celebration in the home. Food and catering, diet and appearance will occupy you now. There could be a new romance; certainly you will begin to feel more attractive and more romantic. There may be some involvement with artists, musicians and artistic work at this time. There will be an increase in business opportunities and good new contacts. You may find yourself dealing with more than the usual number of Taurus or Libra people now.

Moon/Mars Conjunction
You will experience a high level of energy and drive, and you could develop sudden enthusiasms for work projects or energetic hobbies. There will be some kind of fresh start now. There could be a working partnership with a young man and you will have a more energetic and youthful attitude to work matters. If you are in a competitive field or are playing in competitive sports you should be able to win. Your ambition level will be high and opportunities will suddenly come your way. This is not a great time for dealing with women and you will have to watch your temper now, as all your feelings will run high. You may become ill, feverish or even have an accident (especially in the home). If you change vehicles now, the new one will go faster than the previous one did. Your sex drive will be high but you could also fight over emotional and sexual matters. For women, this transit is almost bound to bring a man into your

life; probably young, certainly sexy and energetic. You could be dealing with more than the usual number of Aries or Scorpio people now.

Moon/Jupiter Conjunction

You might rethink your religious and philosophical views now. There will be an interest in travel and dealings with foreigners, possibly in connection with work. There is a feeling of optimism and change for the better although it may not be apparent immediately. You will make new and useful contacts and could have unexpected opportunities at work. Money should become easier to find and doors will open for you. There might be an involvement with legal matters at this time and, if so, you will come out on the winning side, especially if property is involved. This is a good time to deal with women in regard to financial matters, also to invest in property. Domestic matters should go well and you will be given the opportunity to expand your horizons and even to look at yourself in a new way. You may be involved with more than the usual number of Sagittarius or Pisces people now.

Moon/Saturn Conjunction

There will be problems that may relate to your home situation, your parents or other elderly relatives. You could feel depressed and rather lonely, even though you are surrounded by people. You will have extra responsibilities with very little time to rest and, apart from feeling downhearted, you might actually be ill, or just over-tired and run down. Life will feel restricted and rather boring at this time and your love life may also be depressing, it's possible that your loved one is living or working at some distance from you at the moment. Business matters will go slowly, but plans made now will work out well in the long run. Dealings with people in positions of responsibility or with older people may be awkward but should work out well after the progression has passed. There could be the need to make far-reaching decisions with regard to your parents. Money may be short, especially in the home but that will also improve soon. A good time to do some long-range thinking and to chat to knowledgeable and responsible people about your plans for the future. You may meet more than the usual number of Capricorn or Aquarius people now.

Moon/Uranus Conjunction

Sudden changes in mood characterise this progression. This is one of those times when you will suddenly realise that you can no longer bear the job you're in or the person you are living with. This is the kind of situation that brews up slowly, possibly for years beforehand, and then, apparently all of a sudden, changes for good. You may make an unexpected change of house or suddenly decide to tear down and rebuild some part of your home; there could be unexpected family problems or sudden changes with the home set-up. Friends will be more in evidence at this time. You could have some brilliant ideas or you may find answers to questions that have been bothering you for ages. Working life could bring unexpected changes and benefits, almost anything could happen and you will have to study the signs and the houses involved in order to work out all the possibilities. You might even take up astrology! You should have more than the usual number of dealings with Aquarian people at this time.

Moon/Neptune Conjunction

If you fall in love now you will see your loved one through rose-coloured glasses. There will be a strong element of fantasy in any love affair at this time, therefore you could do most of your loving at a distance or even confine it to the inside of your own head. Old half-buried memories will come back to haunt you, and you could find yourself dealing with ancient fears and phobias, possibly facing up to them at last. There will be an increase in your intuition and you could have some interesting psychic experiences. You will be re-examining your philosophical views and religious outlook and could even go so far as to change your religion. You may spend much time daydreaming or you may go in for some inspired forms of meditation. You will feel atmospheres acutely and could well develop clairvoyant and precognitive abilities.

Business matters could become confusing and you might find out that you have been dealing with dishonest people. You may have some great ideas but will have to wait until the progression has passed before putting them into practice. There may be travel to the sea or over it for you, and there should be renewed contact with family and friends overseas. You may rearrange the method of water supply in your home or you may become interested in or work with fluids, gasses, oil and photography. There could be increased contacts with mystical people, those born under the sign of Pisces or who have strongly Piscean birthcharts. Love affairs could be wonderful, inspired or they could really screw you up but you will definitely be awash with emotion and hardly able to think straight. You might be involved with hospitals especially in connection with family members. There may be work in a hospital or institution for you at this time. You may develop a taste for alcohol or develop strange allergic ailments.

Moon/Pluto Conjunction
This is a transforming progression that could change your whole life, and it will certainly change your outlook on life and your view of yourself. You will be emotionally wrought up, possibly because you are coping with some pretty monumental problems. There will be financial matters to sort out and these may stem from a previous divorce, a legacy or some kind of outstanding tax problem. There could be outstanding business finances to sort out and even liquidation is a possibility. You will want to alter a bad family situation and perhaps clear the air with a really terrific argument. You could even walk out for good. There may be dealings with the police, the courts or hospitals, and the matters that are involved could be quite serious. There may be births and deaths around you now, certainly there will be figurative ones. There is even the possibility that your life could be affected by geological upheavals or by war! There could be a connection with mines and miners or explosives. There may be some rather strange occult and psychic experiences. Any kind of subterranean rumblings of discontent that have been going on in your life could erupt explosively now.

Moon/Chiron Conjunction
When the progressed Moon conjuncts Chiron, a major healing process is set in motion. You probably instigate this by making decisions to change your life for the better, but things can happen of their own accord that also bring changes for the better.

This is not an easy time to live through though, because the run up to it is reminiscent of an increase of heat and pressure inside a volcano, and when the Moon meets Chiron, the volcano explodes. This may affect any area of life, but let's say that your adult child's behaviour has become increasingly destructive, and you now reach a point where you say enough is enough and refuse to bail them out any more.

Other scenarios might be the end of a bad marriage, leaving a rotten job, moving to a new area or even a move to a new country. You may dump a friendship that has always been based on you doing all the giving, or you may have a much-needed operation. You may even have a wakeup call that makes you change your own behaviour for the better.

Whatever the scenario, the problem comes to a head, and that brings it to a close. The doors of opportunity may open for you, causing you to consider whether you want to continue with you life as it is, or throw caution to the wind and go with the flow, even though it means leaving other people and places behind. The result will definitely be to your benefit.

Chiron rules wounds, and while these might be painful psychological wounds that have been left over from the past, this conjunction can also refer to actual wounds, such as those caused by an accident or an operation. Take very good care of your health at this time and get all the medical attention and advice that you need.

Moon/Ascendant Conjunction
This is a time of new beginnings as the Moon moves from the twelfth house to the first. You will want to come out of the shadows and be noticed. Your personal and domestic affairs will change for the better now although it might be uncomfortable while this progression is in operation. You will probably change your appearance and your attitudes soon.

Moon/Midheaven Conjunction
This is the culmination of a phase of your life. You should feel that you have reached as far as you can in your present job and now want to change direction. You could become more involved with the public or find that your status and public image is improving. You may achieve some long-cherished dream regarding your career. Domestic matters will go well, and if you move house, you will make money on the deal and will like your new home. Domestic matters will influence your professional life either indirectly, via changes in your home and family arrangements or directly, as a result of working in industries related to food and household goods. A woman may influence your thinking in regard to your objectives in life.

Moon/IC Conjunction
This could bring you closer to your family, especially your mother, and will

bring you closer to your home. You may begin to work from home now. Any lingering emotional or relationship problem in the home can be sorted out for good now. You will be drawn to the past and you may meet up with people from your past, or sort out some issue that stems from the past.

Moon and the Nodes
When the Moon crosses the nodes, you may move, redecorate, have interesting visitors or go on holiday to a completely different place than the one you usually visit. You make take up some special project in the home or start working from home. You could re-appraise your direction in life now. You may have some kind of Karmic experience at this time.

Moon Phases

When you were born, the Moon may have been in the first, second, third or fourth quarter. Fortunately, if you have your birth chart to hand, this is very easy to work out - even for an absolute non-astrologer, as you will see in a minute. Start by photocopying or sketching the illustration below.

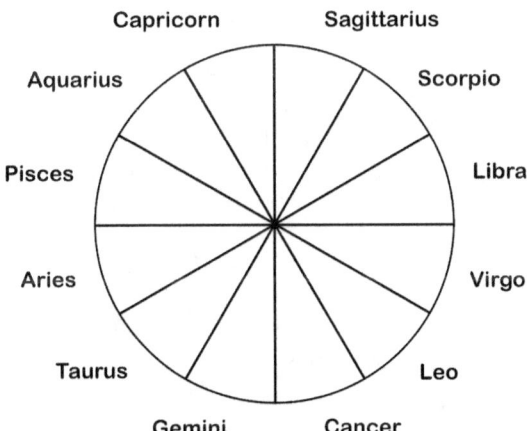

Now, write the Sun symbol in the segment for your Sun sign, and the Moon symbol in the segment that your Moon occupies.

The following example is for a person born with the Sun and Moon close together in Aries, in the first House. This is a birth at the time of a New Moon, and the aspect is called a Conjunction.

Remember that what we are looking at in this chapter is only the relationship between the Sun and Moon - not the Sign or House that they occupy.

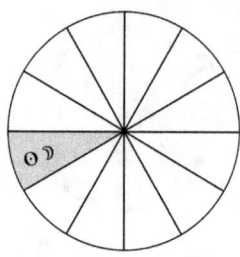

Here are the typical Sun and Moon symbols:

Sun: ☉
Moon: ☽

If the Moon is to the right of the Sun, but less than 90 degrees from it, it will be in the first quarter. At 90 degrees, it's in Square aspect.

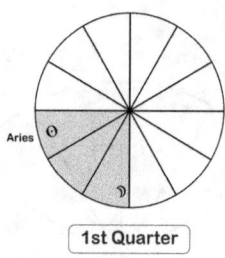

If it's between 90 degrees and 180 degrees, it's in the second quarter. At 180 degrees it's Full, and in Opposition:

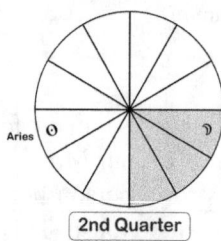

If between 180 degrees and 270 degrees, it's in its third quarter. At 270 degrees, the planets are again, in Square aspect:

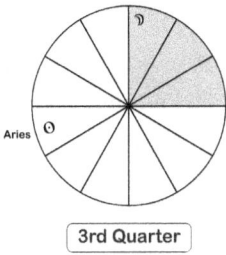

3rd Quarter

If between 270 degrees and 360 degrees, it's in its fourth quarter. At 360 degrees, the Moon is again in Conjunction with the Sun, and it has become a new Moon:

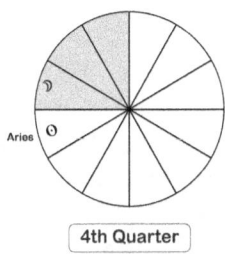

4th Quarter

Moon Phases

First Quarter
Whatever sign you were born under, wherever your other planets are placed, you will have an underlying sense of youthful enthusiasm, a touch of Aries at the heart of your nature. You probably prefer to take the initiative, especially in romance and you will always be ready to look for new interests in life, new people and new ideas. Your lively outlook and optimistic approach to life is an attractive feature but you have to guard against selfishness. You can see how things can be made to work and how situations can be improved. You will spur others into action but then leave them to finish the project. You could be self-employed. You should get off to a good start and become quite successful when young, but other factors on the chart will indicate whether this early promise will be maintained throughout. No-one can make you do something if you really don't want

to, and this may stand in the way of successful relationships. You should try not to react too fast or to take others too much by surprise.

Second Quarter
You are ambitious and sociable with an underlying touch of Cancer and Leo in your nature, you are locked into your own goals and your strong need to create something which will be seen and remembered by other people. You need a place of your own where you can express your own personality and this may be your home or your workplace. Your rather charismatic personality will always draw others towards you. You try to be helpful to others but can't be called on to make sacrifices on their behalf for very long. You may use others for your own ends; this behaviour is instinctive rather than calculated. You need the status and outlet of a career but one where your face is out in front, possibly in sales or reception work. You draw attention to yourself and while you can achieve much, you may miss some of the needs of others. You should reach considerable heights of success while still young, other factors in your chart will determine whether you maintain that success. You are slow to anger but formidable when you do lose your temper. You hate to be hurried, and may be slightly suspicious of methods and ideas that are presented to you as a fait accompli. You don't mind hurrying other people, as you know that it puts them slightly off balance and tips the odds in your favour.

Third Quarter
You are sensitive to the needs of others and you want them to be equally sensitive to your needs. There is an underlying watchfulness with this quarter rather reminiscent of Scorpio. You need friendships, colleagues and relationships and you relate well to individuals within a group. You like an exciting life but want others to share the excitement. You are aware of what others think of you and may not be entirely sure of yourself unless acceptably reflected in the eyes of others. You are drawn to more active, more successful people and can help them to achieve their aims; this phase of the Moon suggests that you will be a supreme achiever in your own right but you would still need the help and encouragement of others. There is a nerviness about you, a kind of coiled-spring tension that can lend you originality and wit, but also a short attention span and a hungry search for new people and new experiences. In some peculiar way, sex could have a

special importance to you and it may transform your life in some way. Your most successful time of your life is in your middle years.

Fourth Quarter
Whatever else there may be on your chart, there is an underlying feeling of Capricorn or Pisces here. You finish the projects that others start, and you reorganise and sort out problems left by others. You may never start projects of your own. You have clairvoyant insight and may follow hunches rather than work things out logically. You are aware of all kinds of undercurrents and can become upset by the demands of others. You have to try to let their feelings flow past you and always trust your basic instincts. You can be too inclined to sit back and let things happen around you. You are probably at your best when helping a group to achieve something beneficial. You can blend in with a large group or work entirely alone. You are probably not too materialistic but you do need job satisfaction. You may be very slow to grow up, happy to sit back and allow things to change around you, however, you are likely to go through some kind of metamorphosis later in life and achieve success in something unusual and completely individual.

Romany Tradition and Moon Phases
- Those born between the new Moon and the first quarter will have a long life.
- Born in the first twenty-four hours of a new Moon brings luck.
- Born on the second day, you will be exceptionally lucky.
- Born on the third day, you will have important and influential friends.
- Born on the fourth day, life will be up and down, with some luck and some reverses.
- Fifth and sixth day, pride could be your downfall.
- Seventh day, you have to hide the wishes that you want to come true from others.
- Those born between the first quarter and the full Moon will do better in life than your parents did.
- First day, prosperity.
- Second day, easy life.
- Third day, wealth through travel.
- Fourth and fifth days, charm.
- Sixth, easy success.

- Seventh, many friends.
- Those born between the full Moon and the last quarter will have difficulties but will overcome them by doggedness.
- First day, you will succeed in another continent.
- Second day, you will do well in business.
- Third day, success as a result of (and probably foreseen by) intuition.
- Fourth day, bravery.
- Fifth day, care must be taken with money.
- Sixth and seventh, great strength.
- Those born between the last quarter and the new Moon will be affectionate and honest.
- First and second days, you will be happy in your home.
- Third day, you are dependable.
- Fourth day, you are sensitive.
- Fifth day, you will make ideal parents.
- Sixth and seventh days, you will acquire money (or maybe non-material wealth) through loyalty.

Progressed Moon Phases

Use the same system as for natal Moon phases to work out the progressed phase. For instance, if the progressed Moon passes the natal Sun's position, it will be new. From the progressed Sun/Moon position you can easily work out whether the Moon is in the first, second, third or fourth quarter, and then you can read the natal information to get a feeling of what these quarters will bring. If you want more detailed information than this, there is some advanced professional astrology software that carries fine details of lunar progressions.

Transits

Check out the actual Moon in the actual sky from time to time. If you notice a New Moon and then check your ephemeris and discover that it's making an aspect to something on your chart, you will probably notice a small fresh start or adjustment to some part of your life. A full Moon often seems to work in a similar way, as it brings a small phase to an end and allows something or someone new to come in.

Eclipses and Occultations

This chapter is probably of more use to those who are already into astrology, but beginners can always consult an astrologer to find out when eclipses and occultations will occur. Professional quality astrology software gives dates of eclipses, but not always of occultations. Neil Michelsen's American Ephemeris of the 21st Century will show eclipses, but you will need Raphael's Ephemeris for the relevant year, to study the occultations.

```
 ☽ Phases & Eclipses
Dy Hr Mn
  5  9:55   ☾   12♊32
 13  6:42   ●☌  20♍10
 ☌  6:55:18 P  0.788
 21  9:00   ☽   28♐04
 28  2:52   ○☌   4♈40
 ☊  2:48    T  1.276

  4 21:07   ☾   11♋19
 13  0:07   ●   19♎20
 20 20:32   ☽   27♑08
 27 12:06   ○    3♉45
```

Eclipses in the Ephemeris
Most of the letters and numbers will become familiar to you as you learn and use astrology, so the only ones I am going into in this book are the symbols relating to eclipses.

Look under the column marked Dy (Day) and find the number 13. Then, track along that line to the right, to the two symbols in the middle of the line. They show that a solar eclipse is exact at that time, on that day. The first symbol, the black circle, represents a New Moon. The next symbol, a smaller black circle with a small "handle" means "Conjunction".

The next line shows that the eclipse is at its greatest at 6:55:18, and that it is a partial eclipse (P), with 0.788 of the Sun being eclipsed.

Now, look down to the 28th, when there is a Lunar eclipse, exact at 2:52a.m. The eclipse is total (T) and greatest at 2:48a.m. with more than the entire lunar surface being covered (1.276).

Note that the exact aspect and greatest visual effect don't need to happen at the same time; in fact, the greatest coverage often happens before the eclipse is exact.

Solar Eclipse

If you were born on a solar eclipse, the Sun and Moon are in the same place, so your inner and outer natures interact well. Your emotional reactions will be fast, so you act instinctively. This would enable you to avoid or get out of sticky situations admirably but it might be hard for you to make plans and carry them out.

Lunar Eclipse

If you were born on a lunar eclipse, the Earth would be standing between the Moon and the Sun, so you would have a less integrated personality, with the inner and outer sides being less harmonious than they might otherwise be. This shows a slower and more careful type of personality because you stop think before you act.

Eclipses in General

The Romans feared eclipses because they brought bad events, and I think they were right, as eclipses do tend to bring unpleasant events, but in my experience, these don't come completely out of the blue. The eclipse effect seems to bring an existing problem out into the open or to bring it to a head.

I have a theory that those born under the signs of Cancer and Leo suffer more from eclipses than other signs, because the Moon rules Cancer and the Sun rules Leo, and by its very nature, an eclipse must temporarily block one or the other of these planets.

Raphael's Ephemeris

Regardless of how much software you buy, you still need to buy the Raphael's Ephemeris for each year. The following illustration shows a couple of days to remember (for all the wrong reasons), as it reveals a solar eclipse and an occultation to Jupiter on the same day, 24 hours after an occultation of Mars!

The section headed Lunar Aspects shows when there will be a solar eclipse, as shown by the solar eclipse symbol on the 26th in the column headed by the Sun (first column).

The same symbol in a column relating to a planet other than the Sun is called an occultation rather than an eclipse, but the idea is the same, because it shows that the Moon is obscuring or "occluding" the light of the planet. In this example, Mars on the 25th and Jupiter on the 26th are occluded.

You only see the opposition symbol that refers to a lunar eclipse in the Sun's column, never in a planet's column.

Occultations

An occultation occurs when the Moon moves in front of a planet. If the planet is an inner one, such as Mercury, Venus or Mars, this may occur for two months running, but when the planet is an outer one that sits in a particular position for months on end, the Moon can occlude the planet month after month. Occultations are never pleasant but the most dramatic effect occurs when it hits an inner planet that also happens to connect with something on your own chart. The effect can be dramatic and very nasty. Here is a true story about a Moon/Venus occultation. (I've changed the names and circumstances of this story to protect the innocent.)

Marianne was enjoying spending time with her new boyfriend, Frazer. Frazer was extremely sympathetic when she started to be plagued by frightening "heavy-breather" and "funny-voice" phone calls. Mobile phones didn't exist at that time and Marianne used her phone for business, so she couldn't just change her number at the drop of a hat without damaging or even destroying her business. So, she was stuck with this unpleasant situation.

One day, Marianne and I were talking about her problem, when my psychic hackles went up. I had never met Frazer but I got the strangest feeling that the calls might have something to do with him. Marianne mentioned that there was an ex-girlfriend who might be at the back of it, but I had the feeling that it was Frazer himself who was making the calls. Marianne's first response was to say that I was being ridiculous, but when I asked Marianne if the calls ever came when Frazer was in the house, or whether they only did so when he was at work. Marianne realised that they only ever came when he was at work. Frazer worked in the electronics field, so he could easily find ways of disguising his voice over the phone.

I checked the Raphael's ephemeris against Marianne's chart, and sure enough, there was a Venus occultation coming up that would occur right on the position of Marianne's natal Moon. I warned her that something would come to light when the occultation hit.

Marianne phoned me a week later and told me that when the next obscene call came, she answered it by saying, "I know it's you Frazer, and if this doesn't stop, I'm going to the police." Later that night, Frazer came to the house and picked a fight, but Marianne had warned the neighbours that this might happen, and she threatened to scream loudly so that they would phone the police for her. Frazer eventually left, and that was the end of the affair.

Weighting and Aspects

Weighting
Weighting is what we do when working out how many items are of which gender, element or quality in order to assess the nature of the chart, and of the person.

When you have discovered the degree and sign of your Ascendant, place it on the left-hand side of the chart and arrange the other eleven signs round the chart in an anti-clockwise direction. Finally, put the Sun and the Moon in their respective positions.

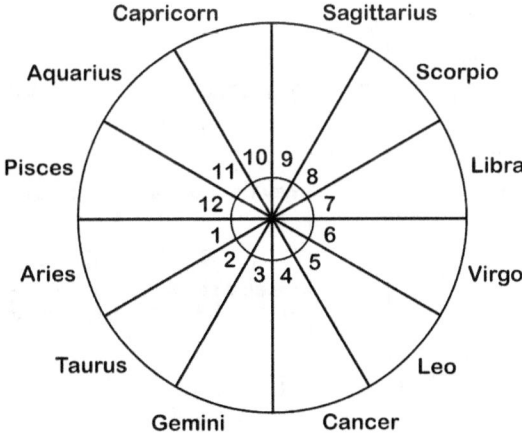

Now check the weighting of the Sun, Moon and Ascendant:
    How many of these are in masculine or feminine signs.
    How many are in fire, earth, air or water signs.
    How many are in cardinal, fixed or mutable signs.

When the Sun and Moon are in compatible signs, the inner and outer personalities are in harmony, but if the two planets are in incompatible signs, the instinctive reactions are different from the outer manner. This is further complicated by the fact that most people actually project the Ascendant or a combination of Sun and Ascendant out to the world, while the lunar side hides away until the emotions come into play or if the subject is ill, drunk or under the influence of drugs. For instance, a modest Virgoan with nervous Gemini rising and the Moon in expansive Sagittarius will become loud and boastful when drunk. An example of someone who has all three features in the same place is Queen Victoria, who had the Sun, Moon and Asc in conjunction in Gemini.

Aspects

Aspects are the angles that the planets make to each other in a chart, and these show how any two features fit with each other. Try this with any combination of Sun, Moon and Asc. The following table defines the main aspects, also showing the normal orbs for each. "Orb" is the technical term for how many degrees of variance from the exact separation is acceptable.

Aspect	Degrees Apart	Orb	Character
Conjunction	0	8	Usually the same sign and house, thus acting in a similar way.
Semi-sextile	30	2	The two signs have nothing in common, but they do share a cusp and that seems to help.
Sextile	60	6	These signs share a gender. The elements are also similar (fire & air or earth & water) so they get on fairly well together.
Square	90	6	Although often challenging, these two signs share a quality.
Trine	120	6	These share a gender and element, so they have an easy relationship.
Inconjunct	150	2	This is a truly awkward aspect, as the signs have nothing in common.
Opposition	180	8	These two share a gender and quality, so although challenging, this aspect is also stimulating.

The Nodes of the Moon

Here are the glyphs for:

The Moon's North Node: ☊   The Moon's South Node: ☋

The Sun, Moon and planets lie along the ecliptic, but the Moon and planets move above and below the ecliptic as they orbit the Sun. The Moon spends two weeks above the ecliptic and then it crosses the ecliptic to spend the next two weeks below it. When the Moon crosses the ecliptic in an upward direction, this point is called the north node, and when the Moon crosses the ecliptic in downward direction, this point is called the south node. For the most part, the nodes move backwards through the zodiac, but every now and again, there are short periods of forward motion, with the whole sequence gradually moving back over a period of time.

Wherever the north node is, the south node is exactly opposite, so when the north node is in Aries, the south node is in Libra. They always share the same gender and quality, but they never share the same element.

North Node	South Node
Aries	Libra
Taurus	Scorpio
Gemini	Sagittarius
Cancer	Capricorn
Leo	Aquarius
Virgo	Pisces
Libra	Aries
Scorpio	Taurus
Sagittarius	Gemini
Capricorn	Cancer
Aquarius	Leo
Pisces	Virgo

The Dates for the North Node Positions

The nodes spend about a year in each sign, and the following tables give you the dates from 1930 to 2031.

Date	Sign
8 Jul 1930	Aries
29 Dec 1931	Pisces
25 Jun 1933	Aquarius
9 Mar 1935	Capricorn
15 Sept 1936	Sagittarius
3 Mar 1938	Scorpio
12 Sept 1939	Libra
25 May 1941	Virgo
22 Nov 1942	Leo
12 May 1944	Cancer
3 Dec 1945	Gemini
3 Aug 1947	Taurus
26 Jan 1949	Aries
27 Jul 1950	Pisces
29 Mar 1952	Aquarius
10 Oct 1953	Capricorn
3 Apr 1955	Sagittarius
5 Oct 1956	Scorpio
17 Jun 1958	Libra
16 Dec 1959	Virgo
11 Jun 1961	Leo
24 Dec 1962	Cancer
26 Aug 1964	Gemini
20 Feb 1966	Taurus
20 Aug 1967	Aries
20 Apr 1969	Pisces
3 Nov 1970	Aquarius
28 Apr 1972	Capricorn
28 Oct 1973	Sagittarius
11 Jul 1975	Scorpio
8 Jan 1977	Libra

Date	Sign
6 Jul 1978	Virgo
13 Jan 1980	Leo
21 Sept 1981	Cancer
17 Mar 1983	Gemini
12 Sept 1984	Taurus
7 Apr 1986	Aries
3 Dec 1987	Pisces
23 May 1989	Aquarius
19 Nov 1990	Capricorn
2 Aug 1992	Sagittarius
2 Feb 1994	Scorpio
1 Aug 1995	Libra
26 Jan 1997	Virgo
21 Oct 1998	Leo
10 Apr 2000	Cancer
14 Oct 2001	Gemini
15 Mar 2003	Taurus
27 Dec 2004	Aries
23 Jun 2006	Pisces
19 Dec 2007	Aquarius
22 Aug 2009	Capricorn
4 Mar 2011	Sagittarius
31 Aug 2010	Scorpio
19 Feb 2014	Libra
12 Nov 2015	Virgo
10 May 2017	Leo
7 Nov 2018	Cancer
5 June 2020	Gemini
24 Dec 2021	Taurus
13 Jul 2023	Aries
30 Jan 2025	Pisces
19 May 2026	Aquarius
8 Mar 2028	Capricorn
25 Sep 2029	Sagittarius
15 Apr 2031	Scorpio

The Hindu View

Hindu astrologers call the nodes of the Moon Rahu and Ketu, meaning the dragon's head and the dragon's tail. The idea is that the tail of the dragon is leaving a previous life, while the head is preparing for the next one. The astrological idea is that certain things come easily to us because we learned them in a past life, while the current incarnation is filled with lessons that help our souls to develop. The south node represents at least one past lifetime, while the north node represents the lessons and tasks for the current one. If you don't believe in karma or reincarnation, you could say that we find it natural to do the things that the south node represents, and difficult to achieve those that the north node stands for.

Politics, Society, Timing and Geography

Leaving aside the ideas of karma, there is a completely opposite view of the nodes, and this is the one that I find useful. The theory here is that the north node represents those areas where the current business, social or political atmosphere runs in your favour. For example, let us say that you wish to open a health-food shop. This would have been a great success at any time during the past twenty years and it would probably do well now. However, if you wanted to open a high street shop selling fur coats, you would need a time machine to take you back to the 1950s, or you would have to move to Russia. It's easier to get something off the ground when a planet transits the north node than when it sits on the south node. This isn't to say that you shouldn't try, but you will have to accept that things will take longer and be more difficult when the south node is being activated.

The Parents and the Past

Because these nodes are linked to the Moon, they can throw light on the experience of being nurtured or mothered - by whoever did the mothering. Sometimes, the nodes tell us something about our own experiences as parents. Oddly enough, the signs that denote a difficult childhood when they are on the Ascendant or as Moon sign are not necessarily so difficult for the nodes. For instance, Gemini is not an easy sign to have rising, but a Gemini node is not bad at all. When planets make aspects to the nodes by transit or progression, events concerning parents (especially the mother) tend to come into focus.

Premises and Property
The nodes seem to have a bearing on home premises and also those that we may rent or buy to run a farm or for any kind of a business or to let out for income. This is not hard to understand, because the home, premises, small businesses, family, heritage and the past are all assigned to the Moon, so these things are bound to have an influence on the nodes.

Connections

A fascinating area of astrology shows the way that charts connect, because one person's Sun sign is often another's Moon or a third's ascendant, and two Sun signs that are apparently incompatible can be eased by these links.

The following is a real family group:

  Mother: Sun Cancer, Moon Taurus, Scorpio rising
  Son: Sun Scorpio, Moon Taurus, Cancer rising
  Daughter: Sun Leo, Moon Scorpio, Cancer rising

Clearly, the mother and son share three signs, while the daughter is only slightly different.

You may find yourself drawn to lovers or friends of a particular Sun sign, and this gets even more interesting when you start to look at Sun, Moon and Asc combinations. One friend of mine has had several husbands and lovers, all of whom had Aries/Capricorn combinations.

People who work together or come together for a common cause often share signs, probably due to the nature of the job:

- I once worked in a major psychic festival where everyone in our group had the Sun, Moon or both, in Pisces.
- A bank in Brighton employed nine accountants, and eight of them had the Sun in Gemini.
- Similarly, a publisher that I used to write for employed nine Sun in Capricorn people.

- A friend once employed a number of carpenters, builders, electricians and whatnot to do some building at her place of work, and every single one of them had the sun in Aquarius.
- I worked on a committee whose members all had watery Moons, with seven lunar Pisceans and two lunar Cancerians.
- Lastly, I remember reading a book by a cat burglar who remarked that he and eleven of his burglar friends were all Sun in Aquarius!

Sun/Moon Combinations

Sun Aries, Moon Aries
An extrovert and self-starter with an endless supply of enthusiasm, quick to think and act. You lack patience and may be too self-centred.

Sun Aries, Moon Taurus
Confident, enthusiastic and lovable, good builder, architect or gardener with an artistic eye. Could be dogmatic.

Sun Aries, Moon Gemini
Dextrous, good engineer or draftsman, full of bright ideas. Clever with words but sharp and sarcastic at times. You may leave tasks for others to finish off.

Sun Aries, Moon Cancer
Very determined, a good business head on your shoulders and a pleasant manner. Home life is very important to you. Sensitive but you hide it from others.

Sun Aries, Moon Leo
A real go-getter, you need the limelight. Enthusiastic and optimistic you may be bossy and domineering. Very creative, but blind to underlying influences at times.

Sun Aries, Moon Virgo
Probing, analytical and clever. Very efficient and clever worker, shy in personal matters. Good writer, harsh critic, may be too fond of nit-picking details.

Sun Aries, Moon Libra
Outwardly confident and ebullient, inwardly calmer. Sensitive to others; also loving and passionate. Good business sense but may be over-ambitious.

Sun Aries, Moon Scorpio
An excellent soldier or surgeon, good concentration level. Single-minded, intense and passionate about everything; you may be too much for anyone to handle for long. Try to relax and let others do the same.

Sun Aries, Moon Sagittarius
Restless and energetic, you are a born explorer on both the physical and mental level. You can fill others with a zest for life and idealism. Tactless and sarcastic.

Sun Aries, Moon Capricorn
Determined, unstoppable, must reach the top but this could be at the expense of your personal life. You seek to dominate others by force of your personality.

Sun Aries, Moon Aquarius
Humanitarian and enthusiastic, you would make a wonderful sports coach or teacher, but you must be careful not to hurt others by thoughtlessly sarcastic remarks.

Sun Aries, Moon Pisces
Outwardly enthusiastic, inwardly shy and lacking in confidence. Kind and well-meaning but could be apt to preach. You need to get away from others from time to time.

Sun Taurus, Moon Aries
Outwardly calm, inwardly ambitious and determined. Could be very creative in a practical way. You may be too fond of your own opinions. Good engineer and builder, artistic too.

Sun Taurus, Moon Taurus
Stubborn, fixed in your views and materialistic, but also creative and artistic with a love of music. You will make things that stand the test of time. Loyal in love.

Sun Taurus, Moon Gemini
Artistic and perceptive, a good media worker or marketing expert. Home-loving but occasional outbursts of restlessness. Affectionate, but not too sensual.

Sun Taurus, Moon Cancer
A real homemaker and family person. You can motivate others to achieve a great deal but you hold back from the limelight. Your imagination can be successfully harnessed.

Sun Taurus, Moon Leo
Very fixed opinions and a definite personality, you find it hard to adapt to change. You love children and are intensely loyal to others. You could be a good singer or dancer.

Sun Taurus, Moon Virgo
A careful worker who can combine detail and artistry. Good family person. Can learn and teach wordy or musical skills. Don't be too critical or pessimistic. A strong interest in nutrition.

Sun Taurus, Moon Libra
Very sensual and also artistic with a good business head. Maybe too lazy to achieve much but when motivated can reach the top. Lovable and kind, but selfish too.

Sun Taurus, Moon Scorpio
Artistic and sensual, you can achieve much. Your opinions are fixed and your nature stubborn. Very loyal and persistent, could be a good sales person, also strongly independent. Extreme stinginess may be a problem.

Sun Taurus, Moon Sagittarius
Outwardly steady, inwardly restless. Could be an armchair traveller. Traditional religion interests you; don't be too old-fashioned or quick to judge others.

Sun Taurus, Moon Capricorn
Determined and ambitious with a strong need for security. A shrewd and practical business head, but inwardly shy and nervous in personal situations. Very loyal and loving. Careful with money.

Sun Taurus, Moon Aquarius
Innovative and artistic you are good company and a hard worker. You need freedom but will insist on others toeing the line. Good concentration and high level of confidence.

Sun Taurus, Moon Pisces
Dreamy and patient, highly artistic you may have difficulty in getting projects off the ground. Your sympathy may land you with the care of lame ducks. Sensual and loving.

Sun Gemini, Moon Aries
Very sharp mind and a great deal of enthusiasm that can carry you away. Good media type, interesting friend but a touch too sarcastic for comfort.

Sun Gemini, Moon Taurus
You have good ideas and the patience to finish what you start. A good homemaker and parent. You need communication and comfort in a relationship and work in a mentally artistic field.

Sun Gemini, Moon Gemini
You have dozens of bright ideas but difficulty in completing anything. Very clever and dextrous but could be a bit unfeeling. Tension is your problem, try to relax and feel.

Sun Gemini, Moon Cancer
Friendly and chatty, usually on the phone. You love travel and novelty plus family life. Don't be put upon by stronger characters. You can make a happy home for others. Your memory is good.

Sun Gemini, Moon Leo
Lively, friendly and good looking you will always be popular. You need to express your ideas creatively. Good with children as you will never quite grow up yourself.

Sun Gemini, Moon Virgo
Inventive, versatile and full of ideas, but lacking in confidence. Your nerves sometimes get the better of you. Good researcher, writer, secretary.

Sun Gemini, Moon Libra
You are full of ideas that may not always get off the ground. Diplomatic, flirtatious and fun, you can be a bit too restless. Inclined to be long-winded.

Sun Gemini, Moon Scorpio
Brilliant and perceptive mind. Outwardly a cool-hearted loner, but burning with secret passions; also emotionally vulnerable. Very creative writer, musician, doctor or spy. Clever with words, sarcastic.

Sun Gemini, Moon Sagittarius
Restless, good sportsman or adventurous traveller. Good scholar and teacher. Might need to get in touch with your own feelings and those of others.

Sun Gemini, Moon Capricorn
Clever and ambitious, literate would succeed in the media. Relationships may bring suffering; you must try to be warmer to others. Capable and businesslike.

Sun Gemini, Moon Aquarius
Broad-minded, good scholar and teacher. Wide-ranging ideas, perceptive. May fear emotional display or even own feelings. Detachment sought, good journalist or traveller.

Sun Gemini, Moon Pisces
Hidden depths to personality, good with children, also sports and dancing. Imaginative writer, but too ready to explain all to others. Bubbly personality, but lacking in confidence; nervous and incapable if under severe stress.

Sun Cancer, Moon Aries
Capable and competitive type with a good business head and the ability to understand others. Would need a good home but easily bored if spending too much time in it. A strange mixture of caring and impatience.

Sun Cancer, Moon Taurus
Kind, caring and cuddly. You love your home and family, you also have a good head for business. Artistic, musical and rather lazy, inclined to brood.

Sun Cancer, Moon Gemini
Clever and businesslike, pleasant and successful. You appear slow but can

be quick and cunning. Good politician, terrific traveller. Could have sporting abilities.

Sun Cancer, Moon Cancer
Strong emotions, strong attachment to family. You tend to be moody and possessive. Kind-hearted, aware of the needs of others. Attached to the past, good historian.

Sun Cancer, Moon Leo
Caring and compassionate, very loving towards your family and friends. Emotionally vulnerable. You have high standards and can cut off your nose to spite your face.

Sun Cancer, Moon Virgo
Good placement for a nurse or doctor, caring in a practical way. Good with details, excellent memory. Will cut off from others when hurt. Good business head, rather dogged, good salesperson. A worrier.

Sun Cancer, Moon Libra
Good business head on your shoulders. Ambitious for self and your family. Love of beauty and harmony, probably artistic. May have difficulty in putting ideas into practice.

Sun Cancer, Moon Scorpio
Strongly intuitive and probably very moody. You would be hard to ignore. Try to keep a positive outlook on life and avoid being too pessimistic or cruel.

Sun Cancer, Moon Sagittarius
This combination makes you a family person who needs emotional freedom. You are idealistic and lovable but you may ask more from life than you could reasonably expect to obtain.

Sun Cancer, Moon Capricorn
You have a very good head for business, and you are shrewd and intuitive. You can succeed as long as you don't try to cut corners or to save money in silly ways.

Sun Cancer, Moon Aquarius
A clever politician with a quirky mind that operates behind a placid facade. You can put your point of view across well. You keep your eye firmly fixed on the main chance.

Sun Cancer, Moon Pisces
Very sensitive and intuitive, you are so tuned in to others that you can forget your own needs. You may prefer to work in a field where you can care for less fortunate people (or animals).

Sun Leo, Moon Aries
You have courage, verve and enthusiasm but you must learn not to ride roughshod over others. If you can see beyond your own needs, you can go far.

Sun Leo, Moon Taurus
You are kind, reliable; dedicated to your family and highly practical but you may be too obstinate for your own good. Traditional outlook on life.

Sun Leo, Moon Gemini
You like to be busy and your mind works overtime. You are independent, creative and clever with good leadership qualities but your sarcasm might be a bit too much for some people.

Sun Leo, Moon Cancer
A real family person with strong need to mother people. Your emotions may overtake you at times. You like the past and tradition. Very caring and kind.

Sun Leo, Moon Leo
Dramatic and outgoing, you need to dazzle others. You are funny and entertaining but might be a bit too self-centred for comfort. Try to cope with details rather than ignoring them.

Sun Leo, Moon Virgo
You could be an excellent employer as you can delegate and also work in a logical manner. Your sharp tongue might be a bit hard to live with. You are very honest and basically kind-hearted.

Sun Leo, Moon Libra
Very affectionate and probably very sexy, you have a great sense of style. You also have a good head for business but you may be too fond of having things your own way.

Sun Leo, Moon Scorpio
Very intense and strong personality, possibly too dramatic. You are very loyal and may be rather possessive but your colleagues will respect you for your honesty and your capacity for work.

Sun Leo, Moon Sagittarius
Very adventurous, you cannot be tied down. You are loyal, proud and kind-hearted. You have high personal standards but will have to curb your sarcasm and think before committing yourself.

Sun Leo, Moon Capricorn
Very organised and ambitious, you are destined to succeed in some traditional field of work. Don't ride roughshod over others or cover up your softness too much.

Sun Leo, Moon Aquarius
You have strong opinions and can throw yourself into a cause. You are loyal, faithful and have a well-developed sense of fair play. Try to develop practicality and a flexible outlook.

Sun Leo, Moon Pisces
A dreamer and mystic who can bring dreams to life. It's hard for you to turn away from those who need your help and strength. Don't become downhearted if all your plans don't work out. Creative and kind-hearted.

Sun Virgo, Moon Aries
Your mind is sharp and so is your tongue. Being quick and clever you can succeed at many jobs. Self-expression in the form of writing is essential for you.

Sun Virgo, Moon Taurus
Interested in the growing and preparing of food, creative in a structured way and kind. You may lack the confidence to get things off the ground. Sensible, helpful and practical outlook.

Sun Virgo, Moon Gemini
You are very quick and clever, your mind and tongue are rarely still. You can gather and analyse information but your intellect may prevent you from getting in touch with your own and other people's feelings.

Sun Virgo, Moon Cancer
Very canny, interested in food and nutrition. Could be a good businessperson in a small way. You worry about your family and can be a bit too fussy and moody for comfort.

Sun Virgo, Moon Leo
Caring, conscientious and organised, you can be relied upon to get things done. You may work with children. Your personal standards are very high but you lack confidence.

Sun Virgo, Moon Virgo
Lack of confidence, partly due to an unhappy childhood. You may pay too much attention to details and worry too much about small matters. Honest and kind, you always try to help others and do your duty in every way.

Sun Virgo, Moon Libra
You are neat and tidy, and you enjoy organising. Could be a good mediator or co-operative worker. Good thinker but slow to make decisions. A good cook.

Sun Virgo, Moon Scorpio
Clever and critical, you would make a very good doctor or nurse. You need to get to the bottom of things but may be too cool for comfort towards others.

Sun Virgo, Moon Sagittarius
Humanitarian and thoughtful, you are interested in education. Warm and friendly and sometimes impulsive, you can also attend to details. Could make a good teacher but an even better travel agent.

Sun Virgo, Moon Capricorn
Good in business but possibly too self-disciplined and serious. You are

capable, conscientious and clever but you need to cultivate a sense of fun and give some attention to the needs of others. Very reliable family member.

Sun Virgo, Moon Aquarius
You could be a wonderful teacher. Deep thinker, very helpful to those in need. Don't let your need for independence deprive you of family life or keep you separated from your feelings.

Sun Virgo, Moon Pisces
You live to serve the needs of others and then wonder why your own needs are not being met. Your mind is good when projected outwardly towards intellectual pursuits. Intuitive, interested in medicine and nutrition.

Sun Libra, Moon Aries
You are a good initiator, but might find it difficult to finish what you start. Others may help you to do this. You are clever and intuitive but can be selfish and impatient. Good in a crisis.

Sun Libra, Moon Taurus
You are attractive to look at and have excellent taste. You love music and art but may be too lazy to become skilled yourself. Good homemaker and family person with practical business mind.

Sun Libra, Moon Gemini
A theoriser with a good mind, you can be superficial. Dextrous and clever you have the ability to put techniques into practice as long as you have help from others. Keep in touch with your feelings and those of others.

Sun Libra, Moon Cancer
Kind but tough, you make a nice home and are a good caring family member. Good personnel manager or accountant. You need to close off from others from time to time to do your own thing.

Sun Libra, Moon Leo
You are in love with love half the time with a romantic and dramatic attitude to life. Clever and creative but could become easily bored. Very clever in business or politics.

Sun Libra, Moon Virgo
Pleasant, charming and sensible, you can do most things as long as they are not messy or dirty. Loyal to friends. Good at detailed work. Literate and musical.

Sun Libra, Moon Libra
You are very attractive both in looks and as a personality but you may be in a bit of a dream half the time. You may need to be more decisive and more energetic.

Sun Libra, Moon Scorpio
Strongly sexed and intense, you would be a handful for anyone who comes close to you. You are determined and businesslike but must watch a tendency to dominate others.

Sun Libra, Moon Sagittarius
You will probably travel quite a bit on business and should be great at dealing with and negotiating with foreigners. The legal profession would draw you as you have a good sense of judgement.

Sun Libra, Moon Capricorn
You are very purposeful and a harder worker, which is unusual for a Libran. You could be very successful as your judgement of people is pretty acute.

Sun Libra, Moon Aquarius
Very independent and also quite clever. You have good judgement and are able to lead others strongly but calmly. Your imagination is strong and it can be used to make your living.

Sun Libra, Moon Pisces
Very artistic and musical, you can be a dreamy romantic. Both your appearance and your nature are attractive. You have a deep level of intuition but may be a bit slow to put things into action.

Sun Scorpio, Moon Aries
You have a strong character but might be too ready to fight everything and everyone. Your feelings are intense and your temper rather short but

you have deep reserves of courage and can achieve a great deal.

Sun Scorpio, Moon Taurus
Sensual and musical you might have great talent for something attractive like horticulture. You may be too obstinate or too practical. Hard to live with, and stubborn.

Sun Scorpio, Moon Gemini
This combination shows a difficult childhood and an early sense of loss. Don't continue to view the world with too much suspicion. Very clever and intuitive about people.

Sun Scorpio, Moon Cancer
Attractive to look at and talk to, you are deeply intuitive but may be able to relate more easily to animals than to people. Your moodiness will be your weak point. Try to avoid stinginess.

Sun Scorpio, Moon Leo
Very fixed opinions. It's hard for you to adapt. Loyal to your family especially your children. You can finish what you start. Guard against over-dramatising everything.

Sun Scorpio, Moon Virgo
This shows a difficult childhood with feelings of alienation. Try to develop trust in others. Clever and dutiful, you could be drawn to a career in the medical profession.

Sun Scorpio, Moon Libra
You are attractive and clever, this combination gives diplomacy and determination, and you would make a good politician. You may either swamp your family with your personality or ignore them while pursuing your career.

Sun Scorpio, Moon Scorpio
You have a powerful personality and feel passionate about everything. Try not to dominate others. You can achieve almost anything, but your resentment and moaning about others isn't attractive.

Sun Scorpio, Moon Sagittarius
Clever and clairvoyant, you would make a good lawyer or businessman but also a good detective. Your sense of humour helps you to keep everything in perspective.

Sun Scorpio, Moon Capricorn
You could be a rather serious and determined person. You would reach the top in any field you set your heart on but could miss out on the personal side of life until your later years.

Sun Scorpio, Moon Aquarius
You are independent and clever with a strong intuitive streak. You are decisive and instinctive but might be something of an intolerant tough guy. Stubborn and determined.

Sun Scorpio, Moon Pisces
Intuitive and artistic, probably musical. You have a strong drive to help others, probably in the field of health. You can withdraw into injured silence or spitefulness if you feel threatened.

Sun Sagittarius, Moon Aries
You are open and honest but may be too quick to jump into exciting new schemes. Your restlessness might take you around the world but may make it difficult for you to hang on to relationships or keep jobs.

Sun Sagittarius, Moon Taurus
You are kind and good-hearted with great enthusiasm for the good things of life. You could be an inspired cook or artist and have the ability to combine practicality with imagination.

Sun Sagittarius, Moon Gemini
You are always busy and restless. You could be a very good sportsman or entertainer. Clever and articulate, you could make a good writer or teacher.

Sun Sagittarius, Moon Cancer
You are intuitive and creative and would make a good medium. There is a split between your need for home comforts and your need for freedom. Childish at times.

Sun Sagittarius, Moon Leo
Dramatic and outgoing, you would do well on the stage. Try to tune in a bit more to the needs of others. Youthful and active, you are great fun to be with.

Sun Sagittarius, Moon Virgo
You have the ability to think both deeply and in an organised manner. You would make a wonderful teacher. Don't lay the law down to others.

Sun Sagittarius, Moon Libra
You would make a fabulous barrister as you have a gift for all things legal. Don't be too hard on others who are not as bright or as successful as you.

Sun Sagittarius, Moon Scorpio
You could make a good detective as you have investigative ability and a legal mind. Don't be too hard on those who don't share your interests or are not as capable as you.

Sun Sagittarius, Moon Sagittarius
You would make a terrific explorer as you love travel and are too restless to sit still for long. Try to tune into ordinary people, as not everyone will understand the breadth of your mind.

Sun Sagittarius, Moon Capricorn
Clever and determined, honest and entertaining, you could go far in life. You should travel and be involved with business but you must have some patience with less capable people.

Sun Sagittarius, Moon Aquarius
Your mind is broad and you can teach others. You tend to live in a world of your own which is out of step with most of the rest of the world. Could be an eccentric genius.

Sun Sagittarius, Moon Pisces
You are intuitive, kind and spiritual and would make a good teacher. You are artistic and imaginative and have much to give others but you may be vague and impractical at times.

Sun Capricorn, Moon Aries

You have a great deal of determination and may be very clever as well. Once you have set your mind on something, you will get there for sure but you may tread on a few toes while doing it.

Sun Capricorn, Moon Taurus

Practical and sensible, you can achieve much both in the artistic and the business world. Guard against stubbornness and try to see the other person's point of view.

Sun Capricorn, Moon Gemini

Clever but organised. Could make a good writer, salesman, and businessperson with the ability to put good ideas into practice and finish what you start.

Sun Capricorn, Moon Cancer

Home-loving family person, very loyal, decent, also extremely businesslike. Can have a tendency to withdraw into your shell. You worry about everything. A good teacher or counsellor.

Sun Capricorn, Moon Leo

Good in positions of authority. A caring boss. Decent, reliable, but also very determined, might be apt to ride over people who are weaker.

Sun Capricorn, Moon Virgo

Very stable, reliable, family person. Probably a good cook. Very good head for business. Could be a bit lacking in humour or too pedantic, and a fusspot.

Sun Capricorn, Moon Libra

A good mixture of stability plus business ability. Can get on with people and also achieve a great deal, but may be a bit over enthusiastic when it comes to money-making ideas.

Sun Capricorn, Moon Scorpio

Great strength of character. Clear idea of where you are going and what you want out of life. Very dependable, loyal, kind, but you have no time for fools. You hate to show your feelings.

Sun/Moon Combinations

Sun Capricorn, Moon Sagittarius
Great stability and ability plus a broad, sweeping mind. Could work in the travel industry or teaching, legal or church work. Good in any sort of concentrated work where you deal with people in authority.

Sun Capricorn, Moon Capricorn
Very shy and withdrawn. Very hard worker, good with the elderly. Could find life very difficult until later on. A creative hobby or outlet would be very beneficial to you.

Sun Capricorn, Moon Aquarius
Good organiser. Able to do things on a big scale. Can be a bit hard on yourself and on other people, but very determined and capable. Original thinker.

Sun Capricorn, Moon Pisces
Deep, kindly, intuitive, very good in a caring profession, particularly dealing with the old, but could be a bit too shy and easily hurt. Rather serious.

Sun Aquarius, Moon Aries
A very broad-ranging mind. Good teacher, engineer, very clever, but might be difficult to live with. Don't judge other people too harshly. Good sense of humour.

Sun Aquarius, Moon Taurus
You can cope with a lot and achieve a lot. You are very steady, determined and reliable, but could be too stubborn. You may be interested in music, art or beauty products.

Sun Aquarius, Moon Gemini
A natural student or teacher, very clever. A bit inclined to flip from one idea to another and also need to develop stability in relationships with other people. Easily bored.

Sun Aquarius, Moon Cancer
A good family person, good with small children and animals. Can teach, a good companion but can be a bit inclined to withdraw into a shell.

Sun Aquarius, Moon Leo
Very lively personality, and you are always busy doing a lot of things at once. Loyal, a bit stubborn, determined, but can be independent and awkward. Probably musical or a good dancer.

Sun Aquarius, Moon Virgo
Clever, studious, able to put ideas into practice in a very detailed way. Probably very good in research but could be a bit eccentric and nit picking, difficult to live with.

Sun Aquarius, Moon Libra
Great fun, easy-going, great friend to everybody, logical mind, but a bit unreliable in close relationships. Good in almost any field that doesn't require too much steady effort.

Sun Aquarius, Moon Scorpio
Full of self-confidence. The ability to be a leader. Can be too inclined to ride roughshod over other people. A very original thinker. Easily irritated with fools. Stubborn and determined.

Sun Aquarius, Moon Sagittarius
Very independent, outspoken, a bit tactless, interested in any kind of novel idea. Intelligent, a good teacher. You have a tendency to rush into things without thinking.

Sun Aquarius, Moon Capricorn
A mixture of seriousness and spontaneity. Responsible, capable, a good family person, a good businessperson. Original ideas and a lot of determination.

Sun Aquarius, Moon Aquarius
Very eccentric, very freedom-loving, independent, great fun. Original ideas and an original lifestyle, but not really a family person. Don't judge others too harshly.

Sun Aquarius, Moon Pisces
Imaginative, intuitive, able to blend common sense and mysticism. Kindly, intelligent, a bit apt to wander off on you're own and go into flights of fancy.

Sun Pisces, Moon Aries
Intuitive, quick and clever, quite determined, great fun and good friend, but not a very reliable family person. You may fluctuate between selfishness and consideration for others.

Sun Pisces, Moon Taurus
Sociable and pleasant, artistic, kind and musical. It's difficult for you to start things but once started you will finish them. You are good looking and graceful. Inclined to be lazy.

Sun Pisces, Moon Gemini
Nervous, talkative, clever, a worrier. You need a stable partner. You're good fun, good looking and interesting, but you never really grow up. Your nerves let you down from time to time.

Sun Pisces, Moon Cancer
Sensitive, kind, thoughtful, very moody, but also kind and caring. You would make a good nurse, doctor or teacher. You may be interested in diets and cooking. Understanding but somewhat impractical.

Sun Pisces, Moon Leo
Generous, imaginative, creative and kindly. You need to be out and about. You like stimulation of new people but your confidence goes very quickly and you can be susceptible to flattery.

Sun Pisces, Moon Virgo
Nervous, thoughtful, deep, intuitive, could work creatively. Can be too fussy, too worrying, would need a strong partner. Interested in food and diets. Impatient.

Sun Pisces, Moon Libra
You will need to keep in touch with reality. Your ideas are good. You could achieve a lot if allied to somebody with strength and practicality. You need other people to encourage you.

Sun Pisces, Moon Scorpio
Perceptive, intuitive, deep, attracted to medicine, police and forensic work. Deep insight into people, can manipulate others. Moody, but also caring and kind. Can be self-absorbed and difficult to live with.

Sun Pisces, Moon Sagittarius
Great traveller with a deep and thoughtful mind. Could work in the religious field or as a conservationist. Unreliable as a family person as your mind is elsewhere most of the time.

Sun Pisces, Moon Capricorn
Creativity, intuition and practicality mixed together here, so you can make achievements on the work front and also be a good family person. The only problem is lack of confidence.

Sun Pisces, Moon Aquarius
Friendly, could start projects and then lose interest. Mystical, a good teacher and a caring person but you need a stable and practical partner, as you don't often have your feet on the ground.

Sun Pisces, Moon Pisces
Very active imagination. You see omens and meanings in things. You prefer to work from home by yourself: You find people tend to wear you out; you soak up other people's problems and find family life hard sometimes.

Information and Suggestions

Here are a couple of things you need to look out for:

Progressions
If you want to do a quick rule-of-thumb, day-for-a-year progression, you need to count forward by one day for each year of your life. For instance, if you were born on the 10th of October 1974 and you want to look at the situation when you reach the age of 35, your progressed date for that year is the 15th of November 1974. Now, all you need to do is look at an ephemeris for the 15th of November 1974.

Remember that April, June, September and November each have thirty days, while all the rest have thirty-one. February has twenty-eight, except when there is a leap year, when it has twenty-nine. A leap year occurs whenever you can evenly divide a year by four, and by 400 as well.

(Leap years get a little bit more complicated than that, so for the full, technical details, one can do an online search.)

Transits
- Look up a date that interests you in an ephemeris, and check out the Moon sign. The Moon takes a mere two-and-a-half-days to transit a sign, so it's only useful if you have something "time-specific" going on, such as a job interview, an important date, or looking into a new venture.
- See whether the transiting Moon is making good, bad or indifferent aspects to your natal Sun and Moon. For instance, if your natal Sun is in Scorpio and your transiting Moon is in Aquarius, it may be making an unpleasant square aspect, signifying that the event will be stressful and tiresome. It might just work to your advantage if you push hard for what you want, but equally, it could turn out to be an upsetting waste of effort.
- Review the chapter on phases of the Moon to judge whether your important date coincides with a new Moon (fresh start), a full Moon

(other people involved, for good or ill), or an old Moon (nothing will come of it).
- Check whether the Moon is "Void of Course", as this also means that nothing useful will come of your event.

And Finally...

Don't become neurotic about all the above. If you really do have some seriously important date to consider, it's worth checking the Moon and as much else on your chart as you can, before the event. However, in the normal run of things, it's usually better for your mental health just to live yorr life and let things happen as they will. It's also interesting, if you've had a particularly good or bad day, to check the status of the Moon (and much else) after the event.

The BIG
Astrology Guide

Volume Two

PREDICTIVE ASTROLOGY

Introduction and Beginners' Section

Now, I will show you how to predict trends and events, starting with the most popular methods and moving on to other popular techniques. After that, I demonstrate less commonly used methods so that you can consider the different approaches.

When I started as an astrologer, there was only one way of working: calculating the natal charts by hand, looking up the transits in an ephemeris, and finally calculating the day-for-a-year progressions by hand. Fortunately, nowadays there are many accessible routes.

At this point in the book, you need to be comfortable reading a natal chart and probably fairly adept at locating the transits and interpreting their effects. Up to now, you have been able to get away with a cheap astrology App, along with ephemerides for the 20th century and 21st century, plus the annual Raphael's Ephemeris; this book, however, takes you further than that. Now you will need professional-quality software, and I would recommend Solar Fire or Winstar. Over the years, I have bought and used some of the other available software and discovered that most of it is too basic, while one expensive program I tried a couple of years ago is wildly inaccurate! Hence my recommendations of Solar Fire and Winstar.

Check out the internet for astrology information and for courses, and check out YouTube for further details. The problem with the internet is the vast quantity of data available, which is daunting and confusing to a beginner. Take things a step at a time, and don't allow yourself to become swamped. Consult a professional astrologer if necessary.

For Absolute Beginners
If you need to check out your own Sun sign, look at the following list.

SIGN	DATES
Aries	March 21 – April 19
Taurus	April 20 – May 20
Gemini	May 21 – June 21
Cancer	June 22 – July 22
Leo	July 23 – August 22
Virgo	August 23 – September 22
Libra	September 23 – October 22
Scorpio	October 23 – November 21
Sagittarius	November 22 – December 21
Capricorn	December 22 – January 20
Aquarius	January 21 – February 18
Pisces	February 19 – March 20

The Sun doesn't change sign on the same day each year, so if you were born on the cusp of two signs and are unsure which sign you are, a visit to an astrologer or an inexpensive App for your smartphone will show you which one is correct. The above table shows the average Sun sign dates.

You may be aware that you are happier at certain times of the year and unhappy at others, also that there are times of the year when things take off for you and other times when nothing much happens. Some people always have a good Christmas, and others find the festive season disappointing or even unpleasant. Some dread a particular time of the year, and others look forward to seasons they know will be good for them. This is roughly how the situation plays out.

On your birthday, the Sun is where it was when you were born, so this is a time of mixed emotions, such as happiness because it is a special time and sadness due to being a year older.

- One month after your birthday will be a reasonably good time.
- Two months after your birthday is usually good, with companionship and with new ideas kicking in.
- Three months after your birthday, you feel stressed and up against several problems.

Introduction & Beginners' Section 179

- Four months after your birthday is likely to be a happy time when creative projects flourish.
- Five months after your birthday could be trying, from the point of view of health or finances.
- Six months after your birthday is likely to be difficult for health and relationships.
- Seven months after your birthday is a trying time for partnerships and finances.
- Eight months after your birthday is a pleasant time with some luck and the potential for travel.
- Nine months after your birthday will be stressful and bothersome.
- Ten months after your birthday is a successful time with friendships, new connections and good ideas.
- Eleven months after your birthday is slightly good in some ways and a bit depressing in others.
- Twelve months – well, you're back at your birthday once again.

So now, let us move onto the starting point of predictive astrological techniques.

Transits

This is the most popular method of predicting the future because it takes the position of the planets as they are in the sky at any particular date and time and judges them against the natal chart. A version of this is even used in all newspaper and magazine astrology columns, and we will look at how that is done later in this chapter.

On a clear night, look at the sky and remind yourself that the planets don't just live in the pages of your ephemeris or inside the workings of your computer. You will certainly be able to spot the Moon, and early in the morning or as the Sun sets, you may spot a bright planet, which is Venus being close to the rising or setting Sun. Another very bright planet is Jupiter, while a reddish one is Mars and a yellowish one is Saturn. You may even spot tiny Mercury near the Sun just around sunrise or sunset.

These days, you may see passing aeroplanes and even a space station occasionally, so you must make sure that what you are looking at is an actual planet. The more distant planets, Uranus, Neptune, Pluto and Chiron, are too far away to be seen with the naked eye.

Now look at your App or check the transit chart on your software to see where the planets are today and where the ascendant, midheaven and many other features are as well. For those of you who are further into astrology, check out the following example of a natal and a transit chart. The natal chart is the inner wheel, and the transit chart is the outer one. The descriptions here are somewhat technical, but if you work through them bit by bit, you will soon see how it works.

An Example of Transits

The following chart belongs to my late friend, Jonathan Dee, and it marks a time when he suffered a bereavement on the 2nd of June, 1993, in Cardiff in Wales. Jon's partner had been ill with stomach trouble for some time, but neither he nor Jon were aware of the gravity of the situation. In April, a road accident meant the partner spent time in hospital, which brought the underlying problem to the surface. Over the next few weeks, Jon's partner became progressively more ill, and then he died.

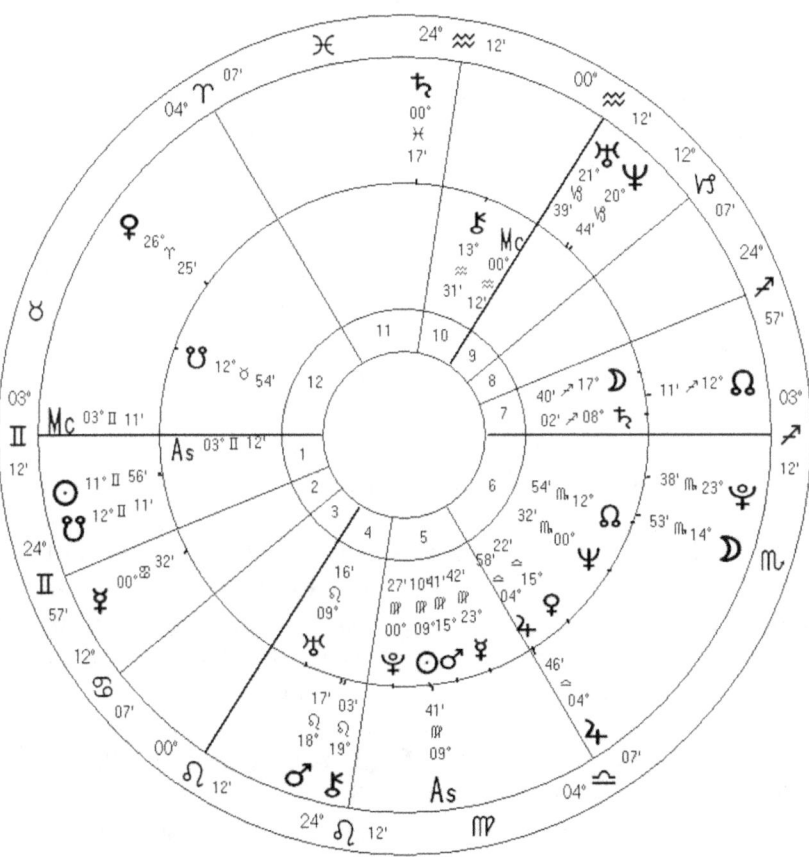

Jonathan's chart showed transiting Saturn slowing down before turning retrograde at 0 degrees of Pisces, opposite his natal Pluto at 0 degrees of Virgo. Saturn brings sadness, and Pluto is associated with death, while both Virgo and Pisces have connections with health – often the health of others as well as our own.

- Transiting Jupiter was conjunct natal Jupiter and moving from retrograde to direct motion. Jupiter is a beneficial planet, but it becomes active at times of significant change.
- Transiting Mars would soon conjunct natal Pluto. Mars and Pluto are considered "malefic" planets, and Pluto is associated with death, while Mars is associated with accidents and the sudden onset of illness.
- Venus was coming into opposition with Neptune, with Venus in the twelfth house and Neptune in the sixth house, both houses being concerned with health issues. Neptune can signify an illness hidden from view, as this one had been until it emerged after the road accident.
- Venus was on the way to a conjunction with the south node, therefore opposing the "karmic" north node.
- The Moon had just crossed the north node.
- The transiting Ascendant was on Jon's Sun.

Interestingly, while progressions show what is going on inside our heads and the changes that we bring upon ourselves, the transits really are the work of fate and the destiny that we cannot control. A combination of changes showing up on both a progressed and a transit chart will mark a definite time of change, which may be for better or worse.

Newspaper and Magazine Astrology

Where media astrology is concerned, there is no natal chart to set the transits against, so the astrologer uses each Sun sign to create a solar house chart. Starting with Aries, the first solar house is on the left-hand side of the chart, Taurus becomes the second house, Gemini the third and so on, with all the other signs ranged round the chart in an anti-clockwise order. For Taurus, the sign of Taurus is on the left, with Gemini as the second house, then Cancer and all the rest ranged around the chart. Gemini starts with Gemini as the first solar house, Cancer as the second house, and so on throughout the system. The astrologer then looks at the planets to see which houses they fall into for each sign and makes a prediction from that. Most astrologers take the new and full Moon and any eclipses into account as well and check into which solar house these events fall.

Transits

The chart shown is a solar house chart for the sign of Virgo, which is placed on the left-hand side of the chart with all the other signs ranged in order around it.

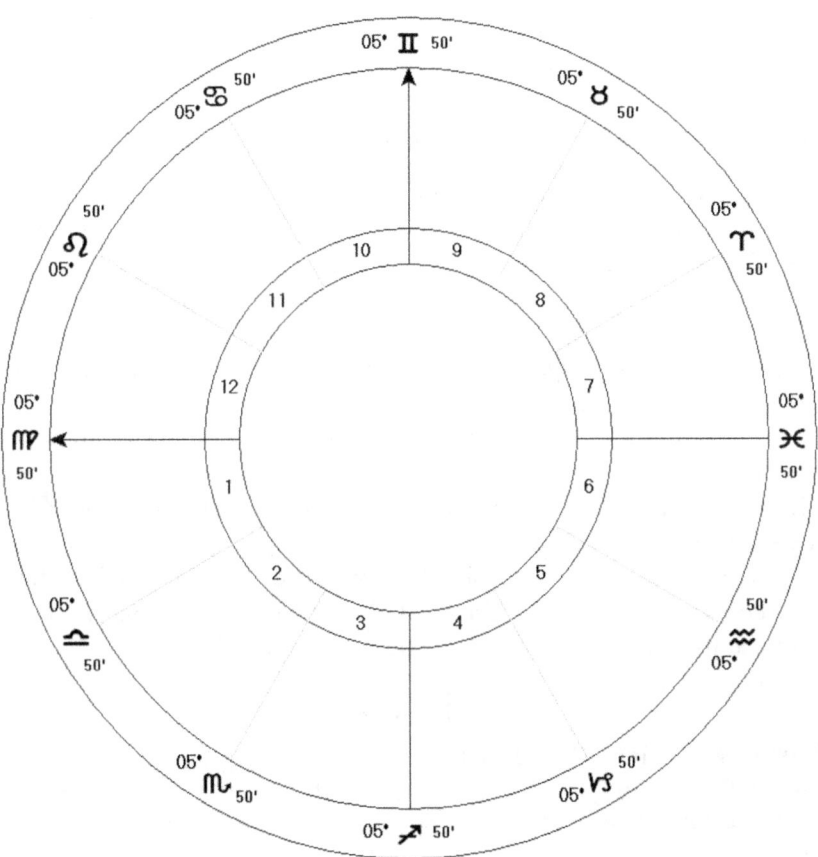

Progressions

Progressions are a mathematical movement of the planets from birth to the moment that you wish to examine and analyse the subject's situation. The biggest problem is the number of different names, many of which mean the same thing, but the following should help clear away the confusion:

Day-for-a-year progressions, secondary directions and secondary progressions are all the same things.

Primary directions, solar arc directions and solar arc progressions and one-degree progressions are all the same thing, while solar arc MC progressions are so closely related to them as to be more or less the same thing.

Some systems are worth using for yourself or your clients, but others may be vaguely interesting for those who enjoy research but not much practical use. Here is the list of progression systems.

Progressions

Day-for-a-year progressions.
Secondary directions.
Secondary progressions.
Primary directions.
Solar arc directions.
Solar arc progressions.
One-degree progressions.
Solar arc MC progressions.
Tertiary progressions.
Minor progressions.
Daily house progressions.
Duodenary progressions.
Converse directions.
Converse progressions.

Progressions

Progressions
This name covers any kind of progression.
Day-For-A-Year Progressions, Secondary Directions, Secondary Progressions

These names all mean the same thing, but most astrologers use the following technique, which most call *progressions*.

The method progresses the natal chart by the number of days of the person's age, so if someone is 38 years old, the astrological program works forward 38 days and makes up a new chart for that time.

It is easy to do this by hand because all you do is find the person's birthday in the ephemeris and then count whatever number of days are needed to move the chart forward from the date of birth.

Now you list the planets and other features and mark them around the outside of the natal chart. For instance, if someone was born on the 10th of June and is 38 years old, their progressed birthday would be the 18th of July, so the planetary positions for that day are what you write outside the natal chart.

Needless to say, the outer planets won't have moved much at all by this method, but the inner ones will, and the Moon will have moved the most. The Moon is the most crucial factor in this kind of progression, as it often acts as a trigger for events.

Interestingly, there are several references to this kind of progression in the Bible, especially in Daniel and other sections of both Testaments. It was known to be a popular method among ancient Jewish astrologers.

Solar Arc Directions, Primary Directions, One-Degree Progressions, Solar Arc Directed Charts

These names also mean the same thing, and most astrologers call this system solar arc progressions or solar arc directions.

These are easy to do by hand and instantaneous on a computer. All you do is move the entire chart forward by the number of years.

For instance, if the subject is 42 years old, you move every planet forward by 42 degrees.

Therefore, if the subject was born with Venus at 10 degrees of Libra, the planet would now be at 22 degrees of Scorpio, and if the natal Pluto was at 15 degrees of Virgo at birth, it would now be 27 degrees of Libra.

Unfortunately, the predictive results of this type of progression are not really reliable, and they don't compare to the results obtained by the day-for-a-year progressions method outlined above.

Solar Arc MC Progressions

This is much the same as the solar arc directions that you see above, but it works out as a little less than a whole degree for a year. So over time, the progressed chart slips back a little, so that someone who is 60 years old will probably have a progressed chart at around 58 or 59 degrees rather than the full 60 degrees.

Other Techniques

Now we start to look at other methods that are useful and others that aren't worthwhile. Here is the list:
Solar returns.
Solar return directions.
90-degree arc.
Lunar returns.
Venusian arcs.
Martial arcs.
Decumbitures.
Horary astrology.
Electional astrology.
Mundane astrology.
Daily house progressions.
The perpetual noon date method.
Physical astrology.

Solar Returns, Solar Return Directions

These names mean the same thing, and this is a handy method to check out the atmosphere of a particular year. It isn't easy to work out by hand, so you need decent software for this. In effect, this is a transit chart, but it is set for the moment when the Sun returns to its exact position, and everything else on the chart must be fitted in for that particular time, day and place. So, if you want to check out your situation on your 35th birthday, you set the Sun back where it was at birth and see where all the other planets and features are now. The first thing to look at is the new Ascendant, as that will give a flavour of what the year will be like, and then look at the planets and houses and see what the general atmosphere will be.

90-Degree arc

This is a very different form of astrology, and while it does have its adherents, those who use this method don't use our familiar forms of astrology at all. I have investigated it, and I can use it, but I can't see any value in dumping our standard forms of astrology in favour of this method. The method breaks the chart down into its component elements of fire, earth, air and water, and then puts all the fire segments together in one area. The method even progresses each of the elemental blocks in turn. Decent astro-software may be able to produce these charts for you.

Lunar Returns

This can be useful when you want to focus on a significant time in your life. This system is like the solar return, but it is the Moon that is doing the returning. This puts the Moon back where it was at birth and fits the planets and other features into the right place. There is a new lunar return every month. If you try this for yourself, you will probably find that the chart only seems to kick in a week or two into each new lunar return month.

Venusian and Martian Arcs

The idea here is like that of the solar arcs, but it is so obscure that even my Solar Fire program can't handle it. Leave this one on Venus and Mars.

Decumbitures

This is a fascinating area of astrology. It is used to diagnose and plot the history of an illness. It is linked to the ancient idea of the humours and ancient herbalism, and the rules for this kind of astrology are very old and very specialised.

Horary Astrology

This is an ancient method of prediction that has come back into use in recent years. It is based on the idea that one makes up a chart for the moment a question is asked and then the chart is assessed to find the answer. This can be done by following standard astrological rules and systems, but actual horary astrology is different and a technique of its own. It takes a lot of study before an astrologer becomes competent to use this system.

To give you a starting point, the planet that rules the Asc. is the person who is asking the question, and one must find that planet and assess which sign and house it is in and the aspects that are being made to it. If anybody or anything else is involved in the subject's life, it is shown by the planet that rules the Dsc.

There are rules to this system that don't exist in traditional astrology; for instance, if Mercury, Venus or Mars were approaching a "hot" planet such as the Sun or Jupiter, the transiting planet becomes "combust" and doesn't work correctly.

Electional Astrology

This is very popular in India, and it is worth using on occasion. The idea is that you pick the best moment for something you want to do. It is used to select the best day for important things, such as marriage, starting a business, buying a home or doing something else important.

Mundane Astrology

The word mundane here means "of the world" and refers to the fortunes of cities, countries, political parties, or any other kind of organisation. Mundane astrology means that one makes up a natal chart to show the character of the organisation, town, country or whatever, then all the usual predictive techniques can be used against this chart. You really should buy two books if you want to study this method, and these are both by Nick Campion. The first is called "Mundane Astrology" and the second is "The Book of World Horoscopes".

Daily House Progressions

I have heard of this, but I haven't a clue what it is or what it does.

Perpetual Noon Date

This is an old method that is difficult and long-winded to work out and not worth the bother.

Physical Astrology

This is to do with the weather and such things as earthquakes, tsunamis and so on. I like this form of astrology, and I find it pretty accurate. One thing worth bearing in mind is that whenever an outer planet sits at around 27 degrees of any sign, something unpleasant is about to happen, either due to some physical event such as a flood or a major fire, or perhaps by war or some other man-made disaster.

Hand Calculations to Progress a Chart

HAND CALCULATIONS TO PROGRESS A CHART

While you are saving up to buy sophisticated software, here is a quick-fix way of progressing a chart using day-for-a-year progressions. The example here is for an imaginary person who I call Fred, born in London in England on the 1st of July, 1980.

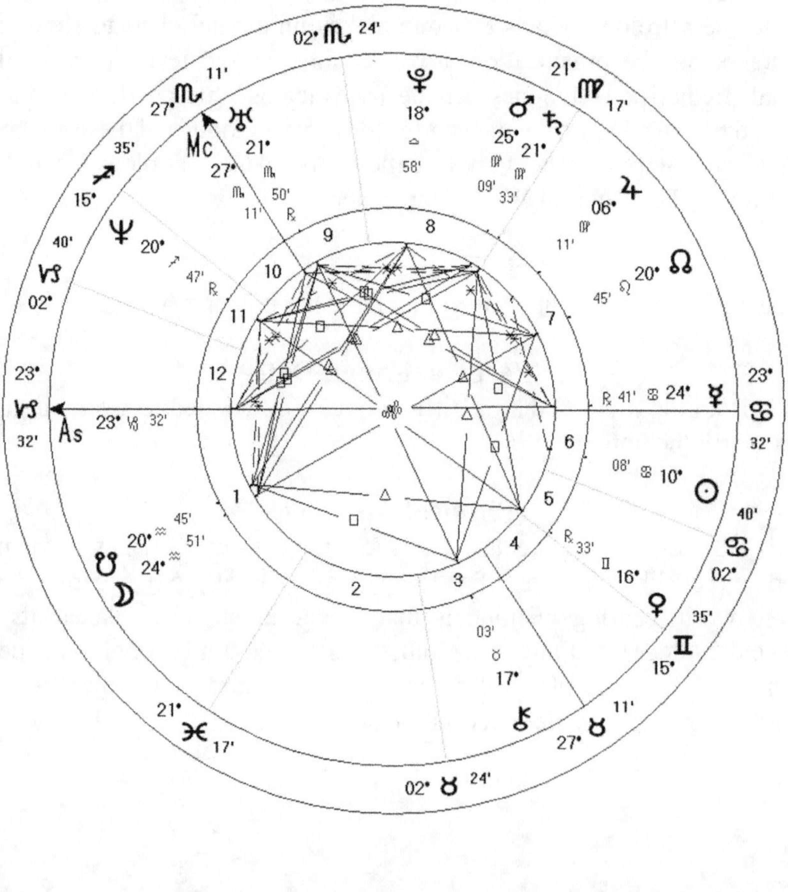

- Decide on the year you wish to examine – for example, 2005, which would make Fred 45 years of age.
- Using an ephemeris for the 20th century, find Fred's birthday and then count 45 days ahead from Fred's birthday. This takes you from the 1st of July, 1980, to the 14th of August, 1980.
- Make up a new chart for the new date and jot down the positions around the outside of the natal chart.
- You can move the Moon backwards and forward from Fred's birthday in 2005 by a degree for each month you wish to examine. For instance, if you want to see what happened in April of 2005, move the Moon back by four degrees, and if you're going to see what will happen in November 2005, move the Moon forwards three degrees.
- Check the progressed planets against the natal ones and see what is going on in Fred's life.

Rectification with the Midheaven (the MC)

This isn't a prediction method, but it is a useful way of rectifying a chart when you don't have a precise time of birth. If you have a vague birth time that gives you something to work with, make up a chart for this and then look at the MC. Move it back and forward until it makes an aspect to another planet and judge what might have happened and the age at which it occurred.

For instance, if you put the MC at 20 degrees of Pisces and your natal Mars was at 25 degrees of Gemini, moving the MC forward five degrees would make a connection, so if you happened to have had an accident at the age of five, you would know the chart is correct. If the accident occurred at the age of seven, you must progress the MC and the ascendant forward two more degrees and maybe move the Moon forward a little to rectify the chart. This makes more sense when you actually do it for real rather than by reading the method in a book.

If you have no idea of the time of birth, check out the rectification information in this book, as it could give you the answer. Some people dowse for the correct rising sign, but I am not sure how useful that is.

Further Methods, Ideas and Information

Here, in no particular order, are some ideas for you to examine.

Midpoints

Midpoints are the halfway point between two planets, between a planet and an angle, or between two angles. Progressions or transits to an important midpoint can be as effective as to a planet itself. If you have a computer program that lists midpoints, print out a list of them by sign and see what you have. If you have ever wondered why a particular spot on your chart seems to be sensitive to transits despite the fact that there are no planets there, a bunch of midpoints may be the answer. A good example of this is in the following natal chart, which has planets in Taurus and Gemini and then in Leo and Virgo, but nothing in Cancer. When planets traverse the sign of Cancer or work their

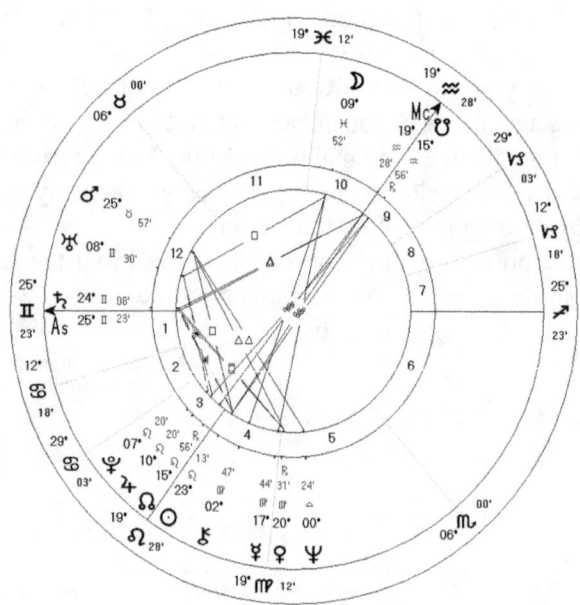

way through the opposite sign of Capricorn, they trigger events in this person's life, due to knocking on one mid-point after another.

The Nodes of the Moon

The path that the Sun and the planets appear to take around our world is called the Ecliptic. The Moon's orbit around the Earth travels slightly upwards and downwards, so it crosses the ecliptic in a northerly direction and then again two weeks later in a southerly direction. The upward junction is called the North Node and the downward one is called the South Node.

Traditional Indian astrologers call the north node Rahu (the dragon's head) and the south node Ketu (the dragon's tail). Indian astrologers consider the nodes to be karmic points, with the south node showing the lessons learned in a previous life, and the north node showing what has to be learned in this one. Some western astrologers consider the north node to be those areas where a subject finds it easy to fit in with prevailing social and political circumstances.

In my experience, the nodes of the Moon link to lunar matters, particularly such things as a change of address or a major domestic upheaval. The same goes for dealings with family members, especially those concerning older female relatives. This is not to say that the karmic or social aspect of the nodes doesn't count, it is just a case of examining the subject's situation and seeing what fits. In some cases, karmic relationships seem to show up on the nodes, in other cases, matters relating to unfinished business seems to be attracted by these points, and in yet others, fame and fortune can be shown when a node is activated.

Planetoids, Asteroids and Moons

Chiron is a planetoid, asteroid, centaur or dwarf planet, depending upon which book you read. I call it a dwarf planet.

You can use asteroids in astrology, if you wish. You do need to know or to look up the legends behind them before you understand them, though. Here are a few to choose from:

Amor, Ceres, Diana, Eros, Hidalgo, Icarus, Juno, Lilith, Pallas Athena, Pandora, Psyche, Sappho, Toro, Urania and Vesta.

Arabic Parts

The Arabs invented a system called "parts". Although these were principally used in natal charting to show the areas of life where a subject would succeed and be happy or where he would experience difficulties, these "parts" were also used in predictive astrology, by watching to see what happened when planets cross them or make other aspects to them.

The one part that has lingered on in modern astrology is the Part of Fortune. This is calculated from the distances in degrees between the Sun, Moon and Ascendant positions in a birthchart. The formula is not difficult, but it can be confusing:

For daytime births,
Count the number of degrees anti-clockwise from the position of the Sun to that of the Moon.
Then, starting at the ascendant and going forward anti-clockwise, count the same number of degrees forward. For example, if the number of degrees between the Sun and Moon is 83, count 83 degrees forward from the ascendant and put the symbol for the Part of Fortune there.

This gives you the position of the Part of Fortune.

For night time births,
Count the number of degrees anticlockwise from the Moon to the Sun, then count this number - still moving anti-clockwise - from the Ascendant. Put the Part of Fortune there.

This isn't as complicated as it looks, and if you are used to geometry or to using a compass, this will come easily. However, you will find the Part of Fortune is available in any decent astrology software these days.

When you've located your Part of Fortune, note the house that it's in, as this will show you how you make your way in life. For instance, if it is in the Seventh house, you will make successful relationships with others. These will bring you joy, and perhaps wealth as well. If this also happens to be in the sign of Gemini or Sagittarius, you will have a lot to teach one another, and you won't run out of things to talk about with each other.

A Part of Fortune in the Second house would bring wealth, which would be personal if the sign was Aries or Taurus, or a wealthy business if it was in Capricorn.

The Vertex

This is an extremely sensitive point in the chart, especially where relationship matters are concerned. If you think you might find this interesting, I have written a book about it, called "Understanding the Astrological Vertex". You definitely need a good quality software package to be able to show the Vertex.

Further Methods, Ideas & Information

Fixed Stars

Ancient astronomers / astrologers called stars "fixed" because they didn't appear to move around the Earth in the way that the Sun, Moon and planets did. Nowadays we know that our own Sun is a small star, close to the outer edge of a huge galaxy that we call the Milky Way. We also know that the whole galaxy is on the move and that the positions of the stars are not fixed at all. Good astrology software gives the position of the main stars and probably an interpretation of their meanings as well. There are books available that describe the fixed stars.

Just to show how "unfixed" the fixed stars actually are, the Alpha star, Regulus, moved into Virgo while I was adapting this book, after spending goodness knows how many centuries in Leo!

The Interpretation Maze

The best way to interpret a chart is to do it logically - also to find a routine that suits you. Until you get so deeply into astrology that you want to experiment with unusual features, I suggest that you use the obvious features and stick to the major aspects.

From here on, it would be a good idea to get used to the common abbreviations:

The ascendant	The Asc
The midheaven	The MC
The descendant	The Dsc
The lower midheaven or nadir	The IC

Progressions

The normal day-for-a-year progressions show a fair bit of movement of the inner planets, which are the Sun, Moon, Mercury, Venus and Mars. Progressed Jupiter will have moved a little since the subject's birth, especially if the person has lived a long time, while the remaining outer planets (Saturn, Uranus, Neptune and Pluto) will have hardly moved at all. Therefore, you will probably concentrate most of your attention on the inner planets, plus the Asc and MC.

You can work through the chart planet by planet or you can start with the Asc and work your way round the chart house by house. If you work planet by planet, the following order is as good as any:

1. Asc
2. MC
3. Pluto
4. Neptune
5. Uranus
6. Saturn
7. Jupiter
8. Mars
9. Venus

10 Mercury
11 The Sun
12 Chiron
13 Nodes of the Moon
14 The Moon

I suggest that you leave the Moon to the last, because that is the planet that will take up most of your attention when doing progressions. If you decide to start with the Asc and work round, perhaps leave the Moon until last once again. We'll look more closely into the progressed Moon later in this book.

The Planetary Method in Detail

The MC
Check for changes of sign or house and any major aspect to any planet or angle because anything that affects the MC is important. After checking to see if this makes any aspects to anything on the natal chart, check to see if it makes any aspects to anything that is progressed.

The Asc
Check for everything in the same way as per the midheaven. This will probably not be as influential in its effects as the midheaven.

Pluto
This won't move enough by progression during a lifetime to be worth considering.

Neptune
This won't move enough by progression during a lifetime to be worth considering.

Uranus
Unless your subject is very old, this won't have travelled far enough to be worth considering.

Saturn
If your subject is elderly, this will be worth a glance.

Jupiter

Check for sign and house changes, aspects and retrograde motion. Check for aspects to other progressions.

Mars

Check as per Jupiter.

Venus

Check as per Jupiter.

Mercury

Check as per Jupiter.

The Sun

Check as per Jupiter. Remember that the Sun never goes retrograde.

Chiron

Check as per Jupiter.

The Nodes of the Moon

These move around the chart in retrograde motion - which means that they work their way backwards through the chart.

The Moon

This is the most important part of the whole reading, and it will probably take you as long to work through this as all the rest put together. Take your time over this.

Firstly, check to see what sign and house the Moon has progressed into. Bear in mind that the Moon moves at roughly a degree for a month, so it is easy to work out how long it has been in its current sign and house, and how much longer it will be before it changes sign or house. Look this up in the relevant chapter and also in the progressed Moon section of this book. Check out the meaning of the Moon through the signs and houses in any other predictive books you can get your hands on as well.

Now, check the actual degree of the progressed Moon and work it forward until it makes an aspect to another planet or to some other feature on the natal chart. Bear in mind that the Moon moves one degree per month.

Next, continue to move the Moon forward and check each event in turn. You may find that several months go by with nothing much happening, followed by a period when a whole bunch of aspects come hard upon each other's heels. Note down the dates and the interpretations. If you want to check that this works, try moving the Moon backwards and check what happened when it made previous aspects.

Transits

Where the transits are concerned, the situation is exactly opposite to that of the progressions. You will find that the inner planets and Moon move much too quickly to be of much importance, while the outer planets are important.

Once again, you can run around the chart from the Asc if you prefer, or you can work planet by planet. Either way, the following will help you.

Pluto

Check for the sign and house this is in and any aspects that it makes to any planet or angle. Pluto's orbit is eccentric but very slow, so it will affect a sensitive spot on a chart for a couple of years at the very least, and longer if Pluto retrogrades over a particular spot. Pluto spends many years in each sign. Its effect is generational as well as personal.

Neptune

When Neptune makes an aspect to a personal planet or to some other planet or feature on your chart, its effect can be felt for a couple of years. Neptune spends around twelve or thirteen years in each sign.

Uranus

Uranus's effect can be felt for a year or more. Uranus spends around seven years in each sign.

Saturn

Saturn's effect can be felt for several months, sometimes up to a year. Saturn spends about two to two and a half years in each sign.

Jupiter

Jupiter's effect can be felt for a few months. Jupiter spends just over a year in each sign.

Mars

Mars's effect usually only lasts for a matter of weeks but when it is in retrograde motion, the effect will be felt for several months.

Venus
Venus transits are usually so swift that they are hardly worth bothering about but take note of those times when Venus is retrograde, because the effect will last longer and be more noticeable.

Mercury
Mercury's transits are usually to swift to bother with, but watch out for retrogrades when Mercury becomes very noticeable indeed.

The Sun
The Sun takes about a month to move through each sign, bringing the sign and house it occupies at that time into focus.

Chiron
This planetoid has an eccentric orbit but it usually spends a couple of years in a sign, therefore its transits can last for several months, especially when it turns retrograde and back again.

The Nodes of the Moon
These take about a year or so to work through each sign, so their effect can last for a few months. The Nodes move backwards through the zodiac.

The Moon
The Moon takes two and a half days to work through each sign, so its transits are very short lived. However a new Moon, a full Moon and especially an eclipse, will have a powerful effect on anything that they aspect. An eclipse that conjuncts your Sun, Moon or ascendant is always noticeable.

Some General Comments
Not all astrologers bother to use progressions, but I have always used them, and I find the progressed Moon extremely important. The fact that progressions work best for the inner planets and the transits for the outer ones means that using each method in turn results in everything getting covered.

When I was in the early stages of working as a professional consultant, I read anything and everything I could get my hands on. Many of the books were written in the pompous, pseudo-psychological style that was in vogue in the 1970s. All the wonderful (usually American) astrologers went to great pains to explain that they prepared a pile of charts and made copious notes, well in advance of their clients actually turning up for their appointments. I came to the conclusion that they were talking through their hats, or they were extremely lucky. If I was stupid enough to prepare a chart in advance of the appointment, the client would invariably turn up and tell me that she had given me the wrong details, cheerfully announcing, "I phoned my mum this morning, and she told me that I wasn't born at three in the afternoon, but at two thirty in the morning. Does that matter?" Another popular one went, "I thought I was born in Birmingham, but it was my sister who was born there, I was actually born in Kuala Lumpur!" Very few people seem to know the difference between a.m. and p.m., and don't see that it can matter very much. I often asked a client to phone her mother or other relative from my office while she was sitting there, and I always made up the charts with the client sitting alongside me.

Oddly enough, the clients actually enjoyed watching me put their charts together. I think that it gave them a feeling that I was working on their lives and their stories in a very personal manner. I also think that sitting quietly and watching this process unfold helped them to relax and forget the cares of the world for a while. It seemed to put them in a meditative frame of mind. It's likely that looking at their charts opened a Chakra or two in the same way that looking at Tarot cards being laid out does, and perhaps that helped me to reach into them psychically as well as astrologically!

A far more frustrating, and all too common situation, was to actually do the job and see the client happily off the premises, only to have them ring back the next day. The tentative voice on the phone saying that mum has now told her that the birth time (or date or place - or all three) was wrong! They took it very badly when I told them that if they wanted the job done again, they would have to pay for it again. They couldn't see why I should happily throw away a few hours of my working life due to their error.

Oddly enough, if the birth time as given is wrong, this isn't quite the disaster in predictive work that it is in natal charting, because most of the time, you are looking at planetary movements rather than worrying too much about the nature of the person. Events are fairly easy to spot, even with a mistaken birth time.

The same goes for cases where the birth time is not known, because it is still possible to get some useful information from a "flat" or "natural" chart where your ascendant or starting point is zero degrees of Aries. In these cases, you won't have the houses to play with and the Moon position could be out by a few degrees, but it is surprising how much information you can glean out of even this kind of half-boiled job. You may even find yourself rectifying the chart and actually locating the ascendant as you go along.

The moral of all this is not to become upset when things aren't perfect, and to be prepared to "jiggle" a dodgy chart in order to get things right. Time and practice will give you a feel for this kind of work.

Other Types of Progressed chart

If you are dealing with a solar arc type of chart, where all the planets and other features have been moved forward by one degree, you need to find a working order that seems logical. If you want to be sure you haven't missed anything out, use the planetary order outlined earlier in this chapter and go through the planets and angles one by one.

Progression & Transit Aspects

It makes sense to judge a progressed chart against a natal chart and check out the aspects formed between the two charts. If you are used to looking at planets that transit a natal chart, use the same method and the same interpretations for a progressed one.

Solar and lunar returns, electional charts and any kind of horary are best used as stand-alone charts.

Aspects

Progressed or transiting aspects work in the same way as natal aspects and the terminology is the same for both. The difference is that a natal aspect relates to the character of your subject, while progressed or transit aspects show trends and events.

Astrologers are allergic to the terms "good" and "bad", so good aspects are often referred to as being easy or beneficial, while bad ones are often called challenging. This kind of astrological political correctness may be irritating, but there is a good reason for it. Nothing in astrology is truly black and white and no planet or aspect can be considered to be wholly good or bad. The trick is to take into account the energies behind each planet and the modifying effects of the signs and houses that are emphasised. This sounds complicated but it soon becomes second nature.

Orbs

Astrologers have different opinions as to the size of the orbs, and there are no hard and fast rules. The table below shows the orbs that I tend to use, but when I am doing a reading, I am likely to be quite flexible about the orb, especially if some important transit or progression is involved. An aspect can often be felt coming for a long time before it actually connects on a chart, and it can fizzle out very quickly once it has passed the point of exactitude.

When a planet does a retrograde dance backwards and forwards over a sensitive point, its effects can be felt for months or even years until it finally passes away. If one planet conjoins another, retrogrades back over it and then crosses it again in a forward motion, this is called a triple conjunction. Other astrologers call a natal stellium of three or more planets in one sign or house a triple conjunction.

Symbol	Aspect	Distance (Degrees)	Orb (Degrees)
☌	Conjunction	0	8
☍	Opposition	180	8
△	Trine	120	8
□	Square	90	8
✱	Sextile	60	6
⚻	Inconjunct (quincunx)	150	6
∠	Semi-square	45	2
⚼	Sesquiquadrate	135	2
⚺	Semi-sextile	30	2
Q	Quintile	72	2
±	Bi-quintile	144	2

Many astrologers use tighter orbs when dealing with features such as the nodes, the Part of Fortune, the Vertex and so on. At this point in your astrological studies, I suggest that you only use the major aspects of conjunction, opposition, trine and square until you get the hang of things. Later you can add any or all the other features.

Reading the Aspects

Conjunction

This extremely powerful aspect can register a wonderful event or an unpleasant one, depending upon the planets involved. You must also take into account the signs and houses in which the conjunction occurs. It is also worth noting that a conjunction in one place in a chart means that something else is being opposed, even if it is only an unoccupied house.

There is a first house feeling to a conjunction, so it always engages the attention of the subject in a very important way. Even an unpleasant conjunction usually has a good outcome in the long run.

Opposition

This is considered to be a difficult aspect, but I feel that it is where a subject has to cope with the decisions and the behaviour of others, and this doesn't have to be bad. For example, if a subject is lonely, the movement of planets into opposition to his ascendant or to something else on the chart can signal a time of meeting someone new. It is also worth noting that planets in opposition will also enhance the sign and house that they are passing through.

There is always a seventh house feeling to oppositions, and they can be quite fortunate in the long run. These progressions and transits are easier to bear if the subject understands that life is likely to be difficult while they last, and if he is prepared to learn from the experience.

Trine

This is always a pleasant, easy and rather lucky aspect, and the worst that can happen is that it goes unnoticed. A trine will set off a period of creativity, love and fun, which is in line with the fifth house feeling to which it relates. Alternatively, it can bring freedom, the chance of exploring new horizons or of learning something new in a ninth house manner.

Square

This is probably the most challenging of all aspects. In a natal chart, a square is considered to be character building, but where progressions and transits are concerned, squared planets can make the individual extremely unhappy. This may bring a fourth house feeling of investigating the roots of the matter, or a tenth house feeling of hardship moving on and leaving something behind.

Sextile

This is a pleasant aspect that brings luck and happiness. This is supposed to be more mental and third house in character than the trine. Therefore, one would expect pleasant news or ease of communication related to the planets, signs and houses that are affected by it. This can also bring friendship, group activity, education and exploration of a third or eleventh house kind.

Semi-square

This can be quite challenging.

Sesquiquadrate

This is less challenging.

Inconjunct

Although this is a minor aspect, it is always worth considering both in natal charting and when looking at progressions and transits. It can be extremely awkward and it puts pressure on the subject, either in a kind of sixth house manner by loading him down with duties and obligations, or an eighth house manner by landing him with financial, sexual or relationship problems. The two signs involved have nothing in common, because they are of different elements and qualities. Two inconjuncts at the same time form a "yod" aspect, and this can be extremely trying.

Semi-sextile

Some astrologers see this as a pleasant aspect, rather like a minor sextile, but the signs involved aren't compatible with each other, so it may be irritating. Either way, the events involved are likely to be unremarkable.

Quintile

A quintile aspect is supposed to bestow talent, so I guess that a progressed quintile would bring talents to the fore. This is hard to spot and rarely used.

Bi-quintile

This is much the same as the Quintile, but weaker.

Parallel and Contra-Parallel Aspects

Parallel aspects form when two planets are at the same distance above or below the ecliptic. Contra-parallels form when two planets are at the same distance from the ecliptic, but one is above it while the other is below it. When it comes to interpreting both parallels and contra-parallels, consider them in the same way that you would a conjunction. Indeed, old-time astrologers reckoned that a parallel was a stronger force than a conjunction.

I suggest that if you are in the process of learning your astrology, concentrate on the ordinary major aspects such as the conjunction, sextile, square, trine and opposition, and leave the rest until later.

Solar Arcs & Returns

In solar arc progressions (or directions), all the planets, along with the ascendant and midheaven, move forward at the same rate as the Sun during the course of one day, which is 57 minutes of a degree. If you are doing this by hand, simply progress everything on the chart forward by one whole degree per year and don't worry about the slight discrepancy. Write the new placements outside the natal chart.

Amazingly, solar arc progressions can be worked backwards as well as forwards! If you want to try the converse picture, push each planet backwards by one degree per year. Whether direct or converse, check for changes of sign or house or any aspects that are being made between planets, angles or anything else that looks interesting.

Solar Returns

Solar returns are a picture of the transits at the time when the Sun returns to its position at the time of a person's birth. These are easier to interpret when they are read as a stand-alone chart, rather than trying to put them against a natal chart.

Solar returns are extremely difficult to do by hand, so you need decent astrology software for this. Most programs will ask you if you want the Solar return for the place of birth, or if you want to relocate the return chart to wherever the subject is living now, and you should relocate the chart.

This may be where the expression "many happy returns" comes from.

Precession

Some programs ask you if you want to take "precession" into account. Precession is a slight backwards movement of Earth that occurs over a period of time. Some astrologers use this feature, others don't. I suggest that you try both and see what works best for you.

What to Look For

The Solar return offers a flavour of the year from one birthday to the next. The most important things are the solar return Asc and MC, because these alone will tell you what kind of a year you are looking at.

If the new Asc is in Capricorn, this denotes an excellent year for work and ambition, but it may be a stressful year in which nothing comes easily.

A radical change of MC could signify a change of direction, even if only for the year in question. Otherwise, see what houses the Solar return planets fall into and generally assess the chart for the year in question.

Lunar Returns

Lunar returns are exactly the same as solar returns, but they occur every lunar month. The Moon returns to the exact position that it occupied at birth and the remaining chart is worked out around this. As this occurs every month, this will give a close up view of the month in question in the same way that the solar return does for the year in question.

This is quite a handy astrological tool, because so much astrology is too wide in its scope and timescale to focus itself on the small things that happen from one week to the next.

Moon Phases & Eclipses

A little observation over a period of months will show you the times during each lunar month when you feel low or when you feel good. This may be down to a particular Moon phase, or a particular sign that the Moon is in.

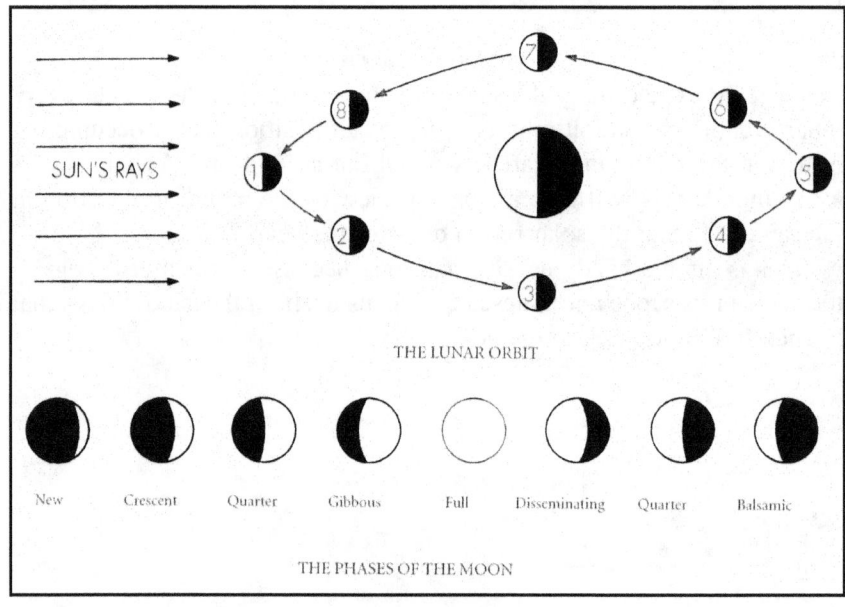

THE LUNAR ORBIT

New Crescent Quarter Gibbous Full Disseminating Quarter Balsamic

THE PHASES OF THE MOON

Eclipses

Eclipses occur in pairs, and at about four to five month intervals. There can be as few as three and as many as six eclipses in a year. Normally, a solar eclipse is followed by a lunar eclipse a couple of weeks later, or vice versa. Some eclipses are easy to see in the sky, but most are partial eclipses and they may only be noticeable in certain areas of the Earth.

From an astrologer's point of view, the fact that an eclipse is partial or full shouldn't make much difference, but we tend to take notice of the more spectacular ones. The Romans considered eclipses to be portents of evil, and modern astrologers tend to agree with this.

Moon Phases & Eclipses

Most eclipses pass ordinary people by without notice, which is just as well, considering their frequency. However, if an eclipse falls on your Sun, Moon or Asc, you will feel its effect.

If you are far enough into astrology to understand a natal chart, you may like to consider the Ptolemaic theory of eclipses:

- An eclipse that occurs on a subject's ascendant can be felt for about three months afterwards.
- An eclipse on the midheaven can be felt for six months afterwards.
- An eclipse on the descendant can be felt for nine months afterwards.

My own observation is that if an eclipse occurs on a subject's Sun, Moon or Asc, it will be felt powerfully within a couple of days, and it will bring an unpleasant situation to a head.

Another personal observation is that eclipses are particularly unpleasant for people born with the Sun in Cancer or Leo, as the ruling planet is always involved.

The Cycles of Time

Wherever the planets were when a subject was born, there are times when they return to the same place. A solar return is a good example, as this happens every year on your birthday. Among the other planets, some move too quickly for their planetary return to be significant, while others move too slowly to make a return during the course of a lifetime. However, even the slowest planet will move a quarter or a third of the way around the chart, sparking off events as they pass tender spots on the birthchart.

All planets have slight variations in their orbits from time to time, and all except the Sun and Moon appear to travel backwards from time to time. Astrologers call this backwards movement retrograde motion.

The Planetary Cycles

The Earth orbits the Sun in approximately 365.25 days (one year).
The Moon orbits the Earth in 27.5 days.
Mercury orbits the Sun in 88 days.
Venus orbits the Sun in 225 days.
Mars orbits the Sun in 1 year 10.5 months.
Jupiter orbits the Sun in 12 years.
Saturn orbits the Sun in 29 years.
Uranus orbits the Sun in 84 years.
Neptune orbits the Sun in 165 years.
Pluto orbits the Sun in 246 years.
Chiron orbits the Sun in roughly 51 to 52 years.

There is absolutely no need for you to memorise these cycles, but there are a few that will become familiar. A point worth bearing in mind is that these cycles affect everybody. If you mix with other astrologers, you will soon become used to the terms "the Saturn return", or the "Uranus half-return".

The Planetary Movements in Detail

The Moon
The Moon travels around the Earth once each month, so there will be one day in every 27.5 days when it returns to the place that it was when a subject was born. This is called a lunar return.

The Earth
From an astrologer's point of view, the Earth stands still while the Sun, Moon and planets orbit round us. We know that this isn't the case, but for the time being, let us assume that the Earth is the centre of the Solar system rather than the Sun.

The Sun
From our perspective on Earth, the Sun appears to move through the whole zodiac once a year. A Solar return is the time when the Sun returns to the position it occupied when you were born. It is often the case that the solar return tends to fall a day before or after your birthday. This is usually a sociable and happy time.

Mercury
Mercury moves very quickly and it is never far from the Sun. In common with all the other planets, (except the Sun and Moon), there are times when it appears to be moving backwards! The term is retrograde motion. Mercury's return occurs once a year, around the time of your birthday. This is a time for thinking and for making plans.

Venus
Venus moves more slowly than Mercury, but it is also never far from the Sun. About once a year, it will spend some time in retrograde motion. However, Venus usually returns to its own place at around birthday time. Venus's return will make you take some time to review your financial and relationship situations. It often sparks off a period of socialising, the desire for a holiday or a bit of luxury.

Mars
A Mars return occurs once every 1 year and 10.5 months. A Mars return can set off noticeable changes, but the outcome will depend upon the signs, houses and aspects that are involved. A return for a Mars that is natally in the twelfth house will bring a great boost to one's psychic powers, while simultaneously bringing some kind of health setback. This

is due to this powerful return occurring opposite the sixth house of health. A Mars return in the first house will boost health, confidence and general lifestyle, but it may have a grim effect on relationships, which are the province of the seventh house.

Because Mars is one of the speedier planets, the effects of its returns, half-returns and other aspects are usually over fairly quickly.

Jupiter

Jupiter takes twelve years to make its return. You should take into account the sign and the house that natal Jupiter occupies, as well as any planets that aspect Jupiter natally when looking at this return. Jupiter is a bit of a double-edged sword; astrology books tell us that Jupiter is "the great benefic", or a planet that bestows all kinds of goodies upon its subjects. Alas, this is not quite the case. You may remember reading that the old Roman god, Jupiter (or Jove, if you prefer), tossed down thunderbolts from Mount Olympus whenever he was out of sorts. Therefore, a Jupiter return can bring sudden and unpleasant changes into a subject's life, but they usually work out for the best in the long run. If the subject loses something or someone from his life under a Jupiter return, it is probably no bad thing.

Jupiter returns at the ages of 12, 24, 36, 48, 60, 72, 84 and 96. At these times, you can expect to form good friendships with people who share your beliefs and outlook on life. You may start a career, find a mate, make a home, give life to a child or find your feet in some way at these times, and you should find something to believe in.

Jupiter half-returns occur at the following ages: 6, 18, 30, 42, 54, 66, 78, 90 and 102.

These can be times of setback and loss, but even so, they shouldn't be too troublesome.

Saturn

This is the planet that all student astrologers mutter about darkly, because the Saturn returns at the ages of 29/30 and 57/59 can take a lot of living through. Oddly enough, these hard times can ultimately bring benefits in their wake, because they set up challenges that bring rewards. The easiest way to understand Saturn's effects is to see them in the form of a table, as shown below.

The trines and sextiles vary in their timing as we get older.

THE SATURN CYCLE		
AGE	ASPECT	PROBABLE EFFECT
7/8	Square	Sadness, loss, realisation that life is not all fun and games.
14/15	Opposition (half return)	Responsibilities begin to weigh heavily. Possible family problems.
19/20	Trine	Often a good time, although extra responsibility is often sought and there may be disappointments.
29/30	Return	Taking responsibility for one's own life. Realising what one really wants to do. Marriage, divorce, parenthood.
37/38	Square	Extra work challenges or other responsibilities may be sought. Women may realise that the biological clock is ticking away.
44/45	Opposition	Middle age. End of childbearing and of some career possibilities. Health may be less reliable.
52/53	Square	The last real thrust towards major work ambitions can be made at this time. Sometimes, the end of a troublesome relationship or serious health issues.
57/59	Return	Health may be an issue. Retirement may beckon. Financial setbacks are possible. May realise that something needs to be dropped for good.

Uranus

The orbit of Uranus is 82 to 84 years. Uranus is the "breakout" planet, bringing issues of freedom and originality to the fore. If you have lived the same kind of life for years, you may kick over the traces when Uranus is active in your life. The outcome will vary according to the sign and house that Uranus is in at birth, and it will be modified by any other planetary aspects that may be involved. From now on, whenever you read your newspaper, take a mental note of the ages of those people who suddenly lose their cool and do strange things, as the chances are that they are being influenced by the Uranus half.

Oddly enough, astrologers don't seem to take much notice of the Uranus squares that occur at 21 and 63, but these also force a subject to reappraise his life, and to make what appear to be sudden and unexpected changes. Astrological theory tells us that squares are challenging, but they aren't always bad. They mark the times when we make decisions based on what has gone before and what we want from the future.

All these outer planets have fairly eccentric orbits, so it is only worth looking in any detail at the aspects that they make against specific, individual birthcharts.

Neptune

Roughly speaking, the good times should occur at around the age of 28 and 52, while the worst times should be at around 42 and 83, give or take a year or two either way. The best aspects of Neptune bring love, unconditional friendship, spiritual happiness, an outburst of artistic or creative talent and an appreciation of the finer things of life. The bad times may bring sadness, strange health problems, confusion and a loss of faith in everything.

Pluto

Pluto's orbit is so eccentric that is has to be looked at against each individual birthchart.

Ages of Change

The following table will make it easy to spot the major times of change in everyone's life. Remember that the planets move at a slightly different rate for different age groups, so be flexible when looking at the list.

The Cycles of Time

Age	Planetary Movement
7	Saturn square natal Saturn.
12	Jupiter return.
14	Saturn opposite natal Saturn (Saturn half-return).
18	Jupiter opposite natal Jupiter (Jupiter half-return).
21	Saturn square natal Saturn.
24	Jupiter return.
29/30	Saturn return.
30	Jupiter opposite natal Jupiter.
36	Saturn square natal Saturn. Jupiter return.
39/42	Uranus opposite natal Uranus (Uranus half-return).
42	Neptune square natal Neptune.
42	Jupiter opposite natal Jupiter.
44	Saturn opposite natal Saturn.
48	Jupiter return.
51	Saturn square natal Saturn.
57/58	Saturn return.
60	Jupiter return.
63	Uranus square natal Uranus.
66	Saturn square natal Saturn.
72	Jupiter return.
75	Saturn opposite natal Saturn.
80	Saturn square natal Saturn.
80/84	Uranus return.
84	Jupiter return.

A very nice couple, Bruno and Louise Huber used to practice astrology in their native country, Switzerland. They looked at astrology with fresh eyes, and came up with several revolutionary ideas; for instance, they decided that Saturn ruled the mother in a person's chart, as it was usually she who laid down the rules in a household, and disciplined the children. The father was represented by the loving Moon in their system.

A second feature was the way they viewed aspects in a natal chart, as they not only took their meaning from the type of aspect (e.g. sextile, square, etc.), but also by the visual shapes the aspects made on a chart. They categorised a large variety of shapes, especially various triangles, into specific meanings. If you are at all interested in examining this variety of astrological systems, search for the Huber System on the Internet.

However, it is yet another highly idiosyncratic "Huberism" that I want to show you here, and that involves the Huber Jupiter Cycle and Half Cycle. This actually left Jupiter behind and became a kind of numerological system, because what you have to do is mentally run through your life, noting the changes that you made or that overtook you every six years. The list may look something like this:

- Age 6 Moving from reception class to proper school.
- Age 12 Change to secondary school, also the beginning of puberty.
- Age 18 College starts, the brain "grows"; maybe the start of a career.
- Age 24 Could be a serious relationship or the start of parenthood.
- Age 30 End of youth, responsibilities loom, often marriage, divorce, parenthood, or finding a better career.
- Age 36 Often a decision to have a child or to have no more children, therefore sterilisation. Career gets serious.
- Age 42 Change of job, opening a business, remarriage, second family, or new child on the way.

And so on...

The weird thing is that this seems to work well, and it marks the passages in many people's lives.

Recap: The Right Method for each Job

The previous chapter was designed to show you what the various forms of progression are and how they work, while this chapter looks at various techniques available to you, and each one's intended purpose.

Transits
This is the most common predictive method of all. Transits can be used to look at any aspect of life, and they are also useful when you want to focus on a specific period of time.

Day-for-a-Year Progressions
This method gives a good overview of a subject's situation and it also gives plenty of specific information. The Moon is the thing to watch, because it shows the general mood and outlook of the subject at the time of the reading and it moves quickly enough by progression for an astrologer to pick out special events. Do the progressions and then use the transits against both the natal and progressed for the best results.

Solar Arc Directions
This is useful for a general look at a subject's life. Try looking at the progressed midheaven and the progressed Sun. I have never used transits against this method but there is no reason why you shouldn't.

Tertiary, Minor and Duodenary Progressions and the Ninety-Degree Arc Method
Experiment with these if you like. I've never used them commercially.

Solar Returns and Lunar Returns
The Solar returns can be used to focus on a particular situation or on life in general, and they give a wonderful flavour of a particular year. Lunar returns give an even closer look, as they show the situation in a particular month.

Venusian and Martian Arcs

Leave these on Venus and Mars!

Decumbitures

If you like horary astrology, you will love Decumbitures. Use these to analyse and diagnose an illness. This is a great aid to astrological herbalists and other health workers. You need to be fully conversant with all aspects of decumbitures before diagnosing anything.

Horary Astrology

Ask yourself a question, such as "Will I get the job I am going after?" Make up a chart for the time the question is asked and see if it answers it. This is best for those who have thoroughly studied this technique, as the rules and terminology in horary are different to standard astrology.

Electional Astrology

This allows you to find the best time to do something important. Try making up a chart of the time and date you think is right as if it were a natal chart, and then judge its chances of success.

Mundane Astrology

This is the astrology of towns, cities, politics and so on. Try finding the chart for a specific country or a political party and work out what is likely to happen to it over the next six months.

Daily House Progressions and the Perpetual Noon Date

Don't bother with these methods.

Astrology and the Body

Check out the following list to see how the signs, houses and planets link to the different parts of the body. This list will come in very handy when you want to check out the state of health on a progressed chart of any kind. The information here is too basic for those who want to make a career of medical astrology, but it is good enough for the rest of us.

Engage your brain before opening your mouth when dealing with this facet of astrology, because the last thing you want to do is to alarm anyone, or to plant the idea in someone's head that they are likely to become ill.

Aries, First House, Mars

Part of body
The head, brain, eyes, skull and upper jaw. Pineal gland, arteries to the head and brain.

Potential ailments
Headaches, acne, fainting, neuralgia, fevers of the brain, blindness.

Taurus, Second House, Venus

Part of body
The lower jaw, the throat - including the thyroid gland, the neck, larynx, chin, ears, tongue, vocal chords, upper (cervical) spine, jugular vein and tonsils.

Potential ailments
Laryngitis, throat inflammation, over/under-active thyroid, tonsillitis and goitre.

Gemini, Third House, Mercury

Part of body
The upper respiratory system, the shoulders, arms, wrists, hands, fingers and upper ribs.

Potential ailments
Bronchitis, asthma, chest disorders, accidents to arms, shoulders and hands. Also the nervous system and the mind.

Cancer, Fourth House, the Moon

Part of body
The lungs, breasts, rib cage, stomach and digestive organs, alimentary canal, sternum, womb and pancreas.

Potential ailments
Gastric disorders, heartburn, diabetes and obesity.

Leo, Fifth House, the Sun

Part of body
The spine - especially the upper back, spinal cord, heart, arteries - especially the aorta, circulation, spleen.

Potential ailments
Back complaints, spinal meningitis, and heart diseases.

Virgo, Sixth House, Mercury & Chiron

Part of body
The lower digestive system, the bowels, the lower dorsal nerves, the skin, nervous system and the mind.

Potential ailments
Bowel diseases, indigestion, colic, intestinal infection. Skin infections and nervous or stress-related disorders. Let us not forget hypochondria!

Libra, Seventh House, Venus

Part of body
The bladder, kidneys, lumbar region, haunches to buttocks, adrenal glands, lumbar nerves, blood vessels.

Potential ailments
Kidney and bladder disorders, eczema, lumbago, abscesses.

Astrology and the Body

Scorpio, Eighth House, Pluto & Mars

Part of body
The reproductive and sexual organs - especially the cervix, lower stomach, lower spine including the coccyx, groin, anus, genitourinary system, prostate gland - and the eyes.

Potential ailments
Bladder disorders, genitourinary diseases, prostate or menstrual problems, piles.

Sagittarius, Ninth House, Jupiter

Part of body
The hips and thighs, pelvis, sacrum, the liver, the sciatic nerve, the arterial system - especially the femoral artery.

Potential ailments
Injuries and diseases of hips, thighs and pelvis. Sciatica, liver disorders, paralysis of limbs.

Capricorn, Tenth House, Saturn

Part of body
The skin, ears, teeth, bones, knees and bones above and below the knees.

Potential ailments
Chronic ailments of any kind. Rheumatism, skin complaints, knee injuries, bone diseases.

Aquarius, Eleventh House, Uranus & Saturn

Part of body
The ankles, calves, shins, breathing, circulatory system - especially to the extremities.

Potential ailments
Calf and ankle injuries, varicose veins, poor circulation, blood diseases, heart palpitations.

Pisces, Twelfth House, Neptune & Jupiter

Part of body
The feet and toes, lungs, lymphatic system and pituitary gland.

Potential ailments
Bunions, chilblains, tendonitis in the feet, gout, drink and drug problems, lymphatic and glandular disorders. Also allergies and strange psychic phenomena.

Signs of the Zodiac

By now, you can see that predictive astrology depends upon a static natal chart, around which (progressed / transiting) planets and other features move, making beneficial or difficult aspects to the natal planets and features as they travel along. However, everything that happens on a horoscope chart also has to move through the signs of the zodiac, and a planet will work differently when moving through one sign than in the next.

For instance, the Sun rules the fire sign of Leo, so it's happiest when passing through the fire signs of Aries, Leo and Sagittarius. It's reasonably happy when in the air signs of Gemini, Libra and Aquarius, uncomfortable in the earth signs of Taurus, Virgo and Capricorn, and unhappy in the water signs of Cancer, Scorpio and Pisces.

The same concept goes for all the other planets. For example, Saturn is associated with the cardinal earth sign of Capricorn, and the fixed air sign of Aquarius, so Saturn can find something to work with in cardinal signs, fixed signs, earth signs, air signs, or the decans that link to Capricorn and Aquarius. It is also comfortable in Libra, where ancient astrology tells us it is "exalted". The lists below show the various ways in which the signs can be divided up and described.

The Genders

Masculine signs are quick and assertive, while feminine ones have more endurance.

>   Aries   Masculine
>   Taurus   Feminine
>   Gemini   Masculine
>   Cancer   Feminine
>   Leo   Masculine
>   Virgo   Feminine
>   Libra   Masculine
>   Scorpio   Feminine
>   Sagittarius Masculine
>   Capricorn   Feminine

Aquarius   Masculine
Pisces   Feminine

The Elements

The signs divide into four elements of fire, earth, air and water. The fire signs are enthusiastic and quick, the air signs are thinkers, the earth signs get things done while the water signs make good use of intuition and empathy.

Aries   Fire
Taurus   Earth
Gemini   Air
Cancer   Water
Leo   Fire
Virgo   Earth
Libra   Air
Scorpio   Water
Sagittarius Fire
Capricorn   Earth
Aquarius   Air
Pisces   Water

The Qualities

The signs divide into three qualities of cardinal, fixed and mutable. The cardinal signs take charge, the fixed signs finish what they start and the mutable signs move things along.

Aries   Cardinal
Taurus   Fixed
Gemini   Mutable
Cancer   Cardinal
Leo   Fixed
Virgo   Mutable
Libra   Cardinal
Scorpio   Fixed
Sagittarius Mutable
Capricorn   Cardinal
Aquarius   Fixed
Pisces   Water

Signs of the Zodiac

Decans

Each sign of the zodiac can be divided into three decans. Each sign contains 30 degrees and each decan comprises ten degrees, the first of which repeats the sign itself, while the second and third decans follow along in the same element. This will make sense when you look at the list below:

The Fire Signs

Aries
First decan	Aries
Second decan	Leo
Third decan	Sagittarius

Leo
First decan	Leo
Second decan	Sagittarius
Third decan	Aries

Sagittarius
First decan	Sagittarius
Second decan	Aries
Third decan	Leo

The Earth Signs

Taurus
First decan	Taurus
Second decan	Virgo
Third decan	Capricorn

Virgo
First decan	Virgo
Second decan	Capricorn
Third decan	Taurus

Capricorn
First decan	Capricorn
Second decan	Taurus
Third decan	Virgo

The Air Signs

Gemini
First decan	Gemini
Second decan	Libra
Third decan	Aquarius

Libra
First decan	Libra
Second decan	Aquarius
Third decan	Gemini

Aquarius
First decan	Aquarius
Second decan	Gemini
Third decan	Libra

The Water Signs

Cancer
First decan	Cancer
Second decan	Scorpio
Third decan	Pisces

Scorpio
First decan	Scorpio
Second decan	Pisces
Third decan	Cancer

Pisces
First decan	Pisces
Second decan	Cancer
Third decan	Scorpio

The Ancient Divisions

The following table comes from older forms of astrology. Some astrologers love these divisions and use them all the time, while others ignore them. Purists would normally only include those planets that can be seen with the naked eye, but some astrologers now include the distant planets, albeit with some dispute over the signs they affect.

Signs of the Zodiac

PLANET	RULERSHIP	EXALTATION	DETRIMENT	FALL
Sun	Leo	Aries	Aquarius	Libra
Moon	Cancer	Taurus	Capricorn	Scorpio
Mercury	Gemini & Virgo	Virgo	Sagittarius & Pisces	Pisces
Venus	Taurus & Libra	Pisces	Aries & Scorpio	Virgo
Mars	Aries & Scorpio	Capricorn	Taurus & Libra	Cancer
Jupiter	Sagittarius & Pisces	Cancer	Gemini & Virgo	Capricorn
Saturn	Capricorn & Aquarius	Libra	Cancer & Leo	Aries
Uranus	Aquarius	Scorpio	Leo	Taurus
Neptune	Pisces	Cancer & Leo	Virgo	Capricorn & Aquarius
Pluto	Scorpio	Aries & Pisces	Taurus	Virgo & Libra

The Sun through the Signs & Houses

It would be lovely to explore every possible progression in detail by examining its effects on the psychology of the subject, looking into all the things that could happen and giving countless examples, but this book isn't big enough, so I'll simply explore the essence of each progression or transit.

The Sun

By day-for-a-year progression, the Sun spends thirty years traversing a sign and it will take the same time to cross a house if you use the equal house method. The Sun takes a month by transit to cross a sign or an equal house by transit. The Sun never travels retrograde.

The Sun corresponds to the fifth house and Leo

Character

Solar progressions and transits always denote important experiences. In theory, this should affect the public aspects of a subject's life, rather than personal feelings or domestic and family matters. Beneficial aspects can bring success in any area of life, happiness in connection with children, holidays, amusements and a fun-filled love life. Adverse aspects can bring great suffering and hardship, but these can be character building and much can be learned from them. Spiritual lessons may have to be learned at such times. The Sun is at its most comfortable and effective when traversing any of the fire signs, whether by transit or progression. The Sun is fairly compatible with air signs, but less so with earth signs and least comfortable when journeying through water signs.

Where to Start

Start by looking at the sign that the Sun is in, then look at the house and then check out the decan. Don't rush: take your time.

The Sun through Aries or the First House

You have reached the end of a phase and are now ready to start something new. New ideas, aims ambitions, renewed energy and a "kick-start" can be applied to your life. There will be satisfaction from looking back over what has been done in the past, but also impatience to get on with the new phase. You will gradually notice yourself becoming more outgoing and Arian in nature. You could start to take an interest in Arian jobs, such as teaching, social work, the armed forces or other large organisations, and you may take up hobbies such as engineering or making things.

Beneficial aspects to the Sun open the doors of opportunity. This would be a good time to seek favours, promotion, advancement and to deal with superiors. Challenging aspects could bring illness, a lack of energy, trouble at work and a loss of position or prestige. Difficult aspects can also bring great benefits, but these will be hard won.

The Sun through Taurus or the Second House

Movement into this sign or house exerts a calming influence and makes you less impulsive, less apt to take up sudden enthusiasms, while growing more reliable and sensible instead. If you have been a bit footloose up to now, you will soon settle into a job and family life, and make as much of a go of it as possible. You will be more stubborn and you may develop a stick-in-the mud attitude but you will also be more inclined to put down roots. Your life will be less eventful, but anything that does occur will be more profound.

Your attitude will be friendly and sociable and you may take up creative Taurean hobbies such as gardening, the fashion trade, building and cooking. You will need to guard against developing a sweet tooth and giving yourself a weight problem. You make an effort to obtain and to keep money and possessions.

You will search for and find your own value system, if necessary, rejecting that of your parents and schoolteachers. Beneficial aspects to the Sun in this sign or house bring money, property and goods. These also bring beauty, harmony and comfort. Challenging ones can temporarily remove these things or make them harder to obtain.

The Sun through Gemini or the Third House
When the Sun moves into this sign or house, you will want to give up some of your more materialistic ways in favour of a more intellectual approach. You will be happy to study and to pass on information to others and you will become more perceptive and critical. Life will hold more variety and you will be more versatile, dexterous, brighter but also more restless.

Local travel will become more important and there will be much contact with neighbours, siblings and colleagues. When the Sun is well aspected, negotiations, intellectual pursuits and contacts with others will progress well. Under challenging aspects, these things will prove to be a struggle but intellectual and other benefits can accrue as a result of efforts being made.

The Sun through Cancer or the Fourth House
When the Sun progresses into this sign or house, you will be less of a rolling stone and more of a stable family person. You could set up a home, open a small business or become more involved with the members of your family under this influence. You may feel more attached to your mother and to other older women.

History and the past will begin to fascinate you and you could start to collect things that have some special meaning for you. This isn't a particularly comfortable placement for the Sun, because your feelings are made more sensitive and painful.

Easy aspects will bring luck with property, family matters and any work that is carried out in the home. Difficult aspects could disrupt these elements of life and or make it hard to achieve a happy family life. The feelings could be very tender when tough aspects occur.

The Sun through Leo or the Fifth House
This being the Sun's natural sign or house, it is at its best here. You should become more centred, happier about yourself and about your way of life. You will be more egotistic or arrogant, but also more successful in everything you do, so you will probably deserve the right become somewhat insufferable! You will become a more powerful figure and you will be happy to display any extra wealth, extra goodies, talents or anything else that you gain under this influence.

You may become concerned with the things attached to this sign or house, such as creative work, show business, dealing with children and young people or working in the leisure industry. Your attitude to business will be less cautious and more flamboyant and entrepreneurial.

Under beneficial aspects, you can reach for the stars and get just about anything that you want from life but, under difficult ones, you could lose most of your gains - for a while at least. However, you won't stay down for long and your optimistic mood will soon return.

The Sun through Virgo or the Sixth House
When the Sun reaches this sign or house, you become more diligent and more concerned with the needs of others. You will quieten down and get your head down in order to concentrate on details. Detailed work such as computing, dressmaking and astrology might appeal. You will be less arrogant and more modest, less confident and outgoing and more cautious. In some ways, life becomes harder.

You may become interested in sixth house matters such as, health and healing. You may also feel the urge to take up issues that are attached to the terms and conditions of other people's employment. You may take on voluntary work in a hospital or a trades union. Try to keep your confidence level high by avoiding negative or critical people and try to avoid criticising yourself too much.

Another problem area is the Virgo habit of destroying anything that looks as if it is likely to be successful before it really materialises. Under beneficial aspects, you will turn into a good employer or employee and you will also make money and learn how to keep it. Under challenging aspects, health or business setbacks can occur.

The Sun through Libra or the Seventh House
This connects you to other people and makes you less self-centred or self-reliant. Marriage, partnerships and working partnerships become important now and you may find a partner, split from someone or make changes within working partnerships. If you have any enemies, they will come out into the open. You will look at value systems that are different from those that you grew up with and you will strive to put your life into balance again.

Libran jobs and interests may attract you, possibly leading you to take up a career as an agent or a go-between. Issues of justice and fair play also begin to play a role, and you will want to fight for what you think is right. You may have to get involved in legal dealings, either in connection with work or as a result of changes in your personal life. You will become more laid back, lazier and less interested in harsh reality. Under beneficial aspects, marriage, partnerships and work arrangements all do well while under challenging aspects; these spheres of life can become difficult. You may have to fight off enemies.

The Sun through Scorpio or the Eighth House

This planetary movement will make you stronger and more positive about everything that you do and you may even be quite earnest and humourless at times. You will be less inclined to sit back and let things happen or to rely upon others. Psychic or spiritual matters could begin to attract you and issues of life and death with both fascinate you. You may be personally affected by life and death situations.

Guard against becoming despotic, too ambitious or disinclined to take the feelings of others into account. You may take up a job that involves probing or investigating. Possibilities might be surgery, oil exploration, insurance fraud investigation, forensic work, mining and so on. You will deal with legacies, mortgages, divorce settlements, shares and anything else that connects money to yourself and others.

Sex and sexual relationships will become a strong force in your life now and this itself could lead to a firm commitment to new way of life. The key idea here is of merging yourself or your money with others. Under beneficial aspects, you will gain from the some of the above-mentioned ideas and you will receive karmic benefits. Under challenging aspects, problems arise and there may be karmic debts to be repaid. Resentment and even hatred might become a problem now.

The Sun through Sagittarius or the Ninth House

The ninth house and Sagittarius are considered "lucky", and the Sun is comfortable in a fire sign. You will feel the urge to expand your mental, physical and philosophical horizons in a number of ways. There will be a strong desire to break away and to increase your personal freedom. You may travel to distant places, and contacts with people from other lands and backgrounds will become important. You may work in an import/export business and it is even possible that you decide to take up with a foreigner.

Religion, philosophy and the spiritual side of life will start to interest you and you may discover that you have hidden talents as a medium, a healer or even an astrologer. Some people learn a lot about the law under this influence, either through their work or through personal circumstances. Teaching and learning begin to interest you. The most important issue is that you will be forced to examine your beliefs in the hunt for a philosophy of life that works for you. Under beneficial aspects, all the ideas mentioned above would prosper, while under difficult ones, you will find your beliefs challenged and your attempts to expand your mental, physical and spiritual horizons being stifled. There could be legal problems. Guard against attacking those who don't mean you any harm.

The Sun through Capricorn or the Tenth House

You will begin to reach for the top now, becoming more ambitious and serious in your attitudes. This sign and house are very much associated with banking, finance and big business so these will become an important part of your life. You will seek financial security, roots and status and this will lead to a more materialistic attitude.

Politics, publicity and prominence would all become important now. You could become more attached to your parents; especially a father or father figure at this time, and you will have more sympathy with older people in general. Under beneficial aspects, you reach the top of the heap but under difficult ones, you would fall from grace. Guard against becoming coldly ambitious at the expense of fun or of your personal relationships.

The Sun through Aquarius or the Eleventh House

When the Sun moves into this sign or house, you won't be any less ambitious but your goals will be different. Your outlook will be less self-centred and more universal. You will take an interest in humanitarian or environmental issues or any number of other causes. Groups of like-minded people will appeal and you may become involved with unions, local or national governments.

You will be interested in studying and also teaching, and for some of you, social work will appeal. Astrology and other philosophical systems will interest you and you will become less conventional and more eccentric as time progresses.

Guard against obstinacy and too independent an attitude, and utilise the other Aquarian traits, such as friendliness and helpfulness. Don't allow idealism to make you lose touch with reality. Under favourable aspects, you will be happy, outgoing and fulfilled while, under challenging ones, you could feel isolated and up against it. Avoid becoming eccentric, dogmatic and difficult.

The Sun through Pisces or the Twelfth House

You become kinder and more spiritual under this sign. You probably won't give up worldly ambitions and become a hermit, but there is bound to be a more introspective attitude. You will be more sensitive to others and much more interested in psychic or spiritual matters.

Circumstances may push you into giving up some aspect of your life and to become more self-sacrificial in some way. You may choose or you may be forced to live part of your life in seclusion for a while. This may be the result of karmic debts that need to be repaid.

On a practical level, you will enjoy working on creative or artistic projects and you may learn to play a musical instrument. You could also travel in connection with your work. Under favourable aspects, artistic, creative, musical, poetic or spiritual matters will prosper. Mysterious events could occur that bring help and guidance from strange sources. Under distressing aspects, you will be lonely.

The Moon through the Signs & Houses

Ensure that you learn how to read the progressed Moon, because this gives a marvellous picture of the circumstances that a subject is living through at a specific time. This will show what is occupying his mind at the time of the reading.

The Moon takes about two-and-a-half years to progress through a sign (roughly a degree per month). If the equal house method is used, the Moon also takes two-and-a-half years to pass through each house. If Placidus, Koch or any other method is used, the Moon could take anything from less than a year to about four years to pass through a house. While I'm on the subject of house systems, I suggest that you use whatever system you like for natal charting, but if you are a beginner, stick to the equal house method when doing predictive astrology, because it is easier. As it happens, I prefer the equal house method for predictive work, as it seems to be more accurate than other systems.

A lunar transit will pass by in a matter of hours, but it can be extremely useful when looking at a very critical event that occurs at a specific time. Typical examples would be signing a contract, attending a job interview or making an important phone call.

The Moon corresponds to the fourth house and to the sign of Cancer.

Character

The Moon refers to personal and inner, emotional matters and also the atmosphere closely surrounding the subject. Domestic and family circumstances are important and when the Moon is activated by transit or progression, the individual will be forced to make an evaluation of his or her family and personal life. Petty and unimportant matters may take on a large significance for a while and then subside quickly once the progression has passed. Mothers, motherhood and women in general are ruled by the Moon, as are a whole collection of strange things, such as dealing with the public, travel and restlessness, and health matters that are brought on by stress. Sometimes odd things surface, such as dealings with the sea, sailors, fishing, sewing and cooking.

The Moon can bring out the character of a planet, angle, sign or house when it progresses over or through it, because it reflects the energies from the other features on the chart rather than stamping its own nature on them. Where events are concerned, the Moon really does act as a kind of trigger for powerful events. When you look back over your life, you will notice that situations tend to last for two-and-a-half year durations, while phases of five, seven-and-a-half or ten years are often also important.

Where to Start

Start by looking at the sign that the Moon is in, then look at the house and finally, check out the decan. Don't rush: take your time.

The Moon through Aries or the First House

This is a time of rebirth. You will be forced to abandon old ways of life and to look around for something new. You will feel more passionate about everything, and even if you are normally placid, you will be more enthusiastic and excited about life. The ego comes to the fore and you begin to demand more out of life for yourself. This can lead to conflicts with others, especially with other family members, authority figures and those who seek to restrict you. The emotions rise to the surface, making you more susceptible to love and passion and also to moody feelings and a general dissatisfaction with your past way of life. Your rather raw and tender feelings will be a contributory factor in family arguments. You may have to deal with females in the family in quite a serious manner.

Familiar patterns of life begin to break up. In working life, there will be new contacts, new ideas and many short-term schemes. New ways of working can occur at this time. Travel or connections with the sea are possible now. You will be more self-centred and more inclined to look after your own needs, rather than those of others. Your sex drive will increase and this may also contribute to a change of partnerships. Even if you don't change partners, a move of house and new family groupings and arrangements are likely to happen around you. You will be less able to put up with the limits that your previous lifestyle has set upon you.

The Moon through Taurus or the Second House

This is the start of a more settled and comfortable phase in which you put projects that you started earlier into steady action. Material matters become important now and you will make a start on getting a nice home together or buying land that you can grow things on. You will begin to make and keep money at this time, and any goods that you buy will be durable. You will become reluctant to lend or waste money, while speculative ventures will hold no interest for you.

Anything that you start to do now is meant to last. This is a good time to form business partnerships, especially with women, and these too will last. Emotional partnerships should also be much more durable, but they lack intensity and passion and you will be happier to found a stable family than to flit from lover to lover. You will become keen on art, music, dancing, photography and anything else that has a connection to form and beauty. Building, gardening, cooking, decorating your home and other such creative interests will hold your interest.

The Moon through Gemini or the Third House

You will be more restless than before and you will probably pack as much as you can into your life just to keep yourself from becoming bored. This is a time for mental exploration and you will have an urge to educate yourself. You would be particularly keen to communicate with others and you may begin to use these skills in a job of work. This could lead you into office work, sales, teaching and other forms of communication. Temporary work, short-term jobs or peripatetic may suit you.

Local issues will become part of your life, and you could get together with friends and neighbours in order to improve your area or raise funds for a local school. You can expect plenty of visits to places of local interest and also plenty of people coming to visit you at your home. Love and romance may be put on the back burner for the time being, because you will be more interested in improving your mental processes rather than your love life. However, connections with intelligent and interesting people could enhance your personal life. You may flirt more and be less inclined to stick faithfully to the same old partner. Your emotions may confuse you because they will get in the way of logic and clarity of perception.

The Moon through Cancer or the Fourth House

The Moon is comfortable in this sign or house but that doesn't necessarily mean that your life is guaranteed to be happy throughout the whole progression, because you may become moody and prone to greater emotional highs and lows and it may be hard for you to understand your own feelings at times. The past will draw your attention and you may take an interest in history or in collecting things that have a history attached to them. You may bore your family and friends by frequently referring to things that happened in the past.

Family life comes to the fore under this progression and you may set up a home and a family. A change of address is possible or perhaps the acquisition of a shop or some other kind of premises. You may become attached to someone else's home for a while. Feelings of family loyalty become stronger and you may fancy researching your family tree. The need to identify with a particular group, race or religion will exert a powerful tug. You may retreat from the world and immerse yourself in domesticity or alternatively, you could begin to run a small business from your home.

Your intuitive and psychic abilities will come to the fore. Your emotions will bring periods of jealousy, possessiveness and loneliness, even when these emotions are unfounded. You may want to be alone and yet fear being lonely. In a lighter vein, you will seek out novelties by visiting new places, especially those with a history to them, and travel will become more important to you.

The Moon through Leo or the Fifth House

This progression should bring you into contact with babies, children or young people. There could be babies born into your circle or you may take up a job or hobby in connection with children. Your own behaviour will become more playful and childlike and you will begin to look around for pastimes and hobbies that allow you to play.

Creativity is the watchword now and this need will energise you into creating something important. You may write the definitive novel or creative a painting to rival that of the great masters, but it could just as easily be the creation of a home, a business, a family or a worthy cause that occupies your attention. Creative hobbies will appeal to you now because a creative outlet will be a necessity. You also need the attention that creative success will bring you. You will become bored with mundane jobs and begin to seek a job with a touch of glamour about it.

Your optimistic attitude could lead you to open your own business. You need to be somebody that people notice and your light cannot now be hidden under a bushel. Your feelings will rise to the surface and they may be hard to control. If you have spend your life thus far being kept down, your oppressors are in for a surprise or two. Exciting love affairs may become a feature of your life now, especially if you have been putting up with a dull or meaningless partnership. You will need an outlet for your passions.

The Moon through Virgo or the Sixth House

This is a great time to take up a new career because all forms of work will prosper now. This is especially so if the job is analytical in nature or if it concerns communications or the medical field. Bookkeeping, record keeping and office equipment could become an important feature of your life now. Do-it-yourself work, dressmaking or any other creative craft that requires dexterity and concentration would succeed at this time, as would writing or acting. You may take up farming or gardening.

This is a good time to establish sensible work habits and also to take on staff to help you cope. You may take up some form of training in order to brush up your skills and, even if you don't, you are sure to learn much that will be useful to you in the future. Your mind will become sharper and so will your sense of humour. You may become interested in health and healing, either of the normal medical variety or in the alternative therapy field. There may be an attachment to clinics, hospitals or doctor's surgeries due to family health problems or to finding a job in such a place. You will have to avoid taking on too much and working so hard that your nerves become stretched.

You may become faddy about food. Guilty feelings may plague you and you could become far too critical of yourself and others. Working relationships are more likely to be formed than personal ones. One rather nice compensatory factor for this all-work-and-no play syndrome is that it is a favourable time to buy new clothes.

The Moon through Libra or the Seventh House

Partnerships and relationships are the most significant feature of this progression and you will split away from some of those who have been a feature of your life and form new associations. Your emotions will be strong and they may be at odds with your needs, possibly because you want security and freedom at the same time. This progression is best used for exploring new relationships than for outright commitment, except in the business sphere when it works very well. This is an excellent time for all forms of business; especially where you have to act as an agent or assure that fair play is the rule. You will take care of your appearance and generally behave in an attractive and pleasant manner both at work and in your personal life. Legal matters may need to be attended to at this time, especially partnership agreements.

The Moon through Scorpio or the Eighth House

This progression brings crucial events because it is associated with the most vital aspects of life. There may be births and deaths in the family and among your friends. This is a time when one moves up a generation.

Any form of separation, divorce and other losses will be compensated for by forming new relationships. Business relationships that tie you financially will be formed now and other people's financial situations will be important. There will be dealings with the legal and official aspects of money and business in the form of mortgages, taxation, legacies and corporate matters of all kinds. There may be legal wrangles over property or goods relating to partnerships that have ended.

You could up a new home or place of business with someone new and fortunately, there are great opportunities opening up for moneymaking. Investigations will become important, and these may take the form of medical investigations, police or other types of investigations. Psychic and mystical matters may interest to you and your level of intuition will increase. This is likely to be a very stressful time for both positive and negative reasons and you will end this period feeling wrung out but a new lifestyle will be the outcome. You should make some really good financial gains during this period.

The Moon through Sagittarius or the Ninth House
This progression will expand your horizons. You will be contact with foreigners, foreign goods and ideas that emerge from cultures and backgrounds that are different from yours. You may choose to live in another country for a while and also learn another language, or you could fall in love with a foreigner. This may lead you to investigate religions and philosophies that are different from yours. You may decide to take up some form of higher education, and the subject you choose could well have a philosophical aspect to it. You may be involved with schools, colleges and churches as part of your daily life or you could take online courses.

Legal matters could become an important part of your life now. There should be a lot more fun in your life under this progression. You may take up hobbies and pastimes or become enthusiastic about sports. You may become more than usually interested in spiritual concepts such as mediumship, spiritual healing, reincarnation and astrology. Your values will become more spiritual and less materialistic and your sense of humour will become sharper. You will need to guard against over-optimism or expanding your horizons too quickly.

The Moon through Capricorn or the Tenth House
You will work hard while the Moon is in this sign or house and there will be a number of large and prestigious projects for you to complete. Details will need attention and you may feel at times as though you are being overwhelmed by work and responsibilities. You may suffer setbacks, and

some sphere your life may become limited or restricted. A chronic ailment may surface and you could feel old and tired at times. Older people or those in positions of authority will do much to help you reach your goals and in the end, all the hard work will have been worth it. It will be easy for you to sell a product or a service at this time.

You will learn how to work in a structured and businesslike manner. Your work could bring you into contact with the public. You will take a sensitive attitude to colleagues and employees. Personal and business relationships will become blurred and you may begin to work with someone you love or fall in love with a person you meet through your work. This is not a truly romantic time, and your feelings may need to be kept under a tight control. It may not be possible to be with the one you love as much as you would like.

Domestic life will take a back seat while you concentrate on your career. Parents, older people and authority figures will become an important feature of your life now. You could become a grandparent yourself under this progression. Your attitude will be quite materialistic at this time, and you must guard against becoming hard and calculating, or working yourself into the ground.

The Moon through Aquarius or the Eleventh House

Friends will become an important feature of your life at this time and you will have more dealings with other people than formerly. You will feel the need to be identified with a particular group of people who share your views and represent a lifestyle that you aspire to. There may be a cause or a movement that attracts you now. At work, you will have to work as part of a team or in charge of a group, and you will not be able to achieve too much on your own. You will strive for independence and you could seek to leave a situation that no longer works for you. There will be contact with helpful women but there could also be differences of opinion.

The urge to learn new things will lead you to seek education or to gain new skills. Modern methods and equipment will begin to fascinate you now. You will redefine your hopes and wishes and you may seek a completely different direction to the one you have followed up to now. Guard against becoming destructive, irrational or eccentric, and try not to push those who love you away. The chances are that the situation that you are in at the start of the progression will change radically by the time you end it. During this two-and-a-half year period, you could change your job, partner, home, family or even your country.

The Moon through Pisces or the Twelfth House
This will be a time of reflection and retreat and you may feel like a hermit at times, either staying quietly at home, working from home or not feeling sociable. You will become kinder and nicer but also more vulnerable, and your own personality may have to be suppressed for the sake of others or for the common good.

You will become involved with secrets, possibly due to starting something but not being able to talk openly about it for a while. There could be any amount of secret romantic entanglements, or you may be wrongly accused. Your family may find an excuse to exclude you from the fold. You must strive to keep hold of reality now, and not find yourself falling into a strange emotional morass, so try to avoid drink, drugs and opiates if you can. You may work in a prison, hospital or some other secluded place. You may travel to the sea or even move near water.

Artistic and creative skills will develop and you could learn to become competent at something creative. Metaphysical and psychic concepts will begin to interest you and you could develop a real flair for something different. You will be notice a great increase in your intuitive perception and probably real flashes of ESP. You must try not to become the architect of your own undoing with this progression.

Solar Aspects

It would be nice to look at every transit and progression in detail and then into all the possible events that could occur under each, but in a book of this length, we can only take a generalised view. I suggest that you treat yourself to a few books on transits and use the transit data for every kind of progression as well. Offer to make up charts for your pals and predict events for them, because their feedback will be very informative.

Sun/Sun

Easy aspects
A good time for self-expression.
Health improves.
Creativity comes to the fore.
Children and young people will bring joy.
Romance will be fun and leisure pursuits amusing.

Challenging aspects
This could be a frustrating and lonely time when others seem to be against you rather than with you.
You may become intolerant or you may draw intolerance to you.
This is a bad time to seek favours, especially from those in positions of authority or responsibility, and it is unlikely that you will be able to influence anyone else either.
Children could become a problem to you now, while children who undergo this aspect themselves will feel unloved and misunderstood.

Sun/Moon

Easy aspects
An improvement in domestic circumstances ranging from moving house to refurbishing a home.

Improved family relationships and harmony between the women of the family.
Children do well and there could be something to celebrate on their behalf.
You will contact old friends and could even look up an ex-lover.
Romance will go well as would a holiday on or by water.
Small business interests do well now, especially shops, farms and anything vaguely domestic.

Challenging aspects
Family and home situations are likely to be difficult and older women in particular could be difficult.
You may feel at odds with yourself and it will be hard to become "centred" at this time. Romantic situations could crumble.
Arguments will arise over money and there could be some very different views of who should spend what and how in your household.
Business matters may suffer, especially small businesses of your own.
Creative ventures will be difficult.
The best thing is to keep to a routine, avoid arguments and try to learn as much as you can from this experience.

Sun/Mercury

Easy aspects
A great time to learn something new or teach something to others.
Neighbours, colleagues and friends could figure strongly in your life now, as could brothers and sisters. All of these could come up with great ideas.
A new vehicle is a possibility.
You may take up an intelligent hobby or a creative venture.
Negotiations will go well.

Challenging aspects
Try not to allow pride or intolerance to spoil things for you.
Watch what you say and how you say it, because your mouth may have a tendency to run away with itself.
Avoid being malicious behind people's backs.
Games and gambling are likely to go wrong and this is definitely not the time to take up competitive sports of any kind.

Sun/Venus

Easy aspects
This brings a great improvement in your social life.
Romance, friendship and everything associated with having a good time will be on the menu for you now.
Art, music, dancing, leisure and pleasure will all play a part in your life at this time.
You will use your charm to captivate others and your looks will improve dramatically.
If you have neglected your appearance or allowed your wardrobe to become jaded, this is the time to make changes.

Challenging aspects
You may become lazy under this influence and put on weight.
You aren't interested in exercise, self-control or dedication to hard work at this time.
You may be tempted to spend money, either on your own behalf or on behalf of your children and you may not want to admit the nastier sides of their nature - or yours.
Anything to do with art, beauty and creativity will be delayed now and your social life will be very quiet.
Family celebrations will cause hassle.
Romance may go badly, but curiously, your sex life could take off.

Sun/Mars

Easy aspects
These two fiery and energetic planets can combine to give you a great time.
Your courage will be at its peak and you will feel that you can take on the world.
This is a great time to get involved in anything competitive.
If you decide to do anything really dangerous, make sure that you take extra care, because cutting corners could cost you your life.
Men of influence may enter your life and your own status and financial standing could increase.
You may take up something glamourous or you may simply appear more glamourous than ever before to those who count.
You may make love more frequently and more passionately than usual.

Challenging aspects

You could suddenly become aggressive, impulsive, argumentative and difficult.

A competitive streak could suddenly emerge and you may become keen on dangerous sports.

You will have to guard against accidents associated with weapons or machinery.

Impulsive financial speculation can lead to losses, and uncontrolled desires can lead to almost anything!

Keep control of your temper and of your life.

Sun/Jupiter

Easy aspects

This is a great time to learn something new and to explore new ideas of all kinds.

You may take a course of training at this time.

If you fall in love now, it will be by finding someone who feels the same way as you do and who shares your beliefs.

You will take charge of your life and you may have considerable responsibility and leadership thrust upon you.

Political aims, recognition and support are on the way to you now.

You could travel now or become involved with foreigners, foreign goods or foreign organisations.

Legal matters would also go well.

Challenging aspects

This can lead to arrogance, intolerance and an exaggerated idea of your own importance.

There may be too much expansion in some area of your life and you could go totally over the top in anything from a philosophical belief to a business venture.

Your attitude will be impractical and this will create problems in your relationships with others.

You may become extravagant or there may be unavoidable losses.

Foreigners and foreign travel may prove difficult, as could legal or educational matters.

Sun/Saturn

Easy aspects
Hard work that has been done in the past will bring rewards now.
Older people will be cooperative and those in positions of responsibility or authority will be approachable and helpful.
You may have some extra responsibility thrust upon you.
Sensible people will enter your life and any relationship that has been unsettled will steady itself down into a workable pattern.
Your mood will be rather serious and any groups or organisations that you associate with now will also have a rather serious outlook and purpose to them.

Challenging aspects
Personal ambition and creativity will be stifled for a while and everything will be hard to achieve.
Social life and romance will probably disappear, and illness or depression could limit your activities for a while.
You may become cold, hard and rigid in your opinions and you may try to use your position and status in order to push others around.
You will find it hard to gain recognition and even harder to find love.
Children may be a burden to you at this time and, children themselves who are under this progression will feel unloved.

Sun/Uranus

Easy aspects
You will feel an urge to break out of your usual mould and seek the freedom to be yourself and to do your own thing.
You will wish to develop your creative ideas in many new and original directions.
Friends and like-minded groups will appeal strongly to you and these could have a strong influence on you now.
You will wish to look inside yourself and to achieve your own personal goals.
You may become involved with politics or causes of some kind.
Novel subjects may begin to appeal to you or you could become interested in science, engineering, information technology or something similar.
You could fall head over heels with someone to whom you feel a magnetic attraction, but it may not last.
Something you are hoping for will work out well.

Challenging aspects

Your behaviour could become completely incomprehensible under this transit and you may vacillate between one kind of belief and another.

Nobody will be able to work out what you are going to do next.

You will find life unpredictable and unsettled for a while and you may end the transit or progression by changing your way of life forever.

Restlessness and eccentricity will drive you to break out of your rut and make changes.

There will be changes in connection with friends and also with children at this time.

You may leave a group of people who you have been associated with for some time past or you may decide to join a new and different group of people now.

Something you are hoping or wishing for will be a letdown.

Sun/Neptune

Easy aspects

Your creative instincts will come to the fore at this time and you may wish to lend your support to people or organisations in the creative field.

You could deal successfully with hospitals, institutions and homes for the elderly now.

There will be an increased interest in religion, philosophy, spiritualism or even astrology, and you may seek to instruct children in these subjects.

Art and music will appeal to you.

You may wish to delve into your past and discover the patterns that have shaped your life.

Many people experience an increase in psychic experiences at this time, especially precognitive dreams.

Challenging aspects

It will be hard to keep a grip on your life now and you must take care who you trust, or who you help.

Partnerships may be extremely strange or ultimately disappointing.

You must take care in business, romance and just about everything else that is important in life.

You may overdo things in many ways, either by falling in love with the wrong person or by taking a real interest in drink or drug abuse.

Delusions of grandeur or any other kind of delusion could make you hard to fathom.

You may become quite psychic, especially in connection with dreams.

Avoid medical treatments at this time if you can and be very careful about any medication that you take.

Children may drive you crazy at this time.

Sun/Pluto

Easy aspects

This marks an important time of transition in your life.

You may marry, divorce, take up a new career, retire, move to another country or do anything else that represents a major change of life.

Guard against illness at this time and, if you do get ill, then you need to take this into account as part of the changing pattern of your life.

Business matters related to banks, tax, corporations, legacies and shared financial resources are likely to become important now.

You may have to change your personal financial status as a result of the actions of others. Shared resources, such as in marriage could become an issue.

You will want to look more deeply into the meaning of everything and some aspect of investigating will become part of your life.

Challenging aspects

You will have to take care in all business dealings and also in connection with taxes, legal matters, corporate matters and other people's money.

Guard against becoming involved in power struggles at work or within sexual relationships.

Sex, birth, death and the deeper aspects of life could cause you problems.

You will have to make some kind of transformation to your lifestyle but this may work out well in the end.

Sun/Chiron

Easy aspects

If you or anyone in your circle has been ill lately, this will improve.

You may become interested in alternative therapies and all other matters related to health. You could wish to help others by treating or counselling them.

Teaching and learning will become important to you, especially in connection with the development of children.

You may become interested in music or the martial arts, even something like Tai Chi.

Challenging aspects

Watch your health and also the health of those who are around you.

You may want to teach others how to live, only to find that they don't want to listen.

Relationships and work could cause problems for a while now.

Sun/the Nodes

Easy aspects

This would be a good time to move house or to improve the one you have.

Family matters will go well and anything that you try to achieve out in the world will succeed now too.

The atmosphere around you will be conducive to success and the political "zeitgeist" will suit you. You may receive some kind of karmic benefit.

Challenging aspects

It may be hard to get the world to accept your ideas.

Family life will be difficult and anything domestic will be a bit awkward.

There may be some kind of karmic debt to be paid.

Sun/Ascendant

Easy aspects

This is a good time for a fresh start and to assert yourself.

New friends, increased social life and a time of fun should be around you now.

Health should improve with this aspect.

Challenging aspects

There could be problems with children or with creative projects.

Guard against becoming egotistical.

Sun/Midheaven

Easy aspects

This is a great time to seek recognition, to forge ahead with career aims or simply to make up your mind as to what you want from life and then go out and get it.

People in positions of authority should be helpful.

Clean up your home, your office and your act now, you have everything to gain and nothing to lose.

Challenging aspects

Problems associated with authority figures could feature now and your own authority will be challenged.

It will be hard to achieve your objectives for a while.

Lunar Aspects

When doing day-for-a-year progressions, these lunar aspects assume a terrific importance. When coupled with transits, this is probably the most accurate and interesting form of predictive astrology of all. Each progression will last for about a month, but it can have a tremendous impact on your life, with the effects lasting far beyond the month in question. Lunar progressions are the triggers of your life, setting off trains of events that are fascinating to watch and to live through.

Moon/Moon

Easy aspects
This would be a good time to change your address or to invest in property.
Family matters will go well as will anything that involves women or women's interests.
You may be emotional and rather restless at this time.
Travel is well aspected now.

Challenging aspects
Domestic and family matters are likely to be strained, and this is a bad time to call in the builders or to try to move house.
Your emotions will be stretched and you may go down with some kind of ailment as a result of stress.
Travel is not well starred, although you are restless enough to try it anyway.

Moon/Mercury

Easy aspects
Your curiosity will be stimulated and the harnessing of your imagination to your intellect could have very interesting results.
Travel around your locality will be well-starred.
Business matters, especially those that require negotiation, trading or communication will go well.

This is a good time to enjoy sporting activities, and also the company of younger people.

You will enjoy the company of brothers and sisters.

Challenging aspects

The car may let you down, your local buses and trains may go on strike or your bike will spring a puncture.

Your temper will not be at its best.

Domestic matters will become screwed up and some piece of machinery that you depend upon may suddenly develop a bad case of the gremlins.

Older women will get you down and business matters will be delayed or difficult.

Your brothers or sisters could aggravate you.

Moon/Venus

Easy aspects

This is a wonderful time to fall in love!

Be careful, because your feelings are vulnerable and close to the surface.

There may be family celebrations and happy events of all kinds, especially those that bring you into contact with others in a social setting.

Holidays, dinners and other outings will please you.

You may become involved in something to do with music, beauty or other pleasant subjects.

The money situation should improve but you may also be in a mood to spend, and if so, you will buy goods that are attractive, lasting and a little luxurious.

Challenging aspects

Partnerships will be difficult and a romance may suddenly go wrong.

You may fall in love with someone totally unsuitable because your feelings are vulnerable and you may not be able to think straight.

Family celebrations and events will be a source of irritation and anything to do with domestic life will be fraught.

Don't buy anything important now if you can help it, especially if it is something for the home.

Women will be a source of aggravation and your health may not be the best.

There may be more work than play for a while.
Try not to become involved in any business dealings or money transactions now.

Moon/Mars

Easy aspects
This aspect will heighten your feelings and it may make you rash or impetuous.
You will find it hard to keep your temper and you may fly off the handle all to easily.
It would be best to take your time now over any important decisions.
Dealings with men will be very interesting and this can mark the start of an important love affair.
Family and domestic matters should go well but your impatient attitude may make you irritable towards those who are close to you.

Challenging aspects
You may lose your temper.
Guard against accidents through rashness.
Family matters will be extremely irritating.
There may be health problems, even an operation or dental treatment.

Moon/Jupiter

Easy aspects
This is a good aspect if you want to deal with property or premises, and a move or refurbishment would work well.
Legal matters related to property or the family would also succeed.
You may become involved in religious or spiritual matters, possibly through coming into contact with interesting new people who introduce you to new concepts.
This is a good time to learn or to teach and if you need to take an examination, you should be successful in your endeavours.
Finances should pick up and there should be some excellent business opportunities with such matters as publishing or broadcasting being especially successful.
Foreigners, foreign travel or anything to do with foreign goods are all well starred.
Most of your schemes should succeed at this lucky time.
This can bring losses in one area whilst bringing gains in another.

Challenging aspects
This could be an expensive time with unexpected bills and few opportunities of finding any extra cash.
Dealings with property or legal matters will be difficult to manage.
Any business that involves farming, food, women's issues, publishing, broadcasting or the general public will be awkward.
You may find that your beliefs are being challenged and you may temporarily lose faith in your guardian angels or in yourself.
Educational matters will go slowly.
This is a poor time to travel or to deal with foreigners.

Moon/Saturn

Easy aspects
This will heap a certain amount of extra responsibility on to your shoulders and it may be a time of very hard work.
You could be a bit off colour at this time or just tired and feeling that you are being overworked and underpaid.
You will finish all that you start now and you will be well rewarded for anything that you do.
This is an excellent time in which to deal with those in authority over you and also to sort out anything regarding older relatives.
Your own authority and status should improve.
You must pay some extra attention to the home and to your family at this time and you will also take a serious attitude to domestic problems.
Your emotions will be under control and you shouldn't be swept away by your feelings.

Challenging aspects
A time of hard unremitting work and the rewards may not be obvious or quick to materialise.
A chronic illness could suddenly assert itself.
People in positions of authority could be very hard on you and life in general is likely to be unfair and difficult for a while.
Parents and older relatives will be demanding and family life may be depressing.
You may long to move house or to do something about your surroundings but you could be short of the time, money or the opportunity to do so.

Moon/Uranus

Easy aspects
Uranus always brings the unexpected, but at least the surprises should be pleasant ones.
This should bring good news in connection with family and domestic matters, and it could bring unexpected visitors or an opportunity to visit other people in their homes.
You will make new friends and you could also join a group or an organisation that looks like being fun.
Any business that concerns food, women's interests or domestic matters will go well.
You may be a bit over emotional and over excited at times.

Challenging aspects
There could be sudden events in connection with your home and family or among your friends.
If you have been involved in a group activity for some time, there will be sudden changes.
Nothing is certain now and your own mood is strangely rebellious, eccentric and awkward.
You may want to make a bid for freedom and to cut those ties that have become just a little too comfortable, familiar and boring.
If other heavy aspects are involved, you will change your way of life quite dramatically.

Moon/Neptune

Easy aspects
You will become a really sensitive soul.
Neptune will make you compassionate towards the sufferings of others.
Artistic and creative endeavours will do well; you could become keen on photography, poetry, music or anything else that evokes memories and feelings.
You may find yourself looking back over your past and even reliving something that happened to you years ago.
You will become more receptive to your inner feelings and you will notice an increase in your intuitive powers.
Precognitive dreams are possible at this time.
Daydreams are also possible and you may lose yourself in a time of dreaming and drifting for a while.

Challenging aspects
- You may feel as though your life is on a kind roller coaster with the chief victim being your own emotions.
- The past could come back to haunt you in some way and you may have to face up to some pretty awful memories or feelings that have been buried away for years.
- You will become over sensitive and terribly vulnerable.
- Guard against deception in financial and business dealings and if possible, leave any important decisions until well after this progression has passed.
- Artistic and creative ventures will be especially badly affected.
- Avoid self-sacrifice.

Moon/Pluto

Easy aspects
- You may decide to change your domestic circumstances, or even to move house.
- If this occurs when other important progressions or transits happen, it could be life changing.
- Important matters relating to births, deaths, beginnings and endings can go your way now and if you have to deal with legacies, taxes and other joint matters these should prosper now.
- Family matters are important at this time.
- There may be something in the offing, relating to mothers or motherhood.
- Your sex life may suddenly pick up and both secret and open liaisons are likely to move into a more passionate phase now.

Challenging aspects
- You may find yourself facing up to something that in your heart of hearts, you have known was wrong for a long time.
- You may bring an affair of the heart to an end or make a start on a new one but whichever way this goes, there will be pain and soul-searching on a deep inner level.
- You may suddenly become frightened by psychic experiences or by people who are sinister.
- Don't become involved in business matters or partnership matters that involve shared resources.
- Legal and official matters can bring problems at this time and there could be family wrangles over wills, tax bills and so on.

This is a poor time to buy property or to have major work done at home.
Family life is likely to be a bit tense.
Your sex life could become an issue and this too could lead you to take some difficult decisions.
Dealings with births, deaths, beginnings and endings may bring problems.
Old resentments may resurface.

Moon/Chiron

Easy aspects
If you or anybody close to you has been ill lately, this should begin to improve rapidly.
Your compassion for those who need help will be stimulated at this time.
There could be some kind of strangely karmic or emotionally important event in your life, and you could learn a lot from this.

Challenging aspects
This could bring health problems for you or your loved ones.
If you work in the health or healing field, things may be tough for a while.
Teaching or learning may present difficulties

Moon/the Nodes

Easy aspects
This is likely to bring joy and happiness to your home.
Business matters may go well and there may be a karmic feeling to everything that is going on.
If you deal with the public, it will be a success.

Challenging aspects
Your mother or other older relatives could be demanding now and your mood is not a happy one.
Home, household or domestic matters go badly.
There may be some kind of karmic debt to be paid now.

Moon/Ascendant

Easy aspects
Happy family life and a good mood all around you typify this event.

You will feel optimistic and outgoing and anything that you start now should go well in the future.

Domestic and family matters are well starred as are any business matters relating to farming, food, women's interests or the general public.

Challenging aspects

Logic and intuition will be at odds with each other.

You won't relate well to others and you may not understand yourself either for a while.

This is not a great time for business, domestic life or matters of the heart.

Moon/Midheaven

Easy aspects

If you need to improve your public image out in the world, this is the time to do it.

Public relations and sales or marketing of any kind will succeed, as will domestic and family matters.

This would be a good time to entertain important people at your place of work or in your home.

Challenging aspects

This aspect will bring difficulties with your aims and ambitions.

Business matters will not go well and there could be a conflict between your work and your home, with plenty of pressure coming at you from both sides.

Your parents may not approve of what you are trying to do.

This is a difficult time for real estate transactions or for working in anything that is supplied to women or which deals with the public.

Planetary Aspects

Mercury/Mercury

Easy aspects
It's easy to learn something new or to teach others now.
Your curiosity will be stimulated and you will need to stretch your mind.
Relationships with neighbours, colleagues, brothers and sisters will be good and any local or family events will go well.
Something to do with vehicles will go well.

Challenging aspects
Your mind may become temporarily blocked but this will simply lead you into other ways of thinking.
Your vehicle may break down.

Mercury/Venus

Easy aspects
This is great for business, romance or social life.
Negotiations and anything to do with finances will succeed, as will dealings with women.
You will want to spend money on your appearance and this will pay off both in personal and professional life.
You could become interested in art, beauty or music and anything to do with the preparation and enjoyment of good food.

Challenging aspects
Misunderstandings with siblings, neighbours and even those you love could occur.
You will find it hard to express yourself clearly, especially to those whom you love.
This is the wrong time to ask for a raise or spend much money.

Mercury/Mars

Easy aspects
An intense period of work.
Good business ideas.
You will think and act very quickly and can put this to good use in a business context.
This should be a good time to sign papers and to work in partnership with men.
Attraction to a person who shares your sporting and spare time interests is possible.
Anger and aggression can be diverted into action but you may become somewhat sarcastic and cutting.
Confidence increases.

Challenging aspects
A bad time to be involved in any kind of business with others, or to sign important papers.
There will be disagreements over work methods and new technology may be hard to get to grips with.
Anger, biting sarcasm and bitter arguments are possible.
A possible split from a man in business or personal life.

Mercury/Jupiter

Easy aspects
This will be an educational phase in which you seek information and ideas on a big scale.
Philosophy, religion and psychic matters will be put under the microscope and ministers of religion could enter your life.
You may decide to expand business enterprises and the chances of negotiating good terms are excellent.
New people in your life will open your eyes to great possibilities and travel of all kinds will be favourable.
Legal matters will be successful.
This is a great time to study, write or teach and foreigners could be a source of inspiration.

Challenging aspects
You become muddled and confused about your beliefs.
Conflicting ideas could confuse you.

This is a bad time to become involved in legal matters or to agree to anything big that involves business negotiations.
Don't sign anything important.
Travel may be difficult. Foreigners or foreign goods could cause problems.

Mercury/Saturn

Easy aspects
This is a good time to get your head down and concentrate on a course of study or on new work practices.
Anything that is started now should be finished properly in due course.
Nothing will happen quickly but progresses will be made.
A realistic and methodical approach will pay off and there may be an interest in scientific or detailed work of some kind.
Older people may be influential in business matters and an older relative could help you out.
Family matters will be sorted out and there could be some travel to and from family members or on business.

Challenging aspects
You may feel tongue tied and stupid at this time but if you can find a way of expressing yourself, you can succeed.
Guard against losing your confidence.
Hard work, especially in a scientific field can bring results and writing may be especially successful.
Guard against problems due to sloppy financial or business practices.
Avoid overwork or allowing a health problem to get out of hand.

Mercury/Uranus

Easy aspects
This will stimulate your mind and take you into new realms of thought.
Original and unusual ideas can be successfully pursued.
You should make new friends and become involved in institutions, groups and social clubs that are stimulating and amusing.
You may get new job or discover a new way of doing a current one.
You may become involved in alternative therapies and spiritual healing and your intuition level will increase dramatically.

Challenging aspects
Reliable machinery will be taken over by gremlins.

You may have some very original ideas, but they may be too unrealistic.
Your temper and your mental processes will be erratic and uncertain.
There may be arguments with neighbours and siblings.
Take care while driving or travelling around your locality for some time now.

Mercury/Neptune

Easy aspects
You could fall in love with a dream that does not match up to reality.
If it isn't love that fascinates you, the spiritual side of life will appeal.
You will find it easier to visualise and to conceptualise at this time.
Dreams may become reality now, and travel near or over water will be beneficial.
This is a great time to put creative ideas into action and hobbies such as acting could prove to be fun.

Challenging aspects
If you fall in love with a dream or a vision now, you could be in for a rude awakening later on!
Guard against becoming involved with deceitful people, losers, betrayers or those who seek to destroy your confidence.
Drinkers and druggies may be tremendously appealing but they are all part of the illusion.
There may be scandal, loss and difficulties in dealing with people in business or legal matters.
Try not to travel or become involved with foreigners for the time being if you can avoid it.
Psychic or psychological problems may arise.

Mercury/Pluto

Easy aspects
There will be an increased interest in shared resources or merging with others.
You will want to look behind and beneath every question and it will be easy for you to solve mysteries now.
This would be a great time to write a successful thriller!
You may take an interest in psychic matters and you will want to know how these work.
You will want to improve your education and probably your financial position as well.

You will be able to communicate with others on many levels.
There could be legal dealings, possibly as a result of deaths in the family and siblings may well be involved in these matters.
You will want to look into matters relating to birth, death and sex!

Challenging aspects
Business could go wrong, and legal matters could become a minefield.
You may even have to pay someone to investigate a particular problem or a situation.
This is not a good time to sign anything important, and you should take care over matters relating to taxes, mortgages and so on.
Avoid becoming involved in strange psychic experiences or practices.
There may be difficulties in connection with siblings and neighbours.
Sex may bring problems.

Mercury/Chiron

Easy aspects
Study, teach and take up any interest in health or healing.
Sporting interests are favourable.
If you or anyone in your family have been ill lately, they will soon recover.

Challenging aspects
Health is the big problem here and any ailment that occurs now could hang around for long time.
Studying, teaching and sporting interests would be problematical.
Take care of any sick people who are around you.

Mercury/the Nodes

Easy aspects
Depending upon the node that is involved, past experiences or completely new ideas could be very successful.
Anything that you do now will fit well with the public mood, and any form of public relations or image polishing would be a great success.
Property and family dealings will succeed.

Challenging aspects
Property matters will bring problems and family life is not easy now.
Don't take chances in business now.

Planetary Aspects

Mercury/Ascendant

Easy aspects
Your confidence is on the increase and your sense of initiative and enterprise is building all the time.
Your communications ability will be on the increase and all business matters should go well.

Challenging aspects
Guard against over-expansion in business and watch what you agree to.
Think before you speak and don't allow others to sap your confidence.

Mercury/Midheaven

Easy aspects
A great time for business enterprises or for forging ahead in any sphere of life that requires communication ability.
A career change or a change of your direction is quite likely.
If you deserve a raise or a promotion, ask for it now.

Challenging aspects
Difficulties connected with your aims and ambitions are likely to arise.

Venus/Venus

Easy aspects
You will appreciate music, art and beauty in all its forms.
Women could be very helpful to you, and life should be pleasant and easy.
It will be easy to make money and very pleasant to spend it.
People in your circle will be friendly, helpful and sociable and you will be able to impress them with your charm and charisma.
You may fall in love.

Challenging aspects
Difficulties in connection with money or relationships.
Women may pose problems.
You may be unhappy with your looks or your image.

Venus/Mars

Easy aspects
A love affair could be on the cards.
A time to spend money on luxuries.
You might take an active interest in artistic or creative pursuits.

Challenging aspects
Guard against allowing your feelings to run away with you.
Don't allow greedy people to use you as a meal ticket.

Venus/Jupiter

Easy aspects
You can afford to take a gamble.
You should be able to enjoy whatever you are doing.
The culture and beliefs of those you come into contact with will influence you beneficially.
There may be travel in connection with business.

Challenging aspects
Over expansion could lead to losses.
Travel may be expensive.

Venus/Saturn

Easy aspects
Creative ventures may be slow going but, once the work has been put into them, they should be successful.
Friendships and acquaintanceships will be rather pleasant and relationships with older relatives will also be nice.
This is a very difficult time for love relationships, because on the one hand, they could become durable, but on the other hand, they may bring trials and tribulations to follow in their wake.

Challenging aspects
This could mark a difficult time for all relationships.
Money will be hard to come by and you may feel off colour as well.

Venus/Uranus

Easy aspects
Sudden attractions are possible.
New friendships and exciting people and experiences are likely now and live will be pleasantly unpredictable.
Work that involves electronics could prove to be viable.

Challenging aspects
You may fall for the wrong person.
You may take a job, only to find it doesn't work for you.
You get into the wrong crowd.
You may be eased out of a position in a group or an organisation.

Venus/Neptune

Easy aspects
This is a really dreamy and romantic phase.
You may put your lover on a pedestal and not be able to see reality for the mists of romance.
This is a good time to be compassionate and charming towards others.

Challenging aspects
Romance could go wrong and losses can occur in business.
Avoid drugs, sex and rock and roll if you can.

Venus/Pluto

Easy aspects
Powerful feelings will become apparent and you could even find yourself falling in love.
You benefit from a legacy, pension or tax rebate.

Challenging aspects
Watch your heart and your bank account!

Venus/Chiron

Easy aspects
You should be healthy, and sick relatives or friends will begin to recover.

A woman may teach you something useful.

Challenging aspects
Chiron aspects can be difficult for health and relationships.

Venus/the Nodes

Easy aspects
A good time to spend money on property.
A good time for business dealings that benefit the public.
You may meet a soul mate.

Challenging aspects
You may be drawn to something or someone who is wrong for you.

Venus/Ascendant

Easy aspects
Make a start on improving your image, your appearance and your finances.
You will become happier and easier to get along with.
You may look for someone to love, or get involved in something creative.

Challenging aspects
Relationship difficulties and a loss of inspiration.

Venus/Midheaven

Easy aspects
A great time to forge ahead with your aims, ambitions or making money.
Romance could lead to business opportunities or you could meet someone through work.
You will look good and feel good about yourself.
Good relationships with parents, in-laws, bosses and older people.

Challenging aspects
Life becomes a bit of grind and boring for a while.

Mars/Mars

Easy aspects
A very busy phase in which you can get a great deal done.
Your energy level will be high and you will make decisions quickly.
Jobs that are traditionally considered to be masculine, such as engineering, car maintenance and building may become part of your life now.

Challenging aspects
Guard against rashness, accidents and hastily handling sharp objects.
Take care while driving.

Mars/Jupiter

Easy aspects
This brings an expansion in business or cultural affairs.
Business travel, or exploring new faces and places is indicated.
Groups or organisations that are involved in religion, astrology or spiritual matters might appeal to you.

Challenging aspects
Beware of over expansion in any area of your life, and take care while travelling.
Avoid dealing with aggressive men and overtly dangerous situations.

Mars/Saturn

Easy aspects
You can forge ahead very successfully now.
Progress in career matters and an increase in status are possible.
Older people, those in authority or men in general may help you.
You may find yourself dealing in a beneficial way with people who wear uniforms or who work in the fields of engineering or science.

Challenging aspects
You may find it hard to achieve your ambitions and there may be people who try to stand in your way.
You may become resentful and angry and lose your temper as a result.

Mars/Uranus

Easy aspects
Your emotions may be hard to control and a hectic love affair is possible.
You should put your heart into new and original ideas.
You could take up a sport, a course of education or training.
Your confidence level should increase.

Challenging aspects
Guard against accidents or losses through hasty behaviour.
Arguments are likely.

Mars/Neptune

Easy aspects
Your psychic powers and intuition will be on the increase and you could meet people who inspire you to take an interest in spiritual matters.
If you are interested in any kind of creative endeavour, this will begin to go very well.
Behind the scenes work or any selfless help that you give to others will be worthwhile.

Challenging aspects
You could fall in love, become obsessed and get hurt as a result.
Your sexual drive is very high and it could lead you into trouble.
Avoid drink, drugs and the lower levels of life.

Mars/Pluto

Easy aspects
You will want to push things to the limit and your increased will power will enable you to do so.
You may reach a position of influence or power.
This is an excellent time to deal with business matters, especially those that involve joint finances.
Sexual and relationship matters could be spectacular.

Challenging aspects
Power struggles and temper tantrums are possible.

Try to avoid political situations or places that could put you in a dangerous position.

Business matters and relationships with others could be frustrating due to power struggles. Sex could be a problem, or it could cause one.

Mars/Chiron

Easy aspects
You may want to heal the sick, or learn some form of medicine or healing.
You may study or teach some kind of sports.
You may find a mentor for your spiritual interests.

Challenging aspects
Guard against accidents and look after yourself.
Take care of your knees, shins, calves, ankles and feet.
Avoid dealing with weapons of any kind.

Mars/the Nodes

Easy aspects
This is a good time for property dealings.
You may get together with family members and either plan for the future or reminisce about the past.
Anything that you take up now will be well received by the public.
There may be a karmic benefit from good that you have done in the past.
Life is easy for a change.

Challenging aspects
Family and domestic difficulties.
A feeling that you are swimming against the tide.

Mars/Ascendant

Easy aspects
A time to break out of your rut and make a fresh start.
You will be more self-centred than usual, but this is probably a good thing.

Challenging aspects
It is hard to get anything off the ground now.
You may be feeling off colour.
People could be awkward and obstreperous.

Mars/Midheaven

Easy aspects
This is a good time to put all your energies into getting on and making achievements.
A man may help you reach your goals.
Try to rest if you can because the chances are that you are working very hard at this time.
If you want a raise or a promotion, ask for it now.

Challenging aspects
Someone may stand in the way of your progress and there could be a series of frustrating arguments as a result.
This is not a good time to ask for a raise or for anything else that you deserve or want.

The Slower Moving Planets

Here I have only given the positive interpretation, but if the aspect is a negative one, just turn the positive on its head.

For instance, if Jupiter is square to Jupiter, expect a lack of new options, no opportunity to expand horizons and travel to be problematic.

Jupiter/Jupiter
New opportunities, travel and expansion of horizons.
Legal matters go well as do educational and spiritual matters.

Jupiter/Saturn
Expand cautiously, especially in speculative ventures.
Older people or those who have a spiritual outlook may be helpful.

Jupiter/Uranus
A time of massive expansion.
Original and unusual people and ideas can lead you into new directions.
Unexpected luck.
A good time to deal with your local government.

Jupiter/Neptune
A great time for travel over or near water.
Expansion of ideas, especially spiritual and mystical ones will be
    interesting and successful.
Healing and mediumship would be especially attractive at this time.
Money can be made from creative endeavours.

Jupiter/Pluto
Spiritual matters will come to the fore now and you should experience
    an increase in your level of intuition.
You may develop an interest in health and healing or in legal matters.

Jupiter/Chiron
These two planets are both involved in teaching, especially martial arts, sports and in the case of Chiron, music, so the chances are that a transiting conjunction between these two planets will bring some form of studying or perhaps participating in something competitive or sporty.

Jupiter/the Nodes
Luck in connection with property, family life, work affecting the public.
Karmic benefits.

Jupiter/Ascendant
A fresh start with everything to play for.
Great expansion of horizons.

Jupiter/Midheaven
Could be a terrific time for all career matters, progress may be fast or slow but it is ensured.
You may find a spiritual belief that changes your life for the better.

Saturn/Saturn
A time of facing reality.
Your life may change for the better or the worse but there will be a period of hard work and of sorting yourself out on an inner level.

Saturn/Uranus
Uranus wants to forge ahead and Saturn puts on the brakes.
Others notice you, and you can achieve much in something political.
You will be able to put modern techniques to good use and a realistic attitude to original ideas can bring wonderful rewards.
You will take responsibility in some kind of group activity and friends will become an important part of your life.

Saturn/Neptune
You may work on a successful secret project.
You may tap into your spiritual or intuitive abilities in a useful manner.
Creative enterprises will be hard work but they can be brought to fruition
Love affairs can prosper under this progression or transit and they would combine common sense and idealistic romance.

Saturn/Pluto
Your concentration will increase.
You can make progress in a large project that involves large and important organisations.
Ambitions can be achieved.

Saturn/Chiron
This heralds a serious phase of education or training and it is a helpful conjunction to those who are studying or training for something. It helps you to keep your head down and get on with the work, and to do a thorough job on any revision that is needed.

Saturn/Nodes
Steady progress at home.
The political or prevailing situation in your environment will help you to achieve your ambitions.
There may be some karmic benefit from the past or even from a past life.

Saturn/Ascendant
A time of progress if you work hard and concentrate on details.
You may become rather shy and withdrawn or so devoted to your ambitions that you ignore your loved ones.

Saturn/Midheaven
People in authority can help you now.
Forge ahead with your ambitions but avoid becoming cold and hard.

Uranus/Uranus
Take to break out from your mould.
Friends may exert a strong influence on your life now.
Original and unusual ideas will appeal to you and you may become unpredictable and eccentric for a while.

Uranus/Neptune
Mysticism, astrology and the desire to learn characterise this aspect.
You could become caught up in almost anything that is otherworldly.
Guard against drink or drugs.

Uranus/Pluto
Major changes that are happening out in the world may affect your lifestyle in a major way.

You could change direction radically and leave everything behind in order to start again.
Powerful feelings come to the surface.

Uranus/Chiron
You will suddenly feel inspired to learn something new, or become part of a group of people who you don't yet know.
Friends will help you to heal yourself from past hurts.

Uranus/Nodes
You could develop an interest in astrology or spiritual matters.
Friends or groups will influence your life in some way.
Karmic benefits.
You may take up politics or something else that involves the public.

Uranus/Ascendant
A complete change of lifestyle is probable.
You may break out of your mould and leave some important part of your life behind.
Groups of people and friends will have an important bearing on your life.
You may become interested in astrology or something similar.

Uranus/Midheaven
A change of job or a complete change of direction is likely.
You may become attracted to electronics, astrology, computers or other modern techniques.
You may take up humanitarian work.

Neptune/Neptune
This is a good time for creative projects or for art, photography, film or anything else that creates an illusion.
You may fall in love and you won't be able to see straight as a result.
You may come to terms with something that went wrong in your past.
Something could be revealed.

Neptune/Pluto
Some kind of major change is affecting your life, and this could be a political or world situation.
You may fall in love, take up an artistic career or change your life entirely in some way.

The Slower Moving Planets

Neptune/Chiron
Some painful experience in your past needs to be addressed now. This could be a physical problem, especially one that affects the feet and ankles, but it could be a psychological wound that needs to be aired and healed.

Neptune/Nodes
You may decide to move your home close to the sea or a source of water.
Love could affect your lifestyle, your job and your family situation.
You may do something for others that creates karmic benefit.

Neptune/Ascendant
An increase in your spirituality or creativity.
You may fall in love or you may be a prey to illusions.
Film, photography or art may become important.
You may become psychic.

Neptune/Midheaven
A career in an artistic field is likely.
You may become interested in cosmetics, hairdressing, film, photography or art.
You may fall in love with someone whom you meet through work.
You may become psychic.

Pluto/Pluto
You may appear to change your life suddenly but the chances are that this change has been on the cards for years.

Pluto/Chiron
A major transformation is happening in your life right now; it will be painful and unpleasant while it is working its way out, but the end result is that a great deal of past unpleasantness will be addressed and cleared away, ready for a brighter future.

Pluto/Nodes
A change of address and a change of family circumstances are possible.
You may seek to influence events now or you may be influenced by the prevailing political situation.
Karmic benefits might be on the way.

Pluto/Ascendant
A change of direction is likely.
You may feel paralysed and unable to make changes but subtle alterations are going on somewhere deep down inside you.
You could take an interest in big business or in shared or joint ventures.

Pluto/Midheaven
A terrific time for influencing the world that you live in.
Political or other situations may give you opportunities for advancement.
You will deal with taxes, corporate matters and anything that arises through joint financial matters.

Pluto/Chiron
A major transformation is happening in your life right now and it will be painful and unpleasant while it is working its way out. The end result, however, is that a great deal of past unpleasantness will be addressed and cleared away, ready for a brighter future.

Chiron
Aspects to or by Chiron affect health and sometimes one's state of mind. On a positive note, they can also relate to education, sporting achievements and even an interest in music. Check out the other planets or the angles that are involved in the progression or transit to see which body part is likely to be affected, or whatever else might turn up at this time.

Nodes, Asc, MC, Dsc, IC
It is hard to quantify the changes that movements of the angles bring, but you can pick up clues by looking at the natal planets that are affected.

The nodes can be associated with premises, emotions, family, parents and karma.
The Asc concerns the self.
The MC denotes aims, ambitions, reputation and the future. In some cases, it concerns the father.
The Dsc indicates other people.
The IC harks back to the past, to the background to a situation, to the family, the mother and the home.

A MISCELLANY OF INTERESTING FACTS

In this book, I have focused on natal charting and predictive astrology, but there are many other forms of astrology that you might wish to investigate, and you might like to know what some of them are. Let us start with some ideas that exist in western astrology and then move on to other cultures.

Horary Astrology
This is an old form of astrology that looks familiar to us but that works by different rules. You need to take a course in this to begin to understand it.

ACG, Astro-Cartography or Astro-Mapping
These terms all relate to a form of locational astrology which was dreamed up in the USA some decades ago, when computer programming made such things possible. It relates to the movement of the Sun across the face of the Earth and the line where night and day meet, which becomes the rise line. There is also a set line, an MC and an IC line. The same goes for all the other planets, even though they cannot cast a shadow across the face of the Earth. This is a useful form of locational astrology because the lines show where you can find luck, love, money, a good job, and more in the world. Lines that run around the world in "great circles" form parans, which also have a meaning.

It takes a while to get your head around the system and to get used to the confusing maps, but it isn't difficult to work out how the lines will affect you in any place on Earth, should you wish to travel or do business with people in other countries.

If you're interested in this field, I have written a book on the subject, called: "Astrology... On the Move!" By now, there are also many other books on the subject, so a look on Amazon will help you to choose one that appeals to you.

Local Space Astrology
This is another locational form of astrology, which draws lines from the position of the planets at birth. I am not sure how useful this one is, but I have included it in my book as mentioned above if you want to know more about it.

Mundane Astrology
This is the astrology of countries, regimes, politics and so on, and it is fascinating. It follows the same rules as natal astrology. Try making up a chart for Kabul in Afghanistan for the morning of the 16th of August 2021, and see what that tells you.

Physical Astrology
This is an unusual specialisation, as it relates to weather and natural phenomena. Still, as you get further into ordinary astrology, you might find yourself picking up data on this as you go along. One extraordinary fact is that when any outer planet from Jupiter outwards lands at 27 degrees of any sign, something significant will happen – which might be a volcano, earthquake, flood, tsunami or war breaking out. A major outer planet at that position seems to release the four horsemen of the apocalypse, so we must all watch what happens when Pluto reaches that position in the near future!

Arabic Parts
There is a form of astrology called the Arabic Parts. The starting point is a natal chart, then the astrologer calculates the distance between various planets and adds the data to the ascendant to find another "Part". This is easy to do if you have astrological software. Erect the natal chart, investigate the section on reports and select the Arabic Parts.

Here are just a few of the many parts that exist:

Part of brethren
Part of illness
Part of merchandise
Part of water journeys
Part of death

Most of these parts won't connect with any planets on your natal chart, but some will make an aspect. The only aspects allowed are the conjunction and opposition, and the orb is only one degree. A friend of mine fell head over heels with a lad whose Sun was on her part of catastrophe, and he used her, lied to her and then dumped her. In short, the whole affair was a catastrophe!

Distant Planets and Asteroids

More planets are being discovered all the time, and some astrologers are writing about them on the internet. I have investigated one called Eris that has a 500-year orbit due to being so far from the Sun. It recently returned to the place it occupied during the reformation, so it seems to link with major international power changes and all the revolutionary upheaval that implies. Afghanistan? Add Pluto moving into Aquarius over the next few years; I can see the world being in a state of chaos for a couple of decades, and I'm not the only astrologer to see this coming!

Asteroids or planetoids abound, and you can choose to read them or not. Sometimes, I look at Ceres because there is a shortage of "nice" planets, and Ceres brings abundance and comfort, like the cereal harvest named after this goddess.

Fixed Stars

These are simply stars. The word "planet" is ancient Greek for a wanderer, so the idea is that the planets wander around while the stars stay in place. In fact, the whole galaxy is on the move, as is the whole universe, so nothing is fixed, but it does take a millennium or two for a star to shift from one position to another. As it happens, Regulus spent years at the end of Leo, but it recently moved into Virgo. The principal stars, such as Aldebaran, Algol, Regulus and many others, each have a character of their own, which is activated if a natal planet conjoins them or if something transits over them. Software will show if a few of these stars conjunct any planets on your natal chart.

The Ecliptic or Zodiac

We know that the Earth orbits the Sun, but ancient astrologers thought the Sun and planets orbited the Earth, and the apparent pathway of the Sun around the Earth is called the plane of the ecliptic, better known just as the ecliptic. The signs of the zodiac are ranged around the ecliptic, so it is also called the zodiac. Everything in western astrology happens along this line, so it is vitally important to us.

Midpoints
These are the points that lie midway between two planets or between anything else of interest on a chart. Read them like a weakened form of conjunction and check out the transits to these.

Declination, Parallels and Contra-Parallels
Declination is the distance that any planet moves above or below the ecliptic. A parallel occurs when two planets are at the same degree above or below the ecliptic – for instance, if Mercury and Saturn were both at 8 degrees south of the ecliptic. A contra-parallel occurs when two planets are on opposite sides of the ecliptic but at the same degree, such as Venus at 17 degrees north of the ecliptic and Jupiter at 17 degrees south of the ecliptic. You need Raphael's Ephemeris to check these for any day of the year. A parallel operates like a conjunction, and a contra-parallel is like an opposition.

Unaspected Planets
Sometimes, there is a planet on a natal chart with no aspects, so it can be considered weak. Some astrologers actually find the planet important, perhaps because it compensates for its lack of aspects or because aspects aren't hindering it from other planets.

Eclipses and Occultations
There are about four eclipses a year, most affecting the Moon, but some affecting the Sun. They range from total to annular and partial. (An annular eclipse occurs when the Moon leaves a ring of sunlight around it while it eclipses the Sun). These can be disruptive, especially if a total eclipse of the Sun falls on an important planet in your chart. You can look up everything to do with eclipses on astrological software.

Occultations occur when the Moon passes in front of a planet. If the planet is a fast-moving inner planet, such as Mercury or Venus, this will only happen once, but if the planet is a slow-moving one, such as Saturn, the Moon will occlude it month after month until Saturn moves away from the path of the Moon. Occultations can be unpleasant, so they are worth keeping an eye on. The only way that I know of spotting occultations is in Raphael's Ephemeris.

The Vertex and Anti-Vertex
The Vertex is a sensitive point on a natal chart that tends to set off such things as falling deeply in love, highly passionate relationships, obsessions, grief, major gains and losses and much that is the stuff of

novels and films. It also links to the people you attract and those you can't help falling in love with or even just liking. If you can't keep your hands off someone, see if any of their major planets fall on your Vertex!

The Anti-Vertex is the opposite point on the chart, and it is also a very passionate and unforgettable part of a horoscope.

The East and West Points
These are like shadow ascendants and descendants. They are close to the Asc and Dsc on the chart. They may have an effect, but probably not much.

The Black Moon
This is a particularly nasty spot on any natal chart, and it isn't much fun when activated by a transit. Like all these minor features, it can be found on the displayed planets list in an astrological program.

Chinese Astrology
Chinese astrology fascinates me, but wow, is it complicated! The basics are easy enough to understand, as they relate to twelve animal signs, namely:

The Rat
The Ox
The Tiger
The Rabbit
The Dragon
The Snake
The Horse
The Goat
The Monkey
The Rooster
The Dog
The Pig

Each animal sign rules a year, but an animal sign also rules a month, another rules a day, and another for an hour. It is easy to work out the year, month, and hour signs by hand, but you need to access the internet to find the day sign and put it all together.

In addition to this, there are five elements, these being:
Wood
Fire
Earth

Metal
Water

Each element rules two years in turn, one being yang and the next yin, so in any year, you will be born under a specific element and a particular animal sign. The months, days and hours also link to an element. All of this can be progressed to see what will happen at any hour of any day of any year. Furthermore, the system links to Feng Shui, the Magic Square and much more, and it would probably take a good few lifetimes to understand it all.

India

Hindu astrology, also called Vedic astrology, is like Western astrology, but one significant difference is that we use the tropical zodiac and Vedic astrology uses sidereal astrology.

Tropical astrology is linked to the times of the year. The following works for the northern hemisphere, and you need to reverse the pattern for the southern hemisphere:

The spring equinox on the 21st of March occurs at 0 deg. Aries.

The summer solstice arrives when the Sun moves to its northernmost point, which is the tropic of Cancer, and that occurs on the 21st of June when the Sun is at 0 deg. Cancer.

The autumn equinox on the 21st of September occurs at 0 deg. Libra.

The winter solstice arrives when the Sun moves to its southernmost point, which is the tropic of Capricorn, and that occurs on the 21st of December at 0 deg. Capricorn.

The system that we use in the West was worked out by the Greeks and the Egyptians about 2,300 years ago, and Earth has slipped backwards over time. This means that sidereal time (star time) is 25 degrees back from the tropical zodiac, so someone born with the Sun at 15 degrees of Scorpio would have their Sun at 20 degrees of Libra by the Vedic system. This doesn't really change a person's character because Vedic astrology is mainly used for predictive or Electional purposes.

Another form of astrology is also used in India, called "the Mansions of the Moon." This divides the horoscope into 27 sections, the number of days it takes the Moon to go around the Earth. Each section is devoted to a different god or goddess, and each has a meaning. Needless to say, one must track the Sun, Moon and planets through this system to work out what someone was like at birth and what is likely to happen to them at any time.

Aztec Astrology
This is an amazingly complex form of astrology that has wheels within wheels and various forms of calendar. About the only other thing I know is that the ancient Aztecs took a lot of notice of the position and movement of Venus.

CONCLUSION TO VOLUME TWO

This brings the second volume of the BIG Astrology Guide to a close, but it is only half the story, so if you haven't read the first volume, you might fancy buying it for yourself at some point in the future.

I wrote the Aspect section specifically for this book, but the Moon Signs and the Predictive Astrology sections are heavily revised versions of previous books. When I looked at the Predictive Astrology part of this volume, I was not happy with it because it wasn't as easy to understand or as comprehensive as it should have been. It needed much more than a bit of tweaking, so I reworked the book from start to finish and turned it into something better than the original, and it is now something of which I can truly be proud!

Hopefully, these two volumes will sit on your bookshelf, allowing you to dip into them as the years go by. I hope you learn to love astrology as I have always done, and have many years of enlightenment and mind-expanding fascination. Some of you will become professional astrologers, and you will spend time helping people to understand themselves and get through the trials and traumas of their lives. The combination of psychology, intuition, spirituality and the desire to help others can only help you to grow as a person, and it will help your hidden, twelfth-house soul to grow and develop in its turn.

Good luck,
Sasha Fenton

Index

90-Degree arc 188

A
ACG 281
Ages of Change 216
Aldrin 3
Ancient Divisions 228
Angular Houses 96
Anti-Vertex 284
Apollo 11 3
Arabic Parts 193, 282
Armstrong 3
Asteroids 193, 283
Astro-Cartography 281
Astro-Mapping 281
Astrology, Local Space 282
Astrology, Mundane 282
Astrology, Physical 282
Aztec Astrology 287

B
Ballesteros, Seve 48
Bi-quintile 206
Biden, Joe 30
Black Moon 285
Bush, George 60

C
Cadent Houses 96
Carreras, Jose Maria 24
centaur 193

Ceres 283
Chinese Astrology 285
Chiron 193
Churchill, Winston 48
Clary, Julian 79
Cleese, John 24
Clinton, Hillary 93
Collins 3
Conjunction 135, 205
conjunction, triple 204
Contra-Parallel 206
Contra-Parallels 284
Cowell, Simon 73
Cycles 212

D
Daily House Progressions 189, 220
Day-for-a-Year Progressions 219
Decans 227
Declination 5, 284
Decumbitures 188, 220
Dee, Jon 127
Depp, Johnny 79
Detriment 17
DeVito, Danny 73
DiCaprio, Leonardo 60
Dignity 17
Distant Planets 283
Divine 24
Douglas, Michael 79
dragon's head 193

dragon's tail 193
Duodenary Progressions 219
dwarf planet 193
Dylan, Bob 30

E
Eastwood, Clint 48
Eclipse, Lunar 142
Eclipse, Solar 142
Eclipses 4, 141, 210, 284
Ecliptic 5, 283
Eisenhower, Dwight D 66
Electional Astrology 189, 220
Elements 12
Elements, The 226
Emotions 6
Ephemeris 141
Ephemeris, American 141
Ephemeris, Raphael's 141, 142
Equal House 96
equinox, autumn 286
equinox, spring 286
Eris 283
Exaltation 17

F
Fall 17
Fixed Stars 195, 283
Frazer 144

G
Gates, Bill 24
Genders 12
Genders, The 225
Gibson, Mel 60
Grant, Cary 86

H
Hagman, Larry 86
Hearst, Patti 60
Hindu View 150

Hoffman, Dustin 54
Horary Astrology 220, 281
House Systems 96

I
Inconjunct 206
India 286
Inner Motivation 7

J
Jacobi, Derek 60
John, Elton 30
Jones, Catherine Zeta 93
Joplin, Janis 42

K
Kennedy, John F 54
Ketu 150, 193

L
Lewinsky, Monica 30
locational astrology 281
Lopez, Jennifer 24
lunar return 126

M
Madonna 54
Magazine Astrology 182
Mansions of the Moon 286
Marianne 144
Midler, Bette 66
Midpoints 192, 284
Minelli, Liza 42
Monkhouse, Bob 66
Montgomery, Elizabeth 79
Moon, full 173
Moon, new 173
Moon, old 174
Morgan, Piers 93
Mundane Astrology 189, 220

Index

N
Navratilova, Martina 24
New Moon 135
Ninety-Degree Arc Method 219
Niro, Robert De 93
Nodes of the Moon 193
Nurturing 7

O
O'Neal, Tatum 42
Obama, Michelle 93
Occultations 5, 143, 284
One-Degree Progressions 185
Opposition 205
Orbs 203
Osbourne, Ozzy 79
Osbourne, Sharon 42

P
Palin, Sarah 86
Parallel 206
Parallels 284
Parents 150
Part of Fortune 194
Past 150
Perpetual Noon Date 189, 220
Perry, Jimmy 79
Phases of the Moon 4
Physical Astrology 189
Planetoids 193
Precession 208
Presley, Elvis 93
Price, Katie 66
Primary Directions 185
Princess Diana 86
Progressed Moon Phases 140
Progressions 173, 196
Property 9, 151

Q
Qualities 12
Qualities, The 226
Quarter, First 137
Quarter, Fourth 139
Quarter, Second 138
Quarter, Third 138
Quintile 206

R
Rahu 150, 193
Ramsay, Gordon 54
Rectification 191
Redford, Robert 54
Returns 126
Returns, Lunar 188, 209
Returns, Solar 208
Romany Tradition 139
Roosevelt, Franklin D 42
Rowling, Joanna K 54

S
Semi-sextile 206
Semi-square 206
Sesquiquadrate 206
Sextile 206
Sheen, Charlie 73
Shelley, Mary 73
sidereal astrology 286
Signs, Air 228
Signs, Earth 227
Signs, Fire 227
Simon, Paul 42
Solar Arc Directed Charts 185
Solar Arc Directions 185, 219
Solar Arc MC Progressions 186
solar return 126
Solar Returns 187
solstice, summer 286
solstice, winter 286

Spears, Britney 86
Speedy Ascendant Finder 94
Spielberg, Steven 66
Square 205
Stallone, Sylvester 60
Starr, Ringo 48
stellium, natal 204
Streep, Meryl 30
Streisand, Barbra 48
Succedent Houses 96

T
Taylor, Elizabeth 66
Thatcher, Margaret 48
The Home 9
Tides 5
Timberlake, Justin 73
Transits 124, 140, 173, 219
Trine 205
tropic of Capricorn 286
tropical zodiac 286

U
Unaspected Planets 284

V
Vedic astrology 286
Venusian and Martian Arcs 188, 220
Vertex, The 194, 284
Void of Course Moon 125

W
Warwick, Dionne 30
Washington, Denzel 86
West Points 285
Winfrey, Oprah 73

Z
Zodiac 5, 283

www.ingramcontent.com/pod-product-compliance
Lightning Source LLC
Chambersburg PA
CBHW052046220426
43663CB00012B/2461